I Am Newman

I Am Newman
75 Pounds of Muscle & Gas

BOXER U
PUBLISHING

I Am Newman
Rob Stroup

ISBN: 978-1-942545-89-7
Library of Congress Control Number: 2017941823

Copyright © 2017 Rob Stroup
All rights reserved.

No part of this book may be reproduced or transmitted in any form
or by any means without the written permission of the publisher,
except in the case of brief quotations used in book reviews
and critical articles.

Boxer U Publishing
An Imprint of Wyatt-MacKenzie

Foreword

I GREW UP IN A DOG FAMILY. The breed of choice in our household was labs—yellow and black. Our family dogs lived in an outdoor pen, each with a comfortable doghouse. Despite our dogs not cohabitating our living space, they were certainly beloved members of the family. In my youth, the dogs were playing buddies for me, as my two sisters were a bit older than I. When I was interested in Lego blocks and shooting hoops, my older sisters were away at college, and more focused on their studies, music, or boys.

Flax, our yellow lab, was my primary partner in crime. We played everything together: fetch, Frisbee, catch, pretty much anything that could be done outside. I even pretended that I was He-Man and Flax was my Battlecat. Can you tell that I grew up in the 1980s? During summers, we spent nearly every waking moment outside. Even in winters, we enjoyed playing in the frequent snowfalls along the lakeshore of northwestern Pennsylvania. He had a steady, but not frenetic dose of energy to match mine as a youth. Flax never needed walks because we were so active.

He watched me go from infant to boy to being on the verge of becoming a hormonal teenager. I observed him mature from puppy to dog to senior. Seeing him become less physically able was especially difficult for me. We had shared a lifetime together as confidants and I wanted him to live forever.

As is often the case with the Labrador retriever breed, Flax's hips began to fail him, and then his eyesight started to fade. It was evident that each step of his life at age twelve was difficult and increasingly painful.

My parents, the responsible grown-ups of the house, made the difficult decision that his suffering needed to end. The dog that hopped into open car doors at a moment's notice throughout his entire life looked over his shoulder before his last ride as if to say, "Do I really need to get into the car? I can't." It was a real tearjerker for all of us. Dad drove off with Flax to provide him peace. He deserved it, for he had lived a great life. I distinctly recall being given a pamphlet on how to handle the grief of losing a pet. I could never bring myself to read it because his passing hurt so much. I didn't want to forget Flax, but I preferred the idea of grieving on my own terms and not having salt poured into the open wound.

In our suburban neighborhood, I had many great childhood friends. But Flax and I shared more of a brotherhood bond than I experienced with any of the boys. I was twelve, he was twelve ... but really, he had achieved an age into his mid-seventies[1], which was a pretty good run for a large breed where arthritic conditions can impair dogs at a younger age.

As tight a bond as I had with Flax, he wasn't a house dog. We didn't experience the joys and challenges of having a dog that could (and would) follow you EVERYwhere you went.

When I was a young, married man, my wife, Laura, and I both desired to have a family. As our life together began, we both knew that we wanted children. We came from families with siblings; I was the youngest of three, Laura

---

[1] A dog's age is actually based on the size of the breed. Generally speaking, the larger the breed, the more quickly a dog ages.

was the oldest of four. The perfect combination. Laura was the giving oldest sibling; I was the spoiled youngest child. Just ask my sisters.

Our grand plan was to enjoy married life for a few years before having kids. That we did. We were a couple of "DINK"s (double income, no kids) in South Jersey. Laura and I relished our careers. We enjoyed our life together. Although we lived several hours away from our families, our life was busy. It always seemed as though there was something going on: vacations, weekend getaways, graduations, hanging out with friends. It was all good. There wasn't anything that tied us down.

Less than two years into our marriage, the inevitable day came when Laura asked if I was ready to have a baby. I gave it careful consideration. On the "pro" side, I wanted to be a young father, I always wanted to have children (to corrupt), and I certainly wouldn't mind going through the process of trying to get pregnant. After all, I am a guy. On the "con" side, our alone time together would be diminished and our income would be lessened due to child care considerations. But, ultimately, I figured that it might take us a year or two to get pregnant. In my always-calculating mind, Laura and I would have ample time to enjoy life as a couple and save money before losing our DINK cards.

For over a year, we tried on our own. I didn't suspect anything was amiss, but Laura had an intuition that something wasn't right. She has always exhibited a more highly developed sixth sense when it comes to items of consequence. Laura suggested that we use a fertility monitor to improve the likelihood of conception. As the months continued to peel off the calendar, a twofold impact was seen.

    1. The frustration level was rising. We were two reasonably healthy young people. Why wasn't this working?

Our parents had no difficulty having kids (at young ages, too). We were also spiritual people who believed that God would "allow" us the opportunity to have children.
2. When we tried to have children, the preeminent concern was becoming pregnant. We were losing sight of the bigger picture: that we were young, in love, and already a family, if only for each other.

After a great deal of thought, Laura and I discussed the possibility of getting assistance to have children. This meant going to a fertility specialist. We had both come to the realization (or perhaps rationalization) that something was physically wrong. It turned out that this notion was 100% accurate. So, while the desire to have children was present, the biological ability to do so was lacking. We each had our own set of issues. Laura had endometriosis and my sperm motility was low, both of which contributed to our difficulties in conceiving.

It was about this time that a stuffed Christmas moose simply named "Moose" entered our household. Because we were so starved to take care of someone else, this poor moose became the child of the family. Moose had a high-pitched voice, used foul language, and even was a pastor for the local animals. This entire imaginary persona was thrust upon it by the two of us. We didn't have kids or pets and ended up projecting the presence of a living being onto an inanimate object wearing a green sweater, no pants, and made of stuffing and fur. It was painfully obvious that we needed someone to take care of in our household.

While we were undergoing our medical ordeals, we both understood that Moose wasn't going to fulfill our parental needs. Laura said that she needed someone to take care of ... aside from me, of course. As the whole idea of having a child wasn't exactly going to happen imminently, we both gravitated towards the idea of getting a dog.

We had a number of family members and friends with canine critters. We saw dogs that were Labrador retrievers, Dalmatians, Great Danes, Weimaraners, Rottweilers, boxers, and other mixed breed pooches. Given our current predicament, we desired a breed that would be good with children, hoping that someday we would have that opportunity for dog and child to coexist in our household.

After doing reading and extensive research, we focused our consideration on two breeds: labs and boxers. Both of us had had such a great experience with labs growing up that they simply had to be an option. From everything we learned about boxers, they were sweet, vivacious, and good family dogs. I had a close work friend who had a boxer named Zeus. While he wasn't the first boxer I had ever met, he left a lasting impression on me. The dog had such personality: a gravelly whine when he wanted to "talk" and an "in your face" attitude when he felt you deserved it. Of course, dogs' personalities are molded by their caregivers. But, I was sold on boxers.

The following story reveals the personality and impact of a single, solitary boxer dog on a family. This dog's name is ... Newman. It's a name that just fits. Of course it helps to have the comedic delivery of Jerry Seinfeld to properly say the name through gritted teeth with a tone of half-whisper and full annoyance. It was the only name that could possibly be given to the puppy that would warm our hearts once we got past the unbelievable hyperactivity that goes along with boxer puppyhood. As my life unfolded, I never anticipated the effect that a dog could have on me. This is the story of Newman from *his* vantage point.

Table of Contents

The Boxer	1
Sweet Child o' Mine	11
Subdivisions	19
Riders on the Storm	27
Born in the USA	35
Interstate Love Song	40
Disarm	49
Master of Puppets	53
Somebody to Love	66
Sabotage	76
I Still Haven't Found What I'm Looking For	82
Down with Disease	88
Smells Like Teen Spirit	92
Say It Ain't So	104
Dazed and Confused	114
Gotta Get Away	122
Back in the USSR	131
New York State of Mind	141
Man in the Box	147
The Pretender	158
He Ain't Heavy, He's My Brother	164
Ants Marching	171

Touch of Grey	176
Brown Sugar	186
Walk This Way	193
State of Love and Trust	204
Crazy Train	212
Uncomfortably Numb	219
The Times They Are a Changin'	231
Livin' on a Prayer	240
December	250
Higher Ground	260
One More Night	270
It's the End of the World as We Know It	275
Welcome to Paradise	281

The Boxer

EVERY DOG HAS ITS DAY. That's true for me, too. I had my fair share of days, 4,030 to be exact. Day #1 was an unseasonably cool Sunday in June in the thriving metropolis of Intercourse, Pennsylvania. My first day on the planet is in *Intercourse?* Really? It's a rural town in Lancaster County, which many Amish and Mennonite farmers call home, as did I for my first few months.

My mom, Shela, had three other puppies besides me in her litter. They were all girls. Yuck. I was surrounded by way too much estrogen. Four females and me, without a testosterone-laden canine in sight? A pup can't catch a break. My sisters ostracized me because I'm a male and they were a little bigger than me. Often when it was time to eat, I got squeezed out of the way by those nightmares that I called my fur and blood. I usually had to wait for my sisters to finish before I could have my turn, despite my human's attempts to get me equal time with my mom. Well ... I did get to eat, but not as ravenously as my sisters. I couldn't wait until they all went away. I'd rather just hang out with mom. I suppose that's what happens to the runt of the litter.

I grew more slowly than my siblings, but I finally did start to get a little meat on my bones. I have predominantly light brown fur with a slight reddish tinge. My socks are white, gleaming white, if I have the opportunity to adequately clean each of my paws. The mask covering my nose and jowls (similar to human cheeks, only mine dangle freely below my chin) is black, aside from two spots. One of these pigment oddities is located above my left upper lip. It looks like someone took a pink marker and left an indelible vertical stripe on me. My chin also has a small area that is similarly pink. My thick barrel chest is covered by wispy white fur that overshadows many not-so-subtle dark spots that speckle my chest and belly. As a little guy, I also had inordinately large ears. So large that I could have been mistaken for Dumbo. Wait a second, what in God's name happened to my tail? It's a mere two-inch-long nub. I swear it was longer than that when I got here. Are all my parts going to shrink? I sincerely hope not.

You guessed it, I was a boxer puppy; I was an awkward, gangly puppy that has been slightly underfed and under-appreciated by the crew that I guess I should refer to as a family. If that was indeed my family, it was going to be a challenge. My human was a young man who called all of us "Pup" or "Puppy." When we did pay attention to him (which admittedly was rare), we all wondered which of us he really wanted. I couldn't fathom going through life with the same name as those hooligans.

One day, I saw a different human come to pay us a visit. That human could have cared less about me. Pfft. That's fine, I had more important things to do like chew grass, lick my crotch, harass my sisters, and try to get some food while I had more of an opportunity. After the unfamiliar human left, I realized that only two of my sisters were there. Hmm ... is that a good thing? Well, I had one fewer obstacle to get the attention that I so richly deserved. Did the human make my sister shrink or perhaps even disappear? Was she ever coming back? I couldn't hold that thought in my head for very long. Out of sight, out of mind. She's someone else's problem now, thank goodness.

Over the next several days, more humans came, more humans ignored me, and eventually my two other siblings vanished. Good riddance. Then, it was just mom and me. Woo hoo! I didn't need to eat from her anymore, but I still tried. I had this boundless energy that she simply couldn't handle. She didn't really reprimand me, correct any potential behavioral issues, or even connect with me for that matter. Did I make her mad? That's not possible, I'm an *angel*. I thought that she and I would become close once those silly girls all left. But, I was a puppy, so I wasn't overly concerned about forming a profound bond. Life was all about having fun.

One sunny and warm August afternoon, I saw another strange vehicle in my human's driveway. It wasn't the horse and buggy that I saw come and go with regularity. A relatively young guy exited the car to speak with my human. I couldn't be bothered with their doings. My doghouse and play area were far more entertaining. My human called out, "Pup!" to me. I looked around, remembering that my sisters were elsewhere, and realized that he must be talking to me. He approached and opened the wood and wire mesh gate to my outdoor pen. Holy crap! Let me out, I'm so excited. As the gate was unbolted, I saw the stranger get down on one knee and beckon me toward him. I sprinted across the gravel driveway in his precise direction. However, I blew right by the guy. I didn't need to bother with the stranger because there were so many smells and sights to see out here. I sniffed some plants, peed, looked around for Mom, and reveled in the additional freedom that I had been temporarily granted.

The new guy tried to get my attention, but I was paid him no mind. He followed me around, wanting to play with me, desiring me to focus on him. *Not now buddy, I'm busy.* Oh sure, I eventually let him pet me and scratch my ears. What dog wouldn't? But, he was by no means my focal point. Hell, I don't *ever* have a focal point. The thoughts come fast and ferociously, so much so that my body could barely keep up with my frenetic mind.

My human and the unfamiliar man chatted for a bit more before bidding farewell. The new guy ripped some piece of paper and handed it to my human, closing their discussion with a handshake and a smile. I wondered what the stranger wanted. I watched with growing curiosity as the red sport-utility vehicle departed down the gravel path between the rows of corn at my human's house. The new man seemed genuinely interested in interacting with me, but I'm still here. After his departure, my human ushered me back into my dog pen, leaving me to my familiar surroundings and my ever-present random thoughts.

About a week later, I saw the same red vehicle advance up the driveway behind the farmhouse. I barked expectantly as my human once again permitted me the opportunity to enjoy the sights and smells beyond my pen. It was the same guy! I was mildly more curious about what he wanted. My mom was roaming around quietly as I bounced to and fro. The man was exclusively paying attention to me, watching all of my activity.

The two humans conversed while my human handed the stranger a bottle of pills that I had to take on a regular basis to combat a mild infection behind my front left "elbow." After a few minutes had elapsed, the new guy was saying ... apparently to me, "Come Newman, come here boy. Let's get in the crate. Let's get in the car." What in the world does that mean? He pointed to a small crate that was resting on the ground behind his car. Evidently, he wanted me to go inside the enclosure. NO! Stranger danger. I don't know you. Leave me alone.

    The man was able to wrangle my wriggling 18-pound body and placed me within the prison. He positioned the crate in the back seat of the red vehicle. I tried to adapt to my new environs where I had a bird's eye view of the man. We headed down the driveway after saying, "So long," to my human, the dog pen, farmhouse, blue Harvestore silo, and every other sight that I had grown accustomed to for the first ten weeks of my life. My siblings were gone from this picturesque setting. Now, so was I.

    As I glanced back one last time, my mom was completely unaware of what had just happened. Or, perhaps maybe she just didn't care that the last of her offspring had been whisked away. Sadly, I would never see my mom again. As I began to realize that everything was changing rapidly, I decided that now was a completely appropriate time to announce the disdain I had for my new situation.

    I yipped and yapped as we headed in an easterly direction on rural roads, while I looked out through the openings in the plastic crate. My eyes darted all around, but I focused my voice on this new man because, after all, he incarcerated me here. He kept saying things like, "Newman, it's ok." "We're just going for a ride." "We're going home." Home is the opposite direction. It's not ok! Nonetheless, he continued driving. My bark didn't seem to have any effect on where we were going, yet it was still a worthwhile endeavor. The man attempted to talk to me as we continued our drive. He kept saying, "Newman, be quiet." "It'll be ok, Newman." Intermittently, I barked and whined.

    He reassured me that we were getting closer to our destination as our route of rural roads turned into a steady, quicker pace. The motion of the vehicle was something that I hadn't experienced quite like this before. We traveled faster and farther than I had ever before done in a vehicle.

As traffic increased on our eastward trip through Philadelphia via the traffic-laden Schuylkill Expressway, my chauffeur occasionally cursed other drivers for their ineptitude. More importantly, my belly didn't feel right.

As we neared our journey's end, I felt the earth disappear from beneath the road. We were crossing a pale blue-colored bridge over a massive body of water. I felt this nasty cough come up from my stomach. Uh oh. I think my belly just came out of my throat and is sitting in front of me. This pile of brownish-gray liquid mush smelled terrible. The man turned to look at what had happened as we approached the east side of the Delaware River after crossing the Ben Franklin Bridge. His shoulders slumped as he stated matter-of-factly, "Welcome to New Jersey."

I actually felt a little better now that my stomach had spewed out before me. A few minutes later, the man said, "We're just about home." He guided the vehicle around an abrupt left turn in the road that caused my crate and me to suddenly turn on its right side. With wild eyes, I tried to get on my feet. The man tilted the crate back upright as he maneuvered the car further down the two-lane road. I finally had my paws beneath me and was no longer flailing about aimlessly. Thank goodness that I didn't land in my own vomit. A few feet later, we pulled into a driveway that was adjacent to a yellow house with blue shutters. The guy stated, "We're home and it's time to meet Mom." Oh boy, how did my mom get here?

❖ THE MAN LET ME OUT of my crate and promptly fastened something around my neck and held the other end of the line as I scrambled down from the red car to the ground. I was so excited to no longer be confined, but I couldn't go exactly where I wanted. After all, I was only eighteen pounds and that man towered over me. I figured that he must weigh at least 30 or 40 pounds. He would not let go of the leash that was attached to the collar on my neck, so my freedom was limited. We walked toward the yard behind the house as the sun was setting and the high temperature of the August early evening finally began to relent. The man let go of the leash to allow me freedom to move independently and went to get Mom.

I started running crazy figure eights and scouting out the new digs. The backyard was somewhat larger than the play area to which I had become accustomed at the farmhouse. The grassy area was approximately a 60 foot by 40 foot plot surrounded by wooden fences along each side of the perimeter. All of a sudden, I saw the new guy and a young woman. The man struggled to pick me up because of my spastic nature and introduced me to her. He said that this was Mom. Huh? That's not Mom. Mom looks like me. This is a person ... Mom is a *dog*; you know, four paws, fur, lower to the ground, and some sort of tail? I was so confused. She seemed nearly as nervous as I felt. There was so much going on: the car ride, two new people, a new yard, and this God-forsaken collar. What a pain to be under control by someone else!

This person masquerading as Mom petted my head and remarked about my droopy eye. She could see pink surrounding my right eye because my eyelid did not seem to fully cover the area around my eyeball. I can see fine. Stop messing with my eye. That's annoying. The man handed me over to "Mom" as my wild legs thrashed about in the air. Put me down! I didn't need nor did I want to be carried.

They both said to go potty before we go inside. What's inside? Is that another play area? Sweet! I didn't know what "potty" was, so after several minutes, we eventually walked in through the back door of the house. I promptly sprinted through most of the downstairs rooms – a tiled kitchen floor that is waaaay too slippery, along with the furnished dining room and living room. I had so many new things to sniff: couches, tables, carpet, books, and a television.

As I returned back to the kitchen, I found a particularly good spot. My nub of a tail rose, so I squatted. I had to ... you know ... poop and maybe pee a little. I've never been so scared in my brief life because mid-poop, both people loudly were telling me to go outside. What for? Everybody poops, everybody pees (Isn't that an R.E.M. song?). I don't get it. But, I was quickly getting the idea that there is a spot for my business, and it wasn't in the kitchen.

"Mom" cleaned up my stuff, so I gave her a few licks on her cheek to show my appreciation for fixing my apparent mistake.

I took another gander around the kitchen and saw something moving. What in the world was that?! I approached the black, semi-reflective, vertical surface and the object got larger and larger. I couldn't withhold my surprise and confusion, so I barked. Then, I shook my head violently from side to side, which caused my robust jowls to clap loudly. This object appeared to mimic my every move. I whined and could see the surface display a pair of dark eyes, four legs, floppy ears, and a mouth that was moving at the exact same moments that I barked or whined. This being's head also tilted when I turned my head. It was frightening that the dishwasher was showing me another version of myself. When I reached out to touch it with my front paw, I saw an identical foot movement paw back at me. Following alternating bouts of barking and whining over the course of several minutes, I couldn't stand it anymore and needed to find something else to do. Thank goodness that this other dog only appeared in the dishwasher, and not in other places in the new house. I wonder if it's captive in there.

 The guy put forth a few items for me and let me do as I chose with them: a rope toy, a rawhide bone, and a rubber mesh ball. This was a welcome distraction from the poor pooch that was stuck in the dishwasher. All of these toys were brand new and required what attention I could muster. I chewed eagerly on each item in rapid succession, not knowing how to determine which object deserved the most focus. So ... I sprinted in short fits from one room to the next before going back to retrieve a different toy. The man and woman seemed perplexed by my unfettered energy. After that awful ride in the crate, barfing, and being petrified after pooping in the kitchen, creating a toy parade seemed like a great way to spend my time.

 All good things appeared to come to an end. These people told me that it was bedtime. Bed? Sure, you two go to bed. I'll just play. But, that's ostensibly not how this is going to work. Bedtime appeared to be non-negotiable. The man took me outside and I decided that it was a good idea to pee in the grass and not inside. Boy, was that the right choice. The man effusively praised me and "Mom" did so as well, both of them giving me treats for my efforts. She asked me if Newman was a good boy for Dad. Dad? Newman? I'm sure that this will eventually make sense, but I didn't have the first clue as to what the lady meant.

The man told me, "Say good night to Mommom" before guiding me into the one thing that was familiar to me in these altogether unfamiliar new surroundings, and not in a good way: the crate. Reluctantly, I entered the confinement that had soft blankets lining the base. The good news was that my vomit had been removed. The bad news was that I had not yet figured out how to unlatch the crate door, so I gloomily looked through the openings at my new people. While they seemed nice enough, I didn't wish to be imprisoned. They both said, "Good night, Newman," and promised to see me in the morning. They left the kitchen, turned left, and went upstairs.

Note to self – I needed to find out what was up those stairs. I completely missed them on my initial haphazard survey of the inside quarters. I whimpered pathetically for a few minutes before my eyes shut. I began to lose track of time as my busy and life-altering day came to a close.

Sweet Child o' Mine

A FEW SLEEPY HOURS later, my eyes shot open. Where am I? What am I doing here? I looked around and noticed that I was still detained in the crate on the kitchen floor. This was not cool, so I began to bark and bark ... and bark. I heard footsteps coming down the stairs as the young man sleepily came to check on me. He asked me some questions as he undid the crate latch. "Do you need to go potty? Do you need to go outside?" Um ... yeah, let's go with that—whatever it takes to get out of here. I eagerly pawed at the opening as the crate door swung open.

The man did not give me room to go into the dining room or living room. Instead, he quickly ushered me in the direction of the back door. After unlocking and opening the door, I bolted outside onto the patio and beyond into the lawn. Oh boy, play time! I looked around and noticed that the sky was pitch black. I sprinted to and fro as the man whispered, "Newman, go potty," which I wholly ignored because #1—I had no idea what that meant and #2—I'm my own boss.

Being in the yard was so much more freeing than being cooped up in my enclosure. The man was becoming visibly frustrated as more and more minutes passed, so he tried to corral me. Before he could corner me in the yard, I lowered my hind legs and briefly tinkled. The guy was ecstatic. He patted my back and sides and audibly murmured, "Good boy, Newman! Let's go back inside." I dopily followed him inside the back door, hoping for additional time to play. After I was given more affection and a small Milk Bone treat, that's when I realized my mistake.

The man stood in the opening to the kitchen door and prevented me from going anywhere else. Then, he said words I certainly didn't want to hear. "Newman. Crate." Crap. He pointed in the specific direction of the kennel and I glumly moseyed into it, finding the comfortable blankets beneath my paws. I glared at the guy through the holes in the side of the confinement. If I had lasers for eyes, the man would have disappeared, although he seemed rather unsympathetic about my feelings.

He left the kitchen light on and went back upstairs, I presume to sleep. While I seethed silently at being left alone AND being caged, I once again drifted off to sleep, not to be heard from again until dawn broke.

By the light of day, the two people came down to visit me and let me out of the crate. They were genuinely excited to see me. I was more interested in just getting out. They both accompanied me outside for several minutes. This place was still fairly new to me, so I had to scope out everything again now that it was bathed in sunlight. The grass had all of my smells from the night prior. No other critters had been there. I found a convenient place and squatted before pooping in the grass for the first time. Did I just win the lottery? The man and woman were practically beaming, and gave me a treat instantly. Ooohh, I *like* this game. I poop, I get a biscuit. What happens if I pee? Let's try that. Moments later, I strolled around the corner from the garage and took a leak. Same praise, same joy, and most important, same treat! Woohoo!!

I strutted and galloped clumsily through the dewy morning grass back into the house. My parents dropped a cup of food that loudly clattered into a metal bowl on the kitchen floor. You don't have to tell me twice—breakfast! I devoured the puppy chow in a flash, wondering if there was more to come. Not now apparently.

The people tag teamed how things went in the morning; one would stay with me on the first floor, while the other would disappear upstairs where I could hear water churning through pipes behind the walls. About thirty minutes later, both of them said goodbyes, which seemed curious to me. Where were they going? As they had somewhere to go, I was anxious to join them since they were my new pack, at least at the moment. I was very disappointed to learn that both of them were leaving... without me. They steered me into my kennel for the remainder of the morning, vowing to return soon. I was coerced into the confinement of the crate by being given yet another treat. I bitterly accepted my fate and furiously barked as both the man and the lady departed out the front door. Did you bring me here to incarcerate me?

A few hours later, I heard the front door opening. Thank goodness. It was the woman. I was on pins and needles as she made her way to the kitchen to release the hound. I was crazy with anticipation until she opened the latches to let me out. I bounced all over the place, barely able to stay upright on the smooth flooring. We went outside and I had to release the pent up energy from being imprisoned. It was sunnier and brighter, so I exerted my body to the fullest in short fits and sprints. I even squatted to pee a few times on the lawn, which made the woman smile brightly.[2]

After ten minutes of stretching my legs, I realized that my belly was rolling. By some crazy coincidence, the woman dropped food into my bowl, seeming to understand that

---

[2] I didn't lift my leg to urinate, which most dogs do to mark territory with more precision. Often, males do this because of their "equipment" for aiming. The female was pleased to see me crouching to pee because it was less disgusting.

my young body required nourishment. I ate speedily, wondering what was to come next. After a few minutes of dragging toys around the house, the woman said a word I had already begun to dread: "crate." She also sweetly told me that it was time to go into my house. Despite my protests, I eventually meandered to resume my prison sentence. Of course, it helped matters that she gave me a tasty treat, so I couldn't be *too* mad at her, right?

As the lady was preparing to leave the premises again, I saw something that seemed unusual. There were tears slowly sliding down her cheeks. I don't think that I did anything wrong that would make her cry. I overheard her telling someone on the telephone that she did not want to leave me. Hehehehe, what a softie.

I began to wonder if I would ever get out again as the afternoon dragged on and on, when I heard not one, but two vehicles enter the driveway nearly simultaneously. I was boisterous in my barking to let the individuals in the cars know that I was in here, and needed to get out. Much to my surprise and delight, both the guy and the lady came in through the front door and we immediately locked eyes. If it was possible, I was even more excited to exit the crate than during my lunchtime visit. They both came over and asked how Newman was. They asked if Newman had a good afternoon. *Let me out!*

The crate latch was undone and the back door was opened to our yard. Ah yes ... FREEDOM! I loved getting out of that crate and being able to move freely about the yard. I could eat grass, dig up some dirt, and chase bugs. In the background, I heard some harsh words to stop digging and leave the grass alone. Those directives were ignored. I had boundless energy that I needed to burn and could not be troubled with the preferences of two people who I had met only yesterday. After all, digging is a canine instinct.

One of the few methods to ignore this instinct is for us pooches to be too tired. Ha! I was a boxer pup. Plan B was for my brain to become preoccupied with something more intriguing.

Ooh ... there were some flowers that lined the edges of the patio. They looked like they could be tasty. Let's check them out. I sniffed and grabbed the first one and heard a scream, "No!" I bounced away from the reddish-pink impatiens and galloped a few circuitous laps around the yard, then returned to the very same flower. I focused on the flower and started to nibble. I received a sharp, "Stop it, Newman! NO. Bad dog." This time, I lingered and tore off the stem. The man was now chasing me. Oohh ... this is a game. What fun! I was too quick for him. I didn't have an endless yard in which to operate, but I had plenty of space to steer clear of him. Instead of constantly chasing me (as I had hoped), he stood guard near the flowers and refused to allow me easy access to the impatiens. Hmm ... well, I would wait until he wasn't watching. I stalked out a few new scents and covered them with urine to let everyone know that this area was mine.

We returned inside the house without further conflict. Disappointingly, this time I did not receive a treat for going into the yard. The man opened the pantry door and pulled out more dog food for me, which was relatively bland but I was so incredibly famished that the taste didn't matter. Heck, I barely noticed the flavor because I always ate at lightning speed. I thought it would be wise to finish rapidly so that I could beg for more food. As I was in "wolf mode" destroying my dinner, the humans went through a lot more effort to make their own meal. I thought I might join them in tasting theirs. I didn't receive any of their food that night, but I would keep at it. They would eventually crack under pressure.

Prowling near the flowers, waiting for my opportunity.

After dinner, the people got my leash and collar and said that they were going to take me for a walk. If I was going with them, I supposed it was better than the alternative of being left alone again. I fussed and tried to avoid having that blasted collar latched around my neck. I hated things that made noise, including the infernal jingling of my collar. Add to that the fact that I didn't even like sitting still for more than a second, so it was double the torture. After getting outside, the people took turns guiding me along the sidewalks of our development. I preferred to walk in a more random pattern as things piqued my interest. The people preferred to keep me on or very near to the sidewalk going in a generally straight line, which was frustrating. The smells that often demanded my attention were just out of reach of the length of my leash line. I could pull and pull and pull, but would get nowhere with a person on the other end of the leash. I vowed to become stronger so that I could overtake them someday.

When we returned from our walk around the neighborhood, I got a treat from the humans. We settled inside for the evening. I began to do laps around the dining room table and living room furniture as I received bewildered stares from the young couple. They appeared exhausted, while I could go on for hours. So, I decided to settle down and chew on something. Unfortunately, the dining room chair leg is ostensibly *not* on the approved list of chewable items in the house. I learned this lesson the hard way. Dad sternly reprimanded me immediately after my teeth clamped down on the cherry wood of the chair. Easy big fella ... you haven't laid out all the rules yet. I'll figure it out.

A few hours later, I walked around the living room and was scoping out a good spot. My nub pointed vertically, so I began to squat to pee. The humans rushed me out to the backyard, but it was too late. The damage was already done. I was admonished for not getting outside in time, but I felt like I was given a little slack. After all, it was only my second day here. The rules were so different here than what my previous human permitted on the farm.

After we came back inside, I spent time testing boundaries. Could I go on the couch? No. Could I chew the bookcase? No. What about the remote control? Yikes, no. These people were more than willing to play with me if we used one of my toys. However, it was a non-starter when I tried to play with one of their toys. That didn't seem fair. Hours later, the man and lady directed me to the crate and I went a bit more voluntarily this evening. I was finally tired after playing and romping. I just wished that I didn't have to be crated during the day. My second night at my new house was much more restful. I knew where I was and didn't feel quite as nervous about being left alone. It was such a good night's sleep that I didn't even need to wake the humans or go potty in the middle of the night.

As the hours turned into days and days passed into weeks, we settled into a reliable routine on weekdays. Mom and Dad would arise from upstairs, get me out of my crate, and allow me the freedom to exercise my growing muscles; preferably outside if the weather cooperated. After a few minutes of exploring the yard and snouting all the wonderful outdoor smells, I would eat breakfast and gnaw on some of my toys. I quickly learned the distinction of their toys versus my toys.

Unfortunately, both of my people were full-time employees. As such, I spent each morning crate-bound. After approximately four hours in the dungeon, I had pent up craziness that needed to be expended. At least one of my humans would return home to allow me to eat voraciously, do my business outside like a good boy, and bounce around like a Mexican jumping bean. The tough part was getting all of this done in a measly 30-45 minutes before I was led back into my crate. At the end of the afternoon, both parents came home to feed me, play with me, take me for a walk, and pay the overwhelming majority of their attention to me. I expended a lot of energy in the evenings, so I rarely fought the humans when they deemed that it was bedtime.

Subdivisions

I BECAME MORE familiar with my surroundings with each passing day. As a young puppy, I had the good fortune of being in a house where we had living room windows that stretched nearly to the floor. So, if there was a noise in the neighborhood, all I had to do was sprint, certainly not amble aimlessly, over to one of the two front windows and peer out to examine the comings and goings. I could audibly announce my presence to people and pets alike. Often, the fur along my spine would stand on end if I were feeling anxious or antagonistic. There were even occasions during which I could display my adamant disapproval with a particular event by perching up on the sill and taking a more hardline stance.

I kept hearing that word, "Newman." As this was stated, everything else would get still, so I became accustomed to looking at the person uttering this word to see what I was missing. Of course, I could be busy gnawing on a toy or some other more suitable purpose for my frenzied energy. As much as a boxer pup could focus (maybe not 100% of the time, more like thirty), I would do so when hearing "Newman." Oh ... I get it! That's my name!! People were saying that to get MY attention, if I was willing to offer it. Whew ... problem solved. Now I knew how to introduce

I'll admit it, I'm nosy.

myself to others instead of pup. I am Newman.

I just needed to get straight who Dad and Mommom were. The man and the lady were the only two people I regularly saw, so this shouldn't be too hard to differentiate. Both of them say an awful lot of words to me, and none of them make sense. None at all. They keep saying words like sit, stay, down, potty, outside, food, hungry, treat, and eat. I speak DOG, not human. It's like they were trying to take charge of me: what I was doing, where I was going, when I was eating, when I could go outside or inside. Are we sure that's how it works? I'd like to think that I'm in charge around here. We'll work on that when I'm not too busy.

When they would say commands to me and I happened to be paying attention, I would tilt my head to one side trying to comprehend each word. The one word that I quickly understood was "walk." Within the first two weeks, I figured out that Mom or Dad would ask this in the form of a question and I simply had to react. They led with, "Do you want to go for a ...?" My head would swivel sideways at more than a forty-five degree angle after the first few words. I wouldn't even need to hear the final word of that question (walk) to begin a manic sprint back and forth between owner and door, owner and door, owner and leash, owner and door, leash and door. COME ON, LET'S GO PEOPLE!!

Taking a walk rapidly became my favorite pastime. Hearing the jingle of my leash and collar only added to my excitement; a walk was imminent. I could tolerate wearing the collar if I knew that a walk was in the cards. However, my limitless enthusiasm for these thirty minutes each day prevented me from holding still during the preparation. It often took one person to hold me in place while the other person attached the leash to my collar.

Once the humans were *finally* ready a few seconds later, we usually all went together for a lap around the neighborhood. We lived in an area where the houses were fairly close together, so there were inevitably new things to scope out on a daily basis. Our housing development had a sidewalk that pedestrians and pets used, so that's the path that we took. With each new person, pet, or vehicle, I felt obliged to investigate each as a new entity, something which required significant scrutiny. With repeated exposure, I began to develop a fundamental understanding about what to expect from each. If it were up to me, I would take hours to complete the half-mile jaunt, to allow for a thorough examination of everything I deemed worthy along the way. However, that pesky leash and collar were attached to me, so I was at the mercy of whoever was controlling the leash at the time.

The two people started to play games with me to teach me things. The lady would say, "Go see Dad." The guy would sit there with his arms open. I looked at him and slowly meandered toward him. I was told, "Good boy," given a full body hug, and a morsel of a tasty little treat. He would return the favor saying, "Where's Mom? Do you see Mommom?" I loped back to the lady as she held out a piece of food and she praised me similarly. This little game was repeated several times until it started to become second nature. The lady was Mom or Mommom, the man was Dad. Ah ... those were THEIR names! That made sense. Those other commands were still way too confusing to comprehend for someone with my inadequate attention span.

❖ I FELT THAT THERE WAS an invisible barrier that prevented me from going upstairs. This sense was ingrained in me by Mom and Dad. As such, I had a little time to play with my toys downstairs each morning as they got ready for work upstairs. That amount of free time translated to an opportunity for me.

Well, we all know how boxer puppies are: curious, energetic, and mischievous. You may be thinking, "Oh, he's headed upstairs." Nope. Exploration takes a back seat when compared with a chance to get human food, and large quantities of food that I imagined would taste quite yummy.

One morning, I took advantage of several minutes without supervision ... one where a loaf of bread was just close enough to the edge of the kitchen counter. We boxers have "quick twitch" muscles, so rather than being geared for marathon running, what comes naturally are short sprints and, more important, tall leaps with handsy front paws; but they certainly don't come gracefully to us. This prowess came in handy when eyeing up the bread. I leapt vertically with all my might and got my front toenails up onto the counter multiple times. With each vertical jump, I swept my front paws across the countertop. I had repeated the maneuver enough times to inch the unopened Stroehmann King-sized loaf until the wrapper dangled over the edge. From there, it was a simple task of swiping one last time to get the prize onto the floor for a more thorough examination. Knowing I had little time, I briskly tore a snout-sized hole into the plastic wrapping and devoured as much of the grainy goodness as "caninely" possible before the predictable footsteps descended downstairs to discover my sin.

Dad had this puzzled expression on his face as three full slices of bread, a few torn chunks and crumbs, and a portion of the Stroehmann girl remained on the floor. The rest of the loaf and wrapper was hidden from sight, but Mr. Detective somehow sleuthed that the twenty or so slices were somewhere between my esophagus and rectum.

I would give my right ear for a scapegoat, but no such luck. To say that Dad was displeased wouldn't be entirely accurate, although not incorrect either. Shocked is a better word. I was harshly admonished for taking the human food.

Later that evening, my parents were serenaded by the sound and smell of the most noxious gas that you can imagine. The farts that flew out of me sounded like World War II bombs being dropped from a B-17 aircraft. The aroma was something that approximated rotten eggs combined with dead fish. I'm a pretty flatulent dog to begin with, but this was unholy and borderline embarrassing. You could almost taste the stench. The persistent gas left a cloud that hung in the air for most of the evening. Needless to say, the bread was never again within my leaping range.

❖ I ABSOLUTELY DEVOURED my food when it was set before me. I was always in a mad dash to get through with a meal in hopes that more was forthcoming. In the first few weeks of life in New Jersey, I spat out a few of my baby teeth at mealtime. I never paid particular attention to the little Chiclets that came out. Sometimes there was a little blood, sometimes not. I never had difficulty obliterating my hard kernels of food, so it didn't faze me in the least. Surprise, surprise.

For my many shortcomings as a puppy, potty training was not among them. It actually came easily for me after that first night of being scared out of my wits when I pooped on the floor. Mom and Dad only found one other pile waiting for them as they were getting ready for work upstairs. I simply couldn't hold it anymore, and left a big, steamy present for them on the Persian rug in the dining room. When they came downstairs, I was told that this was bad behavior and made to go outside to see if I was done.

I was a quick study about peeing outside, too. I only had a few mishaps when waiting too long to relieve myself. Mom or Dad would take me outside every hour or two in hopes that I would grow accustomed to peeing with grass beneath my feet. We had a fairly small backyard, so Mom and Dad were not too particular about where I went to the bathroom ... as long as I was able to make it outside to the lawn in time.

After the first week with my new people, the potty-training component of my life was making sense. I showed Mom and Dad that I had the propensity to learn. I think that my parents learned from my non-verbal communication, too. When my nub would start to point skyward or when I began to circle with my nose to the ground, they read my body language and quickly guided me outside to take care of business.

I may have gained an ounce (but certainly not a pound) of self-control after our first month together. I would quietly go toward the back door and sit down in front of it any time I had to go potty. Then, I would stare back in the direction of wherever Mom and/or Dad was located, awaiting their acknowledgement of my situation. While sitting there in anticipation of a response, I would relax my gaze so much that you could no longer see the whites of my eyes. Mom and Dad nicknamed this my black eyes. So, I'd give them ol' black eyes any time I wanted to head outside, either to go potty or just to frolic.

Trust me, it was a rare occasion that I displayed the kind of calm that I did while waiting to be let outside. It was a seismic shift in the decibel level when I was noiselessly waiting for something. My rambunctious behavior typically avoided such quiet moments. Mom and Dad emphasized these instances by associating the word potty with going outside. They habitually asked me if I wanted to go outside, if I needed to go potty.

In the hours that I spent in my crate as a puppy, I never, ever soiled myself. I could always hold it until I had the chance to go outside and "water the lawn." Truth be told, I began to look at my crate as a home of sorts. Mom and Dad always kept it well-cushioned and comfortable and included at least a toy or two for my amusement. Even at night, sleeping in the crate wasn't terrible. Mom and Dad would have heard all about it if I were truly frustrated with the situation.

One evening after dinner, Dad told Mom that he and I were going outside. I eagerly followed Dad, and was inquisitive about the device that Dad was pushing. It had a long handle and a squarish looking metal box on four wheels that could be pushed with a reasonable effort by an angular bar. I surveyed the situation with curiosity as Dad poured awful-smelling, clear fluid into it. When he was done funneling the liquid into the device's tank, he yanked on a string near the handle ferociously once, then twice. All of a sudden, the device came to life with an ear-piercingly loud, vibrating noise. Dad pushed it a few inches and I saw grass begin spew out the side of the box in a spray. This thing moved and shredded stuff? I'm outta here!! I bolted through the back screen door that was closed, tearing a Newman-sized opening in the mesh, opting for safety over whatever that beastly thing was. I believed that Mommom would protect me from the lawnmower, and she did.

Riders on the Storm

MOM AND DAD STARTED this dreadful tradition of making sure that I kept clean. I thought I did a fine job of cleansing myself by licking my paws, back, crotch, and ass clean. Why isn't my tongue sufficient? One of my parents would carry me into one of the upstairs bathtubs and douse me with water, scrub me with dog shampoo that smelled like baby powder, and then rinse all of the suds away from my fur. The sole bright spot of these baths was the sight of fresh, running water. I could not help but drink the water streaming from the spigot. It didn't matter that the water temperature was warmer than the typically cool, refreshing liquid that I drank. It made the endeavor almost worthwhile. Well, that and shaking violently to share some of the water that I could release from my coat with Mom and Dad. Ha ha ha.

Another cleansing ritual was started that was appalling. Mom and Dad put this paste on a brush and shoved it into my mouth. I thought it was a treat at first, so I licked it up immediately until it was gone. Again, the toothbrush was topped with toothpaste. I eyed it up as Dad pried my jaws open to work the brush along my teeth. I nearly caused myself to choke as I tried my darnedest to avoid having my teeth cleaned. The actual motion felt unnatural, and I preferred the foul stench of my own breath to the minty fresh toothpaste. Tooth brushing was one activity that I was going to protest and fight, tooth and nail. Mom and Dad were in for a challenge on this one. My tongue could and would be used as a vital weapon to combat clean teeth. I vowed to remain steadfast in my opposition to this venture.

We also made our first visit to see a veterinarian. I had been to one of those places before I lived with my parents, but I don't remember it. It was an excuse to go for a car ride, so it had to be okay, right? After a brief, fifteen-minute drive, we pulled into a wooded parking lot. Mom went into the building to begin the registration process. Curiously, Dad and I remained outside. I put my nose to the ground and found the scent of not one, not two, but what seemed like a gazillion dogs, and maybe even a cat or two. I scoured the area outside the vet's office, from tree to tree, grassy area to bush, random spot #1 to random spot #2 to ... well, you get the picture. I was overwhelmed by the odor of the countless number of animals who had been there before me. I left my mark so that all future pets making visits would realize that Newman had been here, too.

After a few minutes, Mom came out to ask us to join her inside the vet's office. I strained against the leash to expedite matters. Dad tried to curb my enthusiasm, which only resulted in the leash growing taut and increased panting (not from Dad, from me). They both urged me to slow down. How could I contain myself when there would be several dogs to meet just on the other side of that door? It was impossible.

When I walked through the door, I saw two other dogs in the lobby. I immediately tried to sprint toward one of them. This was apparently a bad idea. Dad yanked the leash backward abruptly to prevent me from appearing to be overly aggressive. The other owner asked if I was friendly.

My parents assured her that I was, although I was a very hyper puppy. I was allowed to introduce myself to the much smaller pooch. I walked in circles around the dog, again and again. I wanted to see what she was all about and give her a thorough greeting. Once I had completed my third revolution around the young female, Dad tugged on the leash to get me to retreat because I was invading her space and she felt frightened.

In an effort to distract me, the nurse asked to weigh me. Mom and Dad led me to the scale. This was stupid and boring. I wanted to visit the other canines in the room, so I kept walking away from the scale. Mom and Dad took turns trying to get me in place for an accurate measurement. Easier said than done. After three failed attempts, Dad brusquely picked me up to get our combined weight. He reasoned that they could weigh him separately to calculate my weight by a simple subtraction. I writhed around in Dad's arms with all four paws moving in seemingly four different directions. Dad held me more tightly to his upper body to allow the scale to settle long enough to weigh us. I had packed on some muscle mass and now weighed 25 pounds, a healthy weight for being a little more than three months old.

With little delay, we were led into one of the waiting rooms where a tall man with intense eyes in a white lab coat introduced himself as Dr. Keefe. He crouched and allowed me to bathe his face and hands in my saliva as he continued to speak, apparently to my parents since I was not listening at all. Mom asked the veterinarian if I could be given a basic examination to ensure that I was healthy. Dr. Keefe agreed to do so. My heart was absolutely racing because a new person was paying undivided attention to me. He and a nurse held me still scarcely long enough to look into my eyes with an annoying light, peer into each of my ears, listen to my ridiculously rapid heart, assess my general size and body shape, and check each of my limbs. I tried to free my face and neck from their grips. It was just to lick them, not to do anything malicious! They were intent at checking out all my parts. Before releasing his grasp on me, the kind doctor administered a rabies shot that I barely noticed. I felt a slight pinch, but I paid no mind to the needle being inserted below the surface of my skin. My nub of a tail may have even wagged just a little while I was receiving the injection.

My parents also asked Dr. Keefe to inspect the fur infection that I had before coming to my parents. The vet carefully checked out the area behind my front left elbow, and found no sign of discoloration or bare skin. He deemed that the medication had done its job.

Dad asked when an appropriate age would be to neuter me since they were not intending to breed me. Neuter? That's a funny word. Hopefully, it makes me laugh when it actually happens. The doctor said that I could be neutered within the next few months, but they recommended waiting until I was at least six to eight months old. Mom and Dad both expressed interest in the surgery in hopes that it would reduce my exceedingly excitable nature. Dr. Keefe suggested that neutering me would potentially help, but certainly not eliminate my hyperactivity because #1, I am a puppy, and #2, I am a boxer. The parental units nodded, but were likely mentally circling a future date on the calendar.

All in all, I was a healthy pup. There were no skin ailments, no specific concerns that worried either doctor or patient, or more specifically patient's parents. For I rarely worried about anything.

❖ ONE FALL EVENING after a bath, I went outside and rolled around in the lawn as the sun set. I wanted to smell like something, anything but that disgusting shampoo. For several minutes, I positioned myself upside down in the dewy grass and tried to get that unpleasantly clean stench off me.

The following day when Dad came to play with me at lunch, he was dumbstruck by my appearance. I had massive lumps all over my body, including my eyebrows, cheeks, neck, back, belly, and paws. He was extremely concerned for my well-being. After chatting with Mom, they figured out that I was covered in mosquito bites from being attacked the night before. I guess those bugs were stupidly allured to me by the aroma of my doggy shampoo. Upon consulting with my vet's office, I received a Benadryl to shrink the swelling of the bug bites. The vet cautioned my parents that Benadryl could have a counteracting effect, making my hyperactivity heightened beyond a typical Newman level. Mom and Dad were willing to take the chance of an overly spastic puppy to make me feel better. After taking the little pink pill, I was back to "normal" within a matter of hours, not days or weeks. I reasoned with Mom and Dad that I should never get a bath again. That would solve the problem! No ... such ... luck.

❖ AS A PUPPY, one thing I quickly learned about was the importance of NFL Sunday. For five days each week, Mom and Dad were gone all day long, except that one of them would come to visit me for lunch. They didn't have to work one day per week, which was glorious. This meant no crate and lots of attention for me. Then came Sunday. Mom and Dad often left in the morning for church, so I was relegated to an hour or two of solitude in my crate. I had enough room, but I was so social that I didn't want to be apart from my parents ... ever. When they got home on Sundays, we'd eat lunch, but then Dad would be zoned in to the television ALL DAY LONG. I don't get television or, for that matter, anything in two dimensions. Why did they spend time looking at TV? It's not like the football is in the room. So, each fall Sunday, I would get so bored by Dad's TV watching that I would willingly spend time lying in my open crate to avoid the senseless, mind-numbing supposed "entertainment" that Dad loved so much.

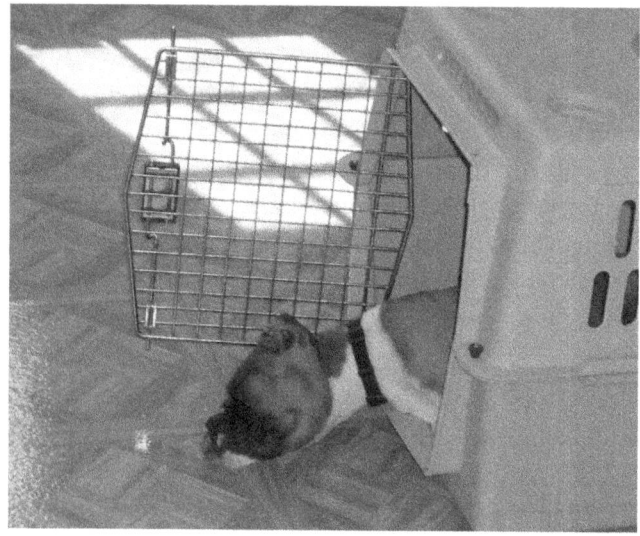

A typical NFL Sunday.

One Sunday when I was pouting in my crate as the Pittsburgh Steelers were shocking the undefeated New England Patriots, Dad looked over at me and realized something. Perhaps it was my head hanging out of the crate that caused this notion to dawn on him: I was really getting big. Because of my seemingly unending growth spurt, the crate was becoming more cramped. Mom and Dad reacted by allowing me to try a few larger crate options before settling on one that would give me ample room to turn around and lie comfortably, while giving me extra room as I was nowhere near fully grown yet.

My ravenous appetite allowed me to quickly put on some weight, to the tune of seven to ten pounds per month for the first few months with Mom and Dad. I went from a skinny, tiny, gangly, awkward puppy with bad manners to a robust, athletic, albeit still uncoordinated older puppy with more aggressive bad manners. My newfound weight meant that Mom could no longer pick me up to control me. Dad could, but he would have to catch me first! I was now able to outrace him, and often did so just because I could. He claimed to be a fast runner, which either means that all humans are slow or he's just lying.

My backyard was adequate for me to stretch my legs and run, although I never managed to show off straight-line speed. Instead, my bountiful energy led me in several minutes of figure eights, arcs, and whatever pattern felt appropriate at the time, only reined in by the boundaries of the fenced-in yard.

❖ MANY OF MY FIRSTS were unexpected, some in a good way while others were scary. One such first was an ominous noise that boomed from beyond the four walls of our house and roused me from the sweet slumber of my dog bed. The noise was a deep, low reverberation that shook my body. I jumped to my feet with a look of dire panic in my eyes. Was something coming through the walls? Were we going to get hurt? Did somebody detonate a bomb? Mom-mom and Dad acted with unbelievable calm. They didn't appear as though this noise was worth fretting over.

Dad pointed to the window and we stared out at the familiar houses of our neighborhood. I had seen rain before, but this was a downpour. The rain pelted the streets, cars, and lawn with such ferocity that it became difficult to see anything through the raindrops. A flash of light illuminated our view briefly, and then came that boom once more. It was louder and briefer than the previous one. I visibly flinched as the blasted thunderclap frightened me again. Mom and Dad tried to reassure me that everything was fine. How could they be so relaxed? The ongoing rolling thunder shook me to my very soul. As the storm continued to rage for the better part of an hour, I begged Mom and Dad to make it stop. They did nothing. The flashes of lightning did not bother me in the least. It was those damnable thunder booms that kept me on high alert. Sudden noises were now enemy #1. If you wanted to get my attention (and ire), go ahead and startle me.

Born in the USA

IN AMERICA, our national pastime is ... no, not licking my own rear end ... but, rather, baseball. I don't get the sport, I don't follow the sport, I could care less about the sport. For some reason, Mom and Dad really like the idea of visiting different ballparks. Dad is a Pittsburgh Pirate fan, through and through. Earlier in the summer (B.N. = Before Newman), they had gone to Boston to see a game at historic Fenway Park.

Mom and Dad had already made plans to go see Old Yankee Stadium for the first time within the first week after bringing home their wonderful, sweet boxer puppy. The team in pinstripes was up against the Los Angeles Angels. I didn't have the first clue about any of that. The only thing that mattered to me was that I got to spend time with someone new! Aunt Ally drove all the way from Rochester, New York, to our house in South Jersey to meet me and take care of me! She must be a Newman fan and we had never even met yet.

When it was time for Mom and Dad to head north to the Big Apple, I wished I was going with them, but I wasn't heartbroken that they left me with one of my aunts. She got right down to my level to play with me and focus on what I wanted and needed. Aunt Ally seemed like she and I were on the same wavelength right from the start. I liked to goof around and cause problems. She seemed to like her own brand of fun, too. Even when I did something wrong, she had a nice way of trying to get me to do the right thing ... or she let things go (shhh, don't tell Mom or Dad). And the treats?! She gave me a small ransom in treats over the course of the day. That's definitely a way to earn the title of "favorite aunt." I could tell that we were going to have a special bond. When Mom and Dad returned home from the Bronx, Aunt Ally had a hard time saying goodbye to me. We had a lot of fun! I would see her again, but it wouldn't be nearly as soon as either of us would like.

Aunt Ally and I had a blast together!

The next road trip Mom and Dad took was to Pittsburgh to meet Dad's parents to see his favorite team do battle. The responsible parents had to figure out what to do with their beloved puppy. They had heard about a kennel not far from home where I would get plenty of exercise, have my own private "run" that extended indoors and outdoors, and be around other dogs. It sounded like the best of all worlds for me, something that would deal with my hyperactivity and accommodate my thirst for companionship.

When we went to the kennel on a Saturday morning, Mom and Dad felt very unsure about leaving me in a strange setting with unfamiliar people and pets because I was their baby. Dad tried to give me a hug as he and Mom were about to depart. I was far too distracted by my new surroundings to pay any mind to either of my parents. I raced up and down the cement 25-foot run as countless dogs had their own separate lanes and joined in the fun. It was a puppy's delight to expend all this energy and have others who wanted to do the same.

After a brief 30-hour excursion, Mom and Dad arrived home in the Garden State to pick me up from the kennel. I was genuinely excited to see them, although there was one problem. Well, actually four significant problems. From countless trips up and down the cement run, the pads on the bottoms of each of my paws were no longer a dull brownish-pink. They were a flaming hot pink color and extremely tender and swollen. Mom and Dad were mortified by my condition. They vowed never to have me return to this kennel, or one similar to this. The cement was far too damaging for my delicate paws. I didn't have nearly enough self-control to limit how often I sprinted the length of the kennel.

Both parents carefully watched me on our trip home and the hours and days that followed. I had nothing to offer because I was purely exhausted. When I roused from sleep, which was seldom, I licked my paws with long, slow licks to try and heal the damage that I had unknowingly incurred by galloping miles at the kennel. The good news was that, after several days, my paws returned to their usual size and color with no permanent harm done.

❖ ON A RAINY SEPTEMBER afternoon just a few days later, Dad left work early with one of his friends (and fellow boxer owner) to watch a doubleheader with his Pirates visiting the Phillies just across the Delaware River in Philadelphia. What the hell is with all the baseball anyway?!

After evaluating the situation, I thought it might make sense to check out upstairs while only Mommom was around. She seemed to be the softer touch of the two. Dad was definitely more of a disciplinarian. As Mom busied herself with something in the kitchen, I got to thinking about those pesky stairs that led up to ... somewhere.

I had been taken upstairs before, but it was as an unwilling participant for a bath. On those occasions, I was carried and not permitted to roam freely. It was Mom and Dad's initial intent to keep me only downstairs. Upstairs was not for Newman, but why? So ... I made a break for it, climbing the first flight of steps to the landing between the first and second floors.

I inspected the area, but was tentative about going further up the last handful of steps. I heard my name being called, which caused me to look down to the first floor. "Newman, where are you?" I stared downstairs as Mommom came into view and I assessed her reaction. If this were Dad, I would be in deep shit. But, it's Mommom. She couldn't be that furious, could she? I raised my ears and cocked my head as she called my name once more and we locked eyes. I didn't budge.

She disappeared as I looked on quizzically. Was she getting something to use for punishment? Oh crap. This can't be good. She returned with a small, silver, hand-held item. I tried to figure out what this item was. No luck. She sat on the landing area next to me behind the silver box that had a clear opening. I focused my eyes on her until I heard multiple clicks and a flash of light that confounded me. I inched closer to get a better look. It didn't make sense—flashing light and clicks. I'm not a fan of the camera, but at least I didn't appear to be in a whole heap of trouble. Mom even jokingly said that she thought *she* might be in trouble. That was the first time that I kinda sorta went upstairs, but certainly not the last.

When Dad returned from watching Pittsburgh get shellacked by Philly in both games, Mommom told him the "news" that I had pressed the boundaries to include going partially up the stairs. While Mom wasn't exactly earning blue ribbons, Dad was not overly scolding of my ventures toward the upper living quarters of the house.

As days passed, my trips upstairs became more exploratory in nature. I found three bedrooms and two bathrooms. I happily sniffed each and every new square inch of the second floor. What's the big deal? Why can't I be up here? One thing I learned from this experience is that the passage of time, along with some maturing on my part had offered me more freedom and opportunity.

Mom and Dad relented to allow me to come upstairs anytime I wished although my crate, bed, food, water, toys, and worldly possessions remained on the first floor. I think that I just wore them down with each day of them being subjected to my cuteness.

Interstate Love Song

I'M NOT GOING TO LIE. I LOVE going for a ride in the car. Next to taking a walk, this may very well have been my favorite activity. Sometimes, we went on short errands. Other times, we ventured further. Our first long road trip was to see Aunt Ally and her steady boyfriend, Cody. It was an exciting time for us to make the nearly six-hour car ride to Rochester.

Mom and Dad loaded up seemingly all of my earthly belongings in the vehicle, including my crate. I didn't care; I was going for a ride. Put me in the crate. It's all good. I hopped into the back of Dad's car into the opening of the crate, looking out the windows. Oh boy, oh boy. Road trip!

By comparison, Mom and Dad loaded a small bag each for themselves and placed it next to my food, treats, leash, collar, gate, towels, toys, and crate with me in it. How do humans pack so compactly for themselves?

The drive through eastern Pennsylvania was fairly uneventful aside from the incessant jingling of my crate latches. It was extremely annoying to hear the non-stop clanging of metal on metal as Dad found bump after bump on Interstate 476 and Interstate 81. I crossed into the third state I had ever visited as we approached Binghamton, New York. Mom and Dad decided that it would be a good idea to stop at the approximate midpoint of our journey and allow me some time to stretch my legs, go potty, and possibly eat.

This situation was brand new to all of us. I saw this as an opportunity to become acquainted with a new area. After a few quick blasts of pee, I scoured the grounds at the rest stop to determine which canines had previously been in each spot. My parents kept after me to eat and to drink, but I wanted no part of sustenance. They gave up after nearly thirty minutes to get me settled back into my crate for the remainder of our trip.

This part of the journey was boooooring. On top of the annoyance of my jingling crate, the sun had dipped below the western horizon and the sky was now dark. There was no scenery to enjoy and very little traffic passing by any of the windows from which I could see. The car ride had become far less enjoyable than what I had envisioned at the outset of the trip.

I felt as though my parents deserved a different noise to round out the cacophony of latch clanking and bumps in the road: my barking. I glared at Dad and began to bark for the better part of an hour because I was done with this car ride. Mom and Dad took turns scolding me, then ignoring me. Neither strategy worked on me. I persisted in yelling at them until I decided that I had had enough. When we passed by the city of Corning, I gave up and lay down for a quick nap, although I wasn't very happy about being stuck in my crate until we arrived.

I awoke to the stop-and-go movement of more urban driving. Dad assured me that we were almost there, so I whined in anticipation of getting out. The car kept moving slower and slower as we approached our destination. That's when I felt it. Uh oh. All at once, my body convulsed as I felt a movement erupt from my stomach. This rumbling ended with the painful exit of something billowing out of my mouth. I barfed up a gigantic pile of stinky puke. Dear Lord, that was disgusting. My parents shined the internal car lamp to see what had happened. They looked on in horror at the sheer size of the vomit mound that was resting on one of my doggy blankets. Somehow, I had managed to throw up about two minutes before we pulled into Aunt Ally and Cody's driveway.

When our car mercifully came to a stop in the driveway and Dad shut off the engine, my eyes were crazed with anticipation. I steered clear of the barf pile and bounced back and forth expectantly, eager to be let out. Thankfully, I didn't get any of the mess on me—just on my crate and blanket. Dad harnessed me with the leash and collar as I jumped down to the ground from the car. I saw a guy approach us as we neared the house. Dad shook his hand as Mom started to unload the car. Dad said, "Newman, this is Cody." He got on the ground and greeted me by vigorously scratching my sides, ears, and belly. I licked his face when Dad warned Cody that I had just thrown up. He didn't seem to mind and continued to play with me.

Cody then helped Dad clean up my mess. What a guy to jump right in and deal with dog barf after meeting me only moments before! Mommom grabbed the leash from Dad and we jetted over to the back door. I had a singular goal in mind: get inside to see Aunt Ally. The hardwood steps were very slippery, or maybe that had something to do with my lack of self-control. I flopped down a few times trying to get up the stairs to find my aunt, but find her I did.

I was excited to see the familiar face of Aunt Ally, who greeted me and allowed me to bounce and jump around in excitement at her waist to try and get closer to her face. Needless to say my intestinal malaise was in the rearview mirror and fading quickly.

I tried to become acquainted with the unfamiliar surroundings as Mom and Dad begged me to finally eat a meal. After getting settled in my digs for the weekend, I still refused to eat until Cody came up with the ingenious idea to coat my kernels of food with peanut butter. What a delicious combination! We would have to remember that for future reference.

I scoped out the scene and showed off my newfound size to Aunt Ally and Cody. They let me have the run of the house, which only endeared them to me even more. Because we had arrived after such a long drive, I only had a short period of time to enjoy their company before bedtime. As usual, I was crate-bound for the night and had my own room. However, I could hear all sorts of subtle, yet foreign noises throughout the night. It put me on edge, so I would whine and paw at the cage. I persisted for minutes and was ignored. It was a fitful period of sleep and at uneven intervals throughout the wee hours of the night. I made noise in the hopes of being let out of the crate. A few times, Dad came to visit me in a vain attempt to keep me quiet. He failed to understand that I was frustrated to be in an unfamiliar environment.

Very early the following morning, Dad took me for a long walk. It was nice to be free and see the brightness of a new day. When we returned, the house had come to life with all the other people awakening. What I hadn't realized was that the majority of Mommom's family was descending on Aunt Ally and Cody's residence. So, Aunt Lindsay, Grandma, and Grandpa all arrived at Aunt Ally and Cody's place for a quick weekend visit. Uncle Adam could not be there because he was serving our country in the Middle East.

Dad, Mom, Aunt Ally, and Cody took turns taking me

outside to enjoy the brisk, yet very sunny late fall weekend. I must have walked more than a few miles that Saturday despite refusing to eat my regular complement of puppy chow. Something told me that the grown-ups were trying to tire me out so that I slept better that night. However, in my mind, what mattered was that there were more people staying in the house. As such, it made sense to me that there would be more options available to help me exit the crate during the night. I was more adamant with my serenades to awaken SOMEbody! For the most part, I was left to my own devices, with only one visit each from Mom and Dad to beckon me and practically beg me to go to sleep. That didn't mean that I kept the noise to a minimum. I was furious with the sleeping situation and I wanted the whole world to know it.

Dad looked positively dead to the world the next morning when we went for a morning stroll with Cody. The walk renewed my energy although my appetite was still lacking. I refused to eat, even though we had slathered my food with more peanut butter. What my parents failed to comprehend was that I was finicky about my habits. We had just traveled all this way to a place I'd never been. It's not that I wanted to go home, but I just felt out of sorts.

After the humans dined on their breakfast and lunch, we took a few family pictures before preparing to depart for home. Each posed photograph was a new adventure, a different set of people who were standing still and smiling. I chose to harass one of the featured participants with each click of the camera. My exuberance may have added a little extra time, but everyone seemed to take my interruptions in stride.

The crate may have been jingling on the way home, but I failed to notice because I slept for the overwhelming majority of the six-hour ride to our home. No potty break was required on our return to New Jersey. I know I made a new friend during this journey.

That Cody guy is ok in my book.

❖ LATER IN THE FALL, we made another lengthy road trip to northwestern Pennsylvania to visit Dad's parents. Once we got past the initial hustle and bustle of the Philadelphia metropolitan area, the remainder of the nearly seven-hour journey was another snoozefest. We stopped about the midpoint of our ride, which was in the college town of Bloomsburg in central Pennsylvania. I needed to relieve myself and relieve some of my pent-up energy. Mom and Dad offered me far less time to take care of business, which truthfully was fine. I didn't need it and wasn't enthused about inspecting the grounds of a gas station.

The cage rattled far less on this venture thanks to some

strategically positioned duct tape covering the latches that otherwise would have driven us all nuts. Interstate driving presented very little to see and I slumbered for the final few hours before we arrived.

When the speed of the car decelerated, I sensed correctly that we were getting close. Dad turned the car into a driveway and I stood up and peered out into the darkness of my surroundings. I shook, which caused my ears to flap noisily. Good news: I didn't barf! My body was seemingly adjusting to car rides.

Dad peeled the duct tape off the latches and freed me from the crate before quickly attaching my leash and collar. I jumped down to the ground and paid no attention to the yard in an effort to get to the door. I could see people waiting to greet us. The door was opened and I spastically sniffed and licked these two new people as they tried to pet me. This proved difficult, given my energy level. I don't know if it was being cramped in a car for most of the night, or if it could be attributed to puppyhood, but I was all lathered up and ready to go.

I sprinted from room to room to see if there were any more people, pets, or perhaps anything else of interest. It didn't take long for me to go through the house to find that Dad's parents were the only ones here, aside from us. Nevertheless, I ran and ran and ran from one end of the house to the other. After two minutes of non-stop action, Dad picked me up and lay down on the floor, holding me tightly to him. He put my head on his chest as my body covered his torso, while my hind legs flailed helplessly below Dad's waist. Dad was quietly begging me to calm down; I think he was concerned that my behavior was too overwhelming for Grandma and Grandpa.

Dad's parents had been dog owners years before; however, their dogs were not house pets like me. So, this was uncharted territory for them, too. Dad released his grip on me and I walked out to the dining room, where I recalled seeing a dish full of water. My sprinting fits had left my tongue dangling inches beyond my lower lip; I ingested several ounces of fresh water to quench my sudden thirst.

I was cooped up in a crate, in a car for nearly seven hours. You had to expect that I had some energy to burn! I could not stop, let alone control my need to exert myself. Mom and Dad decided to just let me go, let me get this lunacy out of my system. I would grab a toy and play with it, then drop it at someone's feet, begging for him or her to play fetch with me. This persisted for the better part of an hour before lethargy finally began to hit me.

Dad set up my crate in one of the bedrooms and I knew what that meant. I had exactly zero interest in sleeping, especially in these new, unfamiliar surroundings. It was well after midnight, but I had slept for hours in the car, so I was far from tired. Grandma and Grandpa bid me good night and went to their bedroom. Mom and Dad also were ready for bed, so they prompted me to take my usual ritual of actually entering the crate for a nightly slumber. It didn't take long for me to start with the whining and barking to beg, plead, and make my best appeal to be let out of the crate.

Despite Mom and Dad's best effort to ignore my pleas, persistence finally paid off. Dad wearily greeted me. He did not appear to be happy. He told me in no uncertain terms that I needed to stop barking and be quiet. I was not granted the freedom that I desired. So, as soon as Dad left the room, I renewed my complaints with more vigor and volume. He didn't get it. I just wanted to have more room to maneuver. I had indeed become very tired, but I was growing weary of the crate. Off and on throughout the night, I voiced my concerns. These were met with silence or harsh rebukes, neither of which suited my needs whatsoever.

The next day, Dad and Grandpa took me on a nice, long walk. While we ambled, I investigated the new environment. There was a lot more wildlife around here: turkeys, deer, woodchucks, raccoons, and more. I didn't get to see any of those animals on this voyage, but my snout could pick up that their scent was nearby. While on our mile-long jaunt, seeing two churches sparked my curiosity. In each case, I walked right up to the main entrance and wanted to check them out more thoroughly. Dad conjectured that I wanted to confess my many sins and hopefully repent from my sinful ways. Nah, I just wanted a new place to examine.

The following night's sleep was once again restless. I was slightly less boisterous, but I chose to speak my mind a few times about the sleeping situation. All I wanted was to be co-located with my people, and have some room to roam. Was that too much to ask for an ill-mannered but well-meaning puppy? Apparently so.

Disarm

AS A SIX-MONTH OLD, my weight had increased to 45 pounds. I was all muscle, bones ... and gas. I was a vibrant, feisty dog that could not hold a thought in my head. I would still bounce rapid-fire from one of my interests to another, with no outward ability to focus on anything for more than a few seconds. The difference between our first days together and now was about 25 pounds of girth and length, along with an increasingly ambivalent mindset toward listening. Long gone were the days of being a runt. I was a solid, overgrown puppy who could no longer be babied because of my size. Quite honestly, I actually needed an outlet for my physical needs. One such need was a growing frustration of being a male puppy without a female puppy ... if you catch my drift.

To compensate, I began a nearly daily ritual of wadding up my thin, rectangular dog bed so that it stood vertically. In such a position, the dog bed was at the ideal height so that it could be used for "frictional" purposes. I stood with my hind legs straddling the bed, as the top of the bed was just below my undercarriage.

Mommom had no issue with this endeavor whereas Dad wanted me to get it out of my system, post haste. He often tried to set a limit on the time that I was able to pursue a "solution." Dad would give me five or ten minutes and avert his eyes in hopes that I would be done within his absurd time constraint. I wonder if he also adhered to such a draconian discipline. Perhaps Mommom kept him in line in a similar fashion.

My bouts of restless energy became more sustained in nature as I grew into my body and strengthened with additional muscle tone. As such, I noticed that Mom had become intimidated of my newfound strength. She was rarely the one holding the leash as we went for our daily walks for fear of being pulled along without the ability to control the direction or pace of our stroll. While she willingly continued throwing toys to play with me, she was far more passive than Dad. He would playfully wrestle with me and slap my paws, ears, and sides to mess with me. Dad even let me gnaw gently on his hands from time to time. I was very tentative with my teeth on him because ... well, he was my Dad, and I think he could kick my ass.

Dad also grabbed my jowls, which I despise. I turned my head to show my annoyance. In turn, he relinquished his grip. When I tried to mouth Dad after retaining control of my jowls, it made a sound similar to the puckering of a Tupperware container. Dad threatened to make a ringtone of the noise.

My parents both loved me in very different ways. Mom was sweet and comforting, often giving me the benefit of the doubt even in times when I likely did not deserve such kindness. Dad's willingness to play rough with me gave him an extra gold star in my book. I needed a playmate. Last time I checked, I didn't see any other canines around here upon whom to expend my puppy power. So, Dad would have to do.

He even kneeled on the ground and put toys up on his back for me to retrieve. Most times, I would just grab the toy and jump back down. Other times, I was of the opinion that Dad needed a little more. I was more than willing to get too rough. Occasionally, I might grip his shirt or his hair between my teeth. It was usually about this time that my playfulness overstepped that mystifying boundary between frisky and too violent. At such times, I would get scolded and occasionally Mommom would have to intervene to save Dad. Haha ... wimp.

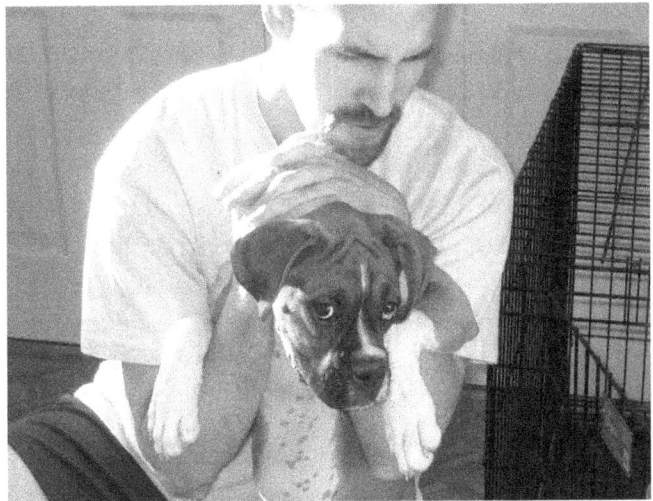

Why the full nelson, Dad?

One of Dad's favorite moves on me was to get me in a full nelson. I always knew it was coming when he circled behind me as we were playing rough. In my youth, I could never figure out how to avoid this predicament. After he locked his hands in place on the back of my neck, I was 100 percent helpless. I would declare "mercy" by allowing my body and paws to go limp. Thankfully, Dad recognized this for what it was and would release me from his death grip. These were the days when I began to presume that all males liked to play rough. Dad did it and Cody seemed genuinely ok with roughhousing, so every other guy did, too, right? Mom disliked this type of play immensely, so that must be correct.

❖ I HAD SEVERAL HABITS that irked my parents. They weren't bad if you asked me. These idiosyncrasies were who I was. When the notion to do something entered my brain, I simply acted on that impulse.

For example, I liked to accompany both of my parents as they moved about inside the house. No big deal, right? One thing I enjoyed doing was walking alongside Mommom as she traversed up and down the stairs. Perfectly acceptable behavior, wouldn't you agree? Well ... in addition to that, I thought it was the greatest thing ever to grab onto one of her pant legs with my teeth and tug on it. Are we still on board with that? Mom usually stopped dead in her tracks to try and get me to relinquish my grip on her clothes. That's her perspective. I would rather shake her pants because it was a ton of fun, especially on the stairs between the first and second floors of our house. I never grabbed onto her leg, bare skin, or anything like that—only her pants. I never considered attempting this with Dad. I saved this for Mom as her special treat.

Dad was concerned that I viewed Mommom as more of an equal than that of a respected parent. The only difference to me between Mom and Dad was an increased level of fear that I felt for the male of the house. Was fear equal to respect? I don't know. I knew that I was more worried about pleasing him than I was her. Dad was definitely the alpha male in my eyes. I wasn't the alpha, but was Mom? Hmm ... I wasn't totally sure. I liked to believe that I was at least middle management, and she was my subordinate.

Master of Puppets

NOT COINCIDENTALLY, Mom and Dad began discussing whether I should attend obedience training. There was a fall session at our local PetSmart store that offered basic commands and socialization with other dogs. Because I wasn't around other dogs on a consistent basis, this would be a great opportunity to see how I reacted.

All that Mom or Dad had to do was to mention a car ride, and I was raring to go. We pulled into the parking lot and I looked excitedly from car to car, store to store, person to person. Oh boy! Where are we?! We walked into the store. Let me tell you something, this was heaven here on earth. I could smell a billion dogs and I could actually *see* several dogs leashed by their humans. I tried to sprint in five different directions all at once. Dad shortened the leash too much for my taste as he struggled to maintain control of where we went within the store. I wanted to meet and greet each and every one of the dogs. The slippery surface of the flooring was not conducive to staying upright, especially with my desire to dash combined with Mom and Dad's preference for me to remain close.

We walked through several aisles. I was hoping to encounter several dogs while my parents were more optimistic for the serenity of vacant space. When we turned the corner to a new aisle, my eyes would dart quickly to see who was there to welcome me. Sometimes I got my wish, sometimes the humans got theirs. I was frantic if I got to be within inches of one of my brethren. I was simultaneously curious, excited, and crazed. This was sometimes met with hostility from older dogs. With younger canines, it was a frothy mess as the two of us circled and the humans tried with little success to keep our leashes untangled. Needless to say, I needed further socialization. I wanted to be around my own kind, my own species. However, I required exposure to situations around other dogs who could handle my puppy behavior.

Mom and Dad had tactfully arrived several minutes early to allow for these preliminary distractions to occur before the training sessions were scheduled to commence. After making our way to the training area, we saw three other pooches: a mutt named Romeo that resembled a small wolf, a Boston terrier named Guinness, and a pug named Sapphire. These pups were tiny! I eagerly greeted each of them with my characteristic "in your face" lack of tact. Guinness was all bark and absolutely no bite. When I confronted him, he backed away and his owner seemed very nervous and protective of his little guy. Mom and Dad took the owner's cue and we kept to our own space. Romeo liked to think that he was all big and bad … until he saw me. We played and pounced around a bit. He was a fun-loving pup, although he didn't like how dominating and imposing I was, compared to him. Then, there was Sapphire. She seemed like a sweet girl, but had very little personality. She was not the least bit curious about me. What was that about?! I sniffed her from head to toe and wanted to play. Sapphire wanted to go lie down, which was very much atypical for her breed.

It was official: I was the class bully. I was bigger than

everyone by a wide margin. I was more aggressive and more curious than my classmates, too. Mom and Dad knew that it was going to be a challenge to get through the training, but also to maintain some semblance of focus with the overall wallflower mentality that the rest of the class employed. I desperately desired to interact with the other dogs.

The young woman who led the training session, Cara, talked briefly about the expectations for the course. Mom and Dad listened attentively while I pondered how to get off the leash and visit my fellow enrollees. She explained that a dog's obedience to his owner's commands would be developed based on his ability to focus on the owner while other diversions were present. Many puppies could not be expected to listen without having proper motivation. This was normal, and each owner should try to find an appropriate method to stimulate his or her dog to listen. Older dogs that have been trained would be able to follow commands through repetition, improved focus, and maturity. But, we puppies would require a little incentive to pique our interest in listening. She subscribed to the theory that owners would benefit from offering a small treat while doing introductory training.

Cara asked Sapphire's owners to relinquish the leash. As they did, Sapphire pitter-pattered across the floor to an open spot in the training area. I thought, "Oh boy ... a new victim." The trainer placed Sapphire in a sitting position. She willingly obliged. My focus drifted from the pug to Romeo, who was barking at something well outside the fenced-in area. Sapphire was fed a morsel of a treat, and then sat still as a stone. The trainer walked about fifteen feet away and held up her hand to halt Sapphire. The pug not only remained still, but she began to yawn and nearly fell asleep. She positioned her body as if she were going to lie down. Sapphire was not paying attention when the trainer called her name until a loud "Come" command jolted her back to reality. Cara waved the treat to finally rouse the lone female puppy in class. Mom and Dad were amazed because pug puppies are typically energetic, not lethargic. Sapphire slowly tapped her little paws over to the trainer to receive her treat for a job well done. Meanwhile, throughout this lesson, my attention rarely diverted from Romeo, wondering what was holding his interest elsewhere.

The trainer said that each of the owners should drop their leashes and mimic the same routine that Sapphire successfully completed. Dad reluctantly released the restraint, and I immediately made a beeline for Romeo to play. Despite ongoing reprimands and rapidly approaching footsteps, I chose to instigate the thick-coated male to playfully wrestle. Mom and Dad hurriedly grabbed my leash to guide me away from Romeo back to the solitude of my corner of the pen.

Mom and Dad subsequently tried to train me in a slightly different manner. Mommom did not hold the leash, but instead, she stood on the leash while Dad tried to put me in a "sit, stay" position. He held a treat over my head and put it so far back from my line of vision that I had no choice but to sit. Mom and Dad fed me the tiny treat that I inhaled without chewing. They praised me and told me to stay. I promptly stood up and lunged in the general direction of Romeo, ready to once more wreak havoc on the training session. Unfortunately, Mommom was standing on my leash, which halted my progress abruptly.

We repeated ... or should I say *attempted* the training multiple times. At first, I would take the treat after being tricked into sitting. While either Mom or Dad was walking away, making direct eye contact with me with their hand held high to halt, my attention drifted to something more important, which was anything but Mom or Dad. The training simply was not my focus. I was so disinterested in the true purpose for our visit to PetSmart that I began to refuse to take the treat. I was progressively more intrigued by the comings and goings of others. Mom and Dad were visibly frustrated that I could not focus for even a cursory command or two. With our collective nub of a tail between our legs, we headed for home. I felt no such remorse for my performance. We had five more weeks to improve. The following few sessions showed the smallest glimmer of hope to my parents. I continued to have difficulty focusing on anything in the training area. My thoughts and gaze often identified items of interest outside of our area.

When I was looking within the fenced area, it was often done so with intent to play, and nothing related to the class itself. It got to the point where a mesh fence was erected in the training area to seclude me from the rest of the class. I guess this method of training was only for the most *special* of dogs.

The other dogs were not getting a fair shake at completing the training with my spazzy dynamic in play. As I peered through the openings in the fence at the rest of the class, I realized that I could not directly interact with anyone other than Mom or Dad. How unbelievably infuriating! The "call to come" commands were issued again and again. When isolated, no one had to restrain my leash, because I could not get to my desired destination. Ever so slowly, I could obey the command to come. Although it was a small step, the order was being ingrained in me. However, it was only possible when I was not otherwise preoccupied.

Without realizing it, sitting on command had become second nature. In early training sessions, a treat in the hand was required. By week three or four, one of my owner's hands drifting overhead prompted my rump to hit the smooth cement flooring. There were occasions when I received my just due: a treat, of course! Other times, I merely got a pat on the head or scratch of the ears. I was still hopeful on each occasion, but I could never discern whether those pesky parents had something for me to ingest. I had to sit ... just in case.

Mom and Dad were gradually working themselves further away from me and lifting their hand. If my eyes weren't furtively darting elsewhere, I found myself slowly alternating light stomps of my front paws and finding a comfortable location for my back side to drop to the ground. The word "sit" was being associated with the hand gesture. There was a lot going on: words, hand motions, expectations. It was substantially easier to just ignore it all and do what I wanted. However, when my fleeting attention could be captured, I felt a desire to actually please both Mom and Dad.

Cara could tell that we had focus and socialization issues based on nearly a month's worth of training sessions. She invited Mom and Dad to spend some time outside class with her four-year-old female black lab. Cara saw that we were making the effort without seeing the full extent of the desired results. She felt that we could benefit from the calming influence of an older dog who would not tolerate the crap that a five-month-old boxer pup would dole out.

Mom and Dad were overwhelmed by Cara's gracious offer, and readily accepted with no hesitation. They saw this as an opportunity for me to mature; I saw it as another car ride to PetSmart. Win-win.

On a Saturday afternoon, we made the now familiar journey to the pet store. I still Scooby-Doo'ed[3] it when I met other dogs as we strolled around the store. We

---

[3] "Scooby-Dooing" is a term that Dad coined to describe my repeated attempts to approach other dogs (or anything) while I was on a smooth surface. It was difficult for me to get my feet to cooperate with my brain's intentions. If you've seen the Scooby-Doo cartoon, it often took the Great Dane a few seconds of running in place before breaking into a sprint. Oftentimes, that was me: paws scrambling wildly before finding traction to run.

approached the training area where a class was just completing its weekly lesson. There was no Romeo, no Sapphire, and no Guinness. Five new puppies were departing the fenced-in area. I was beyond eager to make my introductions to each of the new faces (and asses). However, all the puppies in training departed as their class time had come to a close. There was a silver lining; I noticed that Cara's lab remained inside the fence. Cara welcomed me and invited Mom and Dad to drop my leash as I entered the pen.

I eagerly approached the much larger female and sniffed her from snout to tail. She was also curious about me, but had a much more composed vibe. I bounced back and forth in a playful way. Most puppies reacted to my intensity by panicking. Not my new lab friend. She was a mature woman who could handle me. She placed a heavy front paw on my back to let me know my place. I would scamper away and then return. This was a fun game!

I expended a ton of my limitless energy as I yo-yoed between the black lab and a random spot several strides away. We repeated this "dance" many times for about twenty minutes until I relented a bit because I was beginning to tire. I was dying of thirst, so instead of jockeying back and forth, I followed her around as she loped about aimlessly. Every once in a while, I would paw at her and she returned the favor. The mood had become much calmer as the lab waited for me to act a bit more pacified. Mom and Dad looked on in amazement. If given enough time and another dog that exerted a calming influence, I could actually *settle down*. We parted ways with the promise to return for more fun ... er, I mean, socialization.

We continued our regular training sessions, along with the extra time to interact with Cara's pooch. One conspicuous absence during the last few classes was Romeo. He and his humans stopped attending obedience training for some reason. I don't think that I could be blamed because his humans seemed generally ok with me. I missed having another reasonably-sized pooch in class. I suppose that the other two snack-sized dogs would have to do.

I still needed to be segregated from my two classmates since I was too disruptive in the group setting. It was all or nothing with me. I had surprisingly begun to listen quite well when isolated. The flip side of that was that I could not hear a word that was uttered if there was any sort of distraction.

We employed an interesting technique in the penultimate obedience class. Each family was given our own aisle in the store to work on various commands. Mom and Dad stood at opposite ends of the lane with me between them. Mom called my name to get my attention. The hope was for me to hear her voice and make eye contact. At first, I did indeed hear, "Newman," and looked right at Mommom. I plodded over to her before the come command was issued. You know what they say about young guys: always a little premature. I delightfully accepted the treat despite messing up the timing. Once I was at Mom's side, I tried to peer behind her to determine if there was anything else that I could observe. Anything aside from this training would suffice.

Dad called my name in a terse tone, to which my ears twitched, but I did not turn to acknowledge him. Yes, I heard him. I simply didn't care. There was so much more that I was hoping would captivate my attention. Even if there was nothing present, I anticipated finding something more intriguing than Dad's silly attempt at getting my interest. He repeated my name once again in a more soothing voice with a promise of a treat. Hmmm ... still not interested. My attention span was shot, kaput, bupkis. I needed out of the aisle to see what waited beyond.

Mom and Dad dutifully trudged through multiple issuances of different commands. I tuned them out entirely. Dad asked Cara what to do with a stubborn dog like me. She reiterated that my parents needed to capture my interest. They had to make me want to listen with positive reinforcement. Make me want to do the training to get the end result. Elongate my attention span to make the training have a purpose for me. Day by day, week by week, Mom and Dad should see a subtle improvement in my focus. It wasn't going to happen overnight, as they had hoped but undoubtedly not expected.

Cara suggested that they should do brief spurts of command work at different times throughout the day to follow up on moments where I would be listening. See how I responded in those occasions. Then, mix it up with other times where I was distracted to reinforce that I needed to heed my masters' commands at all times, not only when it was convenient for me to do so. We needed to have positive training moments upon which to build, not only to do more advanced training, but to enhance the relationship between masters and dog. We had to trust and respect each other more to foster my desire to please Mom and Dad into second nature.

Mom and Dad were aggravated because they felt as though I was a puppy who was never going to listen to them. We had one more class, where the three of us canines would be evaluated and hopefully "graduate." Mom and Dad were skeptical; I was apathetic about the whole deal.

When Mom, Dad, and I arrived at PetSmart for the sixth and final Monday in our training series, we entered the familiar training area for the last time in a classroom setting. It was business as usual for me. I was a crazy bundle of energy, enthusiasm, and excitability that was far more interested in inciting Guinness and Sapphire to behave more like me. My parents were nervous; not concerned that I would misbehave, for they had become accustomed to that. Rather, they wondered if I would be the first dog in history who flunked the final exam.

The preliminary hyper shenanigans subsided and each dog retreated to his or her own area of the pen. Cara then welcomed us to the final class and the test that would determine if we graduated or not. She explained the series of commands that we would each perform: sit, stay, come, down, among some other general scenarios that we were to follow. Cara asked if there were any volunteers to go first. Dad shrugged his shoulders and raised his hand. We were going *first*? Mom and Dad surmised that I would do better with less time for distractions.

The three of us moved to the center of the fenced-in area. The trainer told Mom and Dad the order of how she wanted to proceed through the test. Cara advised that one of my caregivers should hold my leash loosely, given my preference for anything other than training. So, Mom controlled me with the leash as Dad began the command work. From about twenty feet away, he raised his closed hand upward pointing to the ceiling and said, "Sit," shortly thereafter. He came toward me and smiled as he rewarded me with a small morsel of a chewy treat.

Dad then placed his hand up with his palm facing me and urged me to "stay." The goal was to remain seated for approximately thirty seconds. After ten to fifteen seconds, I got antsy. As my rear end was lifting off the ground prematurely, Dad hurriedly told me to "come." My attention was about to go elsewhere. Instead, I made my way toward Dad, with Mommom in tow. I wouldn't call it a straight line, maybe more of an arc. My humans were very excited that I had done as well as I had.

I inhaled a few meaty treats, and then Mom had me sit down. My focus was starting to waver, and everyone knew it. Mommom told me, "Down," with the accompanying hand motion with her palm pointing toward the floor, in a downward motion. I jostled my head out of the way defiantly. I didn't really want to lie down. She repeated the command and motion once more, this time with additional emphasis and her hand was considerably closer to my head. I begrudgingly obliged and lay down, but only for an instant before rising. I was done. It had only been three or four minutes, but I could not be expected to follow any more commands.

Guinness, with his eyes looking as though they were going to bulge out of either side of his head, readily accomplished his test and looked to be the valedictorian. Sapphire the sleepyhead also had little trouble in mastering her requirements, although she had to be prompted to actually move off her lazy butt more than once. What would you rather have, a smarty pants, a lazy dog, or lovable, energetic me? That's what I thought.

Cara passed out the graduation caps and diplomas. You know what? I did it! I guess I should have been proud of my achievement. I was certainly worked up and bouncing around because of the energy that Mom and Dad offered via vigorous praise. They were evidently proud that I managed to muddle my way through and pass the class. I couldn't sit still long enough to get a picture with the cap on my head, but that's beside the point. I was a graduate.

Even though I graduated, I needed more socialization. As such, Mom and Dad continued taking me to PetSmart on most weekends to visit Cara's black lab. We were pretty friendly toward each other. Each time we got together, I got used to what was acceptable behavior versus what was unacceptable in a more mature dog's eyes.

Cara had recommended that I use a device that's called a Gentle Leader. This training tool attaches to my collar and loops over my nose to prevent me from pulling my humans when I walk. In essence, the Gentle Leader prevents my full-body lunges from guiding where we walk. Whoever happens to be holding the leash is in complete control of direction and speed of our excursion. Let's say that I wanted to chase a squirrel that I see out of the corner of my eye. If I start to pounce in that direction, Mom or Dad could simply give a quick, effortless tug on the leash, and the strength of my neck, shoulders, and chest would be rendered useless when attempting to pull my humans in a certain direction. I would be halted in my tracks. To add further insult, depending on the torque of my attempted pull, I could even have my face and neck harmlessly turned 180 degrees to face my master instead of looking at the object of my desire.

We tried placing the awful Gentle Leader on my face and around my neck. Mom and Dad needed to be guided through how to place the proper loop over my nose. The extra time it took them to figure out how to operate the device gave me adequate time to determine that I was not going to like this additional restraint one bit!

Once they got the strap clicked into place, I immediately began the process of trying to detach this contraption. It was embarrassing to have such a restriction placed on me. I placed my butt way up in the air and positioned my nose on the ground, while trying to utilize my front paws to forcibly slide the harness off my face. I writhed all over the floor, wanting desperately to be free of this newfound punishment. This was awful! It was bad enough that I could not be trusted to walk leashless, but now I had even less of a say as to where I could go, who I sniffed, and what I could see. Ugh. The icing on the cake was seeing Mom or Dad give gushing gratitude to Cara for the tip on purchasing a Gentle Leader. I had a terrible feeling that my training tool would be sticking around for the foreseeable future.

Somebody to Love

ONE WEEKEND, our trip to PetSmart was more of a puppy play session. There were several of us frolicking about the play area: a few males and a couple females. I noticed a young female pooch with a white soft coat and light brown markings. I never caught her name because she was rather shy. She was fairly meek and mild; the perfect companion to my alpha and nutso. We spent the time sniffing each other, playing with other dogs, but we would always come back to one another. After about twenty-five minutes, I made a return visit. I did what I suspect any hot-blooded male dog with a similarly aged female dog would do: I mounted her. After about three thrusts, I was aggressively pulled off her back by guess who? Dad. Her owner rushed over to her rescue as well. Dad and he conversed, asking if either she or I were "fixed." Both of them sheepishly shook their heads. Dad apologized profusely for my actions. He should be apologizing *to me* ... and my new friend. I didn't get to finish.

We kept coming to puppy play time for the next few weeks to help me socialize with other dogs until the store made a determination to suspend the sessions (no, the company's decision was not based on my attempted sexual indiscretions). The rationale behind this decision was caused by some complaints regarding overaggressive dogs. It's a shame that these bad apples spoiled an otherwise great opportunity for dogs to mix and mingle.

My socialization was certainly still a work in progress. I thoroughly enjoyed having fun. Others may view it as hyperactivity; I saw it as loving life. As we walked throughout our neighborhood development, we often saw two greyhounds with their human. One night, we got close enough to officially meet. I was my typical ebullient self—sniffing, licking, and pouncing—to introduce myself. "Hey, I'm Newman. What are you guys?" Nothing, nada. They stood very still and barely acknowledged my presence. "What the hell, guys? Come on, give me something!" Zero, zilch. Their human gave Dad a holier than thou five-minute diatribe on how to properly socialize your dog. He went on and on and on with pointers on how to get a dog to appropriately interact with other dogs. Dad was incensed, and could not wait for us to get away from this guy. Not because of my silly behavior. No, because he was infuriated with the man.

As we walked away, Dad was grumbling. I felt a vibe of contempt emanating from him, and I was thankful that his disdain was, for once, not directed toward me. Dad asked me, "Do you want to grow up to be a statue?" I cocked my head to try and take in and make sense of his words. A statue? What in the world is that? He had a very one-sided conversation with me about growing up and letting my personality shine through. If he wanted a dog that had no personality, he would listen to the man's advice on how he socialized his dogs. He petted my head a few times and seemed grateful that I was his companion, not the dogs that would forever be known as the statues.

We encountered these dogs a few more times and all parties involved exhibited the same behavior on each occasion. I was adorable with personality and vitality, which anyone could see just by looking into my animated eyes. My ears even emoted how I felt about things: ears up (curious and anticipatory), one up and one down (confused), both ears way back (in trouble), dangling normally (happy and satisfied), one or both ears folded (a hot mess). The greyhounds were dull and dreary with minimal signs of life. Someone should check them both for a pulse. I would, but I was not permitted to get close enough to see if they were breathing.

More often than not, Mom and Dad were reminded by the other human about socialization pointers. There was never a verbal or physical conflict, but it was certainly brimming beneath the surface. It got to the point where we avoided taking a walk at the same time as the statues. Dad was not a fan of repeatedly being told how to raise his dog. I was not a fan of getting no response to repeated attempts at *actually* socializing. Jerks.

It wasn't only in our presence where these supposedly well-socialized dogs behaved this way. We witnessed them at a few of our neighbors' houses when the humans would chat in their driveways. The hounds would just stand still as statues while the conversation lasted. It could have been seconds or minutes, it didn't matter. They appeared as though they were posing for a still life portrait. I, on the other hand, would make an artist dizzy and potentially nauseous if he were to try and capture my still for a canvas.

❖ EVERY ONCE IN A WHILE, Dad would get together with some of his buddies from work to play cards. They played different poker games, rarely for any amount more than a few dollars. They just enjoyed hanging out and letting loose, as opposed to gambling in hopes of winning any serious money. I had not yet been privy to witness such an evening with the boys until Dad took a turn to host the event. The snacks were out, the beer was chilling, and the house was cleaned. Mommom intended to greet each of the guests, but then she wanted to let the boys be boys while she watched the tube upstairs.

The guys started showing up in the early evening hours. I was brimming with exuberance as each knock or doorbell ring announced the arrival of one of Dad's friends. A few of the guys had arrived and were chitchatting in the living room while they awaited the last two guys to show. I quickly recognized that each of his friends was male, so I prompted each of them to play roughly with me. Some guys took the bait while others were a little more passive. They were all dog guys and certainly received a passing grade from me.

Then, Dad's friend Chris, stepped into the house. His boxer, Zeus, was one of the primary reasons that my parents had chosen my breed. Although Zeus wasn't present, I detected his scent immediately. I didn't pick up that Chris carried the odor of my breed. Don't be silly! Breeds don't have their own unique aroma, at least not that I could discern. I just snouted that he had been in contact with another canine. That was enough to warrant Chris receiving some *extra special* attention. He hunched over and willingly accepted my frenetic nosing and licking. He was talking "puppy" to me. "Oh, how's Newman? How's the big boy?" I ate this up and gave Chris a unique treat. As he bent forward to continue talking with me, I unexpectedly jumped straight up in the air with all my might to get at his face. I got all four off the floor by springing more than twelve inches into the air. Chris instinctively latched his arms around me and held me close to his waist. I tongued his face and ears voraciously as he comfortably clasped my body against his torso. It's as though he had experience with boxer puppies or something.

The guys erupted in laughter and Dad could only manage to shake his head in disbelief. He tried to apologize to Chris, who shrugged it off as though it was an everyday occurrence. One of the other guys, Tim, had one of those silent laughs where he didn't make noise and simultaneously could not breathe. Instead, his entire head was red, bordering on the verge of turning purple. After I had bathed Chris in saliva, he set me down on the floor and I had to get a drink of water. Chris likely could have used a shower.

❖ MY LEAPING EXPLOITS were not constrained to just one occasion. No, no ... I showed them off with regularity. I simply could not contain my boundless enthusiasm. What can I say? I am a people dog, in the same way that some of you humans are dog people. Some springs off the floor were more impressive than others. This next little nugget takes the taco.

Mom, Dad, Grandma Diane, and Aunt Lindsay had gone out to dinner on a Friday evening after our out-of-town guests had arrived. As was often the case, I was sequestered to my crate in the kitchen while they were gone. My typical puppy energy would often hit a fever pitch in the moments after being released from hours of crated captivity. Let's add in a sprinkle of fresh meat (I mean out-of-town family) and you have a lethal combination. When the crew returned home to me, I was beyond raring to go.

Mommom unlatched the crate and I sprinted to acknowledge everyone's successful return to the house. First up was Grandma. She desired to keep me at arm's length, but I was moving far too quickly for any of that. I hurtled my body vertically into the air and greeted her by jamming my two front paws directly to her chest with the equivalent of a kangaroo two-handed punch. Grandma was not ready for the full force of the Newman. She immediately lost her balance and started to topple.

Grandma's lower body leaned against the armrest of our couch. As her body began to tilt at an angle less and less vertical by the moment, it became evident that she was going to fall and there was nothing that anybody could do in time to prevent it. Both Dad and Aunt Lindsay were too far away (and too shocked) to make a saving effort to catch her. Mommom was in the kitchen and was far removed from the incident. The saving grace was that Grandma's body was perfectly aligned to land on the couch. She would mercifully miss hitting the floor and the oak coffee table. In a matter of two seconds from the impact of my paws, Grandma was horizontal on the couch with her legs dangling off the armrest. Dad reacted first by asking Grandma if she was all right. She claimed that she was indeed okay, albeit utterly shocked by what had just transpired.

Dad relayed to Mommom what had happened. He said that it felt as though my leap and subsequent punch happened in slow motion, although he was frozen by not believing what he was witnessing. A new certainty could be added beyond death and taxes. I was in *HOT* water. Enthusiasm was one thing, but endangering someone's safety was not going to be accepted. I was told that I needed to clean up my act. There could be no more outbursts that could lead to injury. After the stern scolding that I received, I was banished to the kitchen to ponder my failings.

I quietly stewed in solitude, not wanting to look in the direction of my humans. I just wanted to be everyone's friend. Why couldn't I express myself in this enthusiastic way? People should be grateful to feel so loved.

❖ THE TEMPERATURE GREW COOLER each day, which did not make me very happy at all. When I went outside in December, the cold air chilled my short coat of fur. Where did those warm, summer days go? More important, what in the world was this cold, wet stuff that fell from the sky? Just enough of this white crap piled up in my yard so that it covered my toenails, but our first winter was mild, even by South Jersey standards. Thankfully, we didn't live in a region that was renowned for particularly nasty winter weather.

I nosed the snow that coated our lawn, and felt that it was beyond frigid. Did Mom or Dad make this happen? Were they in control of the weather? If so, they needed to cut it out. I had very little interest in heading outside to go potty when we experienced cold or snowy weather. Fortunately, I had pretty good bladder and bowel control so that I could limit my trips out the back door to just a few times each day if we experienced inclement weather.

What is this white stuff?

I still liked to take walks on a daily basis, even on the coldest of days. Instead of a full lap around our development, I often steered Dad to a shorter route. I couldn't let my little tootsies get frozen. Mommom preferred to remain inside on wintry days because she loathed bitterly cold weather. I'm with her ... although my innate craving for physical activity surpassed my contempt for the cold.

In late December, I learned that we would take a trip to both western New York and western Pennsylvania to celebrate Christmas with both sides of our family. It required the usual long ride, but I had gotten used to slumbering in the car. When we arrived at Mom's parents' house, I was curious to learn more about my temporary accommodations.

My parents let me run around the snow-covered yard as Dad kept control of me with the attached leash. The snow was considerably deeper here, so that was a disadvantage, but one I could certainly overcome. When I was done with my business, we walked into the basement. Dad promptly detached the leash and let me explore my new surroundings. There were no people down here, aside from Mom and Dad. Where was everybody? That's when I heard voices coming from above us. Hmm ....

Mommom gave me a treat and said that she was heading upstairs. I attempted to join her, but Dad grabbed hold of my hips to halt me in my damp paw tracks. Mom told me that she would see me soon, and then departed upstairs into the house. Once the door closed, Dad let go of me. I scurried up the steps in hopes of following Mommom, but I was too late. The door was closed.

Dad tossed some of my toys around the basement to try and engage me to play with him. Playing was the last thing on my mind. Dad started to unpack all of my belongings including my crate, blankets, toys, food, treats, and dishes. Wait a minute. This is where I was staying? Where was the rest of the family going to sleep? My growing anxiety was justified. Dad beckoned me to enter an eight foot by ten foot kennel that now contained my belongings.

Dad begged me to be a good boy and stay quiet. Hold the phone—you're leaving, too? What the hell?! To say that I was upset was a gross understatement. He promised to return shortly to make sure that I was ok. I stood there in shock and rage as both of my people had abandoned me. I intended to let the world know about it.

I raucously announced my displeasure. When I wasn't barking at the top of my never-tiring lungs, I was whining. When I wasn't whining, I was shaking the chain link kennel with my front paws while standing on my hind legs. As none of those seemed to remedy my situation (or even prompt a visit from my humans), I thought that trying to dig through the basement cement flooring was the best remaining alternative. Scraping the smooth floor occasionally made a small piece break off, but I wasn't getting anywhere. Maybe digging into the stone walls would be more productive. Minutes, then hours, passed with no visits (and no progress on escaping, either), although I heard more than one rebuke from Dad to stop making so much noise. He yelled at me without even seeing me?! To put it bluntly, this sucked.

Finally, Dad came downstairs. As we locked eyes, all could have been forgiven. Could we PLEASE get out of here? Dad opened the kennel and set me free. Thank the Lord!! He grabbed the leash then attached the collar. Whew! We were leaving. I bounded toward our car. Instead, he pointed me in another direction. We sojourned in the snowy lawn so that I could take care of business. All done, Dad. Where to now? Home? He knew that I had energy to burn, so we left the confines of Grandma and Grandpa's yard for a slow, steady, and lengthy walk. We trudged along the partially snow-covered sidewalks for nearly a mile along the village streets.

We returned to the scene of the crime after about thirty minutes of vigorous walking. It definitely was a criminal act to leave your Newman. Were we going home now, Dad? No, no we weren't. We ventured into the basement once again. This time, Dad tossed a ball along the floor several times as a pathetic attempt to make me feel better about the situation. My expressive eyes revealed my utter dissatisfaction. I did not want to be appeased by the bouncing of a ball to distract me. I wanted to go home. Instead, I was summoned to enter the kennel and begged to keep the volume to a minimum. Crap. We're doing this again? For how long? Why couldn't I go upstairs? House rules, or so I was told.

Needless to say, I was nowhere near a reasonable decibel level. I was pissed. While my family was eating, playing, or whatever the hell they were doing upstairs, I serenaded them with bark after bark after bark. My voice remained strong for the minutes and hours that I voiced my discontent.

I kept with a steady diet of voicing my complaints throughout the times that I was confined during daylight hours. During the nights, I managed to get in a little shuteye on my blanket-covered beanbag chair. I was still vehemently displeased, so I did not fully give up on speaking my mind no matter what time the proverbial clock on the wall said. Why couldn't I just be with my people?

When Sunday afternoon rolled around, after the better part of two very long and tedious days, I was told that we were driving to visit Dad's parents. Sweet Jesus, that made me feel so much more at peace. I could see my people all day, although I still disliked the idea of being crated while I slept at night. It was still a step in the right direction.

After celebrating Christmas with Dad's family for two days, it was time to head home and get back to our usual routine. I snored for the entire seven-hour ride, and didn't think to awaken, not even to take a leak. Thank goodness things were getting back to normal. That is, until the surprise that my parents had in store for me in the not too distant future.

Sabotage

ONE FROSTY JANUARY DAY, I was told that a blessed event would occur. I was going to the vet to be neutered. That's still a funny word. When I woke up in the morning, I was only allowed to go outside and do my business before being rushed into the car without a meal or even a beverage. What was the hurry? Geesh. Dad looked as though he was going to work because he was wearing his work clothes and badge to enter his office building. But, we were going somewhere. As he pulled into the parking lot, I instantly recognized that we were at Dr. Keefe's veterinary office. We were quickly received without much fanfare because no other dogs were in the lobby at such an early hour.

Dr. Keefe and one of the nice nurses took us into a smaller room to discuss the surgery. The vet mentioned that I would be given an anesthetic so that I would not feel a thing during the surgery. Dr. Keefe said that there would be a few stitches and asked if I liked to lick or gnaw on things. Dad replied, with a look of concern, that I was quite adept in those activities. The vet said that he would aim to do internal stitching so that I would not disturb the affected area. Dad asked how long the surgery would take. Dr. Keefe assured him that it would only take an hour or so, but the effects of anesthesia may persist for the better part of the day, with some time built in for me to recover.

With all questions answered, Dad bent down to talk to me. Dad gave me a big hug that I reluctantly received. He scratched my ears. I wanted no part of any contact from him; I was more interested in where Dr. Keefe was headed. The nurse grabbed the leash from Dad and I dopily bounded behind her. The next time I would see either of my parents, I would not have the same spring in my step.

When I awoke, my eyes could barely open, let alone focus on anything. These drugs were kicking my ass, although I felt this pain that the drugs could not even come close to subsiding. It throbbed constantly beneath the surface of where my testicles used to serve some purpose. I think neuter should be renamed to something more appropriate and a lot less humorous like *crotch pain that makes you want to strangle your parents*. It's a long name, but it could catch on. Neuter is no longer a funny term to this pup.

When Becky, the kind nurse, announced that she was going to take me to see Mom and Dad, I thought that was a fine idea. I wanted to give those two a piece of my mind. Becky led me into the patient's room and I set my dreary eyes on each parent briefly before looking away in disgust. How could they do this to me? What did I do to deserve this unholy pain? The nurse assured my parents that the surgery was successful despite some moderate complications. I was supposedly doing as well as could be expected with the anesthesia still coursing through my system.

Mom and Dad both called my name, but I refused to acknowledge them. My eyes twitched enough to let them know that I heard them, but did not care enough to respond. They petted me and I wanted to summon additional strength to avoid their touch at this moment. Instead, I simply stood stoically. Both of them would need to grovel for forgiveness of their singular and substantial sin. Begging would not even come close to being granted clemency. The act of my parents pleading to get back in my good graces would only result in me placing their forgiveness under consideration at some future date. I wasn't in a very forgiving mood. The nurse left the room, stating that Dr. Keefe would be in to explain the details of my day. I can sum up my day in one word, lady: OUCH!

Mom and Dad showered me with affection. I returned their affection with out-and-out ignorance. I could not even look at them. Someone, please open the door to this patient's room and let me the hell out of here. I wanted to be alone. Dr. Keefe returned and closed the door behind him. My imprisonment within these four walls with these two people who I had considered my family, at least until this day, persisted. Great.

Dr. Keefe reiterated that my surgery went well, but wanted to further explain the procedure. It turned out that I had an undescended testicle that resulted in a lengthier and more invasive surgery, especially considering that the intent was to sew me up with internal stitches. He had to make three separate incisions to locate his target. Maybe I wanted to take my ball and go home. However, the tenacious vet went in and found the hiding little guy. Mom and Dad asked if that could potentially result in any viable sperm finding an egg. Dr. Keefe reassured them that the surgery was a success. I was effectively neutered; there was no mistake about that. I would certainly not be able to procreate. No Newman Juniors or Newmanettes running amok out there. That's the world's loss.

Mommom asked how long my soreness would last. Dr. Keefe thoughtfully said that each dog responded differently to the combination of the surgery itself and the lingering effects from anesthesia, never mind the unanticipated additional incisions that I had endured. He reasoned that it might take a few days for me to feel better. The veterinarian also confided to Mom and Dad that my fun-loving personality would return, despite my current attitude. I gave my parents every reason to believe that such would *not* be the case.

I was leashed, collared, and led out of the office as I mindlessly followed without any interest in interacting with people or pets. I was too depressed and infuriated. We exited into the cold darkness that arrives prematurely on late January afternoons. As we approached the car, Dad gingerly elevated me off the ground so that I did not perform the usual leap to enter the crate. This was presumably to keep me from straining my body and prevent any ruptures to the unwanted addition to my body: stitches. I did not fight Dad's maneuver, although I wasn't thrilled for him to be touching me.

Once we arrived home, I was again carefully lifted so that I did not make the two-foot jump down to the ground. Dad petted my head, asking for forgiveness in his own way. We ventured toward the backyard so that I could tinkle before dinner. I gently eased up the two steps leading up to the back door as Dad looked on with concern, ensuring that I was not unnecessarily straining myself. All was well; there was no more pain than I had already been feeling.

Mommom and Dad did not show any outward signs of ill will towards me, so today's visit to the vet that resulted in such unbearable pain did not make sense. I could not fathom why this had needed to happen.

I did my best to enjoy a quiet evening at home, primarily ignoring my humans. The anesthesia had fully worn off, and I felt the dull aches increase to a new plateau of pain. I wanted to crawl into a ball in the corner and die.

When they put me to bed, I droopily plodded into my

crate. I glared at my caregivers for putting me through this ordeal. I was in sheer agony, and for what? Both of them tried to comfort me, to no avail. I wanted them to go away, and they obliged. I was silent throughout the night, trying to sleep through the agonizing torture of this post-surgery hell. Thankfully, the eventful day left me exhausted and I successfully slept for my customary complement of seven to eight hours.

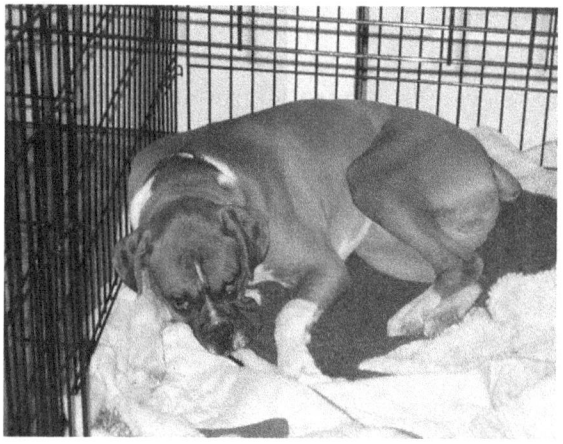

How dare you ... how dare you.

When the dull, gray morning dawn broke, my eyes shot open to the realization that my surgery was not a figment of my imagination. I was still living the nightmare, although the pain had subsided to a moderate intensity. That didn't mean that Mommom and Dad were off the hook. Certainly not. I was going to milk the effects of being neutered for as long as I could. Glare a little longer. Offer a cold shoulder. Pretend to ignore commands and even the gentlest requests. If I played it right, I might get extra treats, extra privileges, and extra love. Unfortunately, the new day was a typical weekday with both parents headed off to their respective employers. So, I couldn't exactly get all my wishes granted at the drop of a hat. One or both of them would actually have to be here to be on the receiving end of my indignant attitude for it to work.

I almost hate to admit it, but by day's end, I was feeling as good as new. That started to bleed across in my attitude at the homestead. I had resumed interacting with Mom and Dad, going so far as to ask them to play with me. I even listened to them a few times despite my most stubborn wishes to stay pissed off. The evening walk had cinched it for me; everything was back to normal. The dissipation of my soreness made me forget my anger. Damn it, I wanted to stay mad for longer but I couldn't. I suppose that was for the best, considering the family struggle that was about to stare us in the face.

I Still Haven't Found What I'm Looking For

MY RAGE AGAINST the parental units had regressed so that our relationship had returned to normal, whatever that was. I was Mom and Dad's only "baby," although they certainly wanted to add to their brood. God knows why, but they weren't in the market for a second boxer puppy. Rather, they wanted one of those small human things: a child.

Before I came along, Mom and Dad underwent infertility treatments because they had not yet been able to conceive a child on their own. They had attempted for over a year without assistance, followed by several inseminations done under the guidance of a doctor who specialized in fertility. Nothing had worked to this point, so they ramped up efforts to increase the likelihood of success.

The next step was to perform an in vitro fertilization. This was a rather invasive method done by fertilizing eggs outside of the womb, then implanting them into Mommom, and hoping that the infantile cells were accepted by her body. It was a lot more complicated than that, but I have never claimed to be a medical professional.

The bottom line was that Mom and Dad had invested a lot of their hopes and dreams into this little venture. They had abandoned their poor, sweet pooch for a continuum of doctor's appointments at all hours of the day across multiple days, weeks, and months, to achieve the highest probability of pregnancy.

Following months of preparation, the day had come to transfer three fertilized eggs back inside Mommom in hopes that at least one would survive "the move." Mom had gone through so much to prepare her body for this moment: endless blood tests, injections with all kinds of medications introduced into her system, and intrusive surgeries. Now that her body was prodded and properly prepped, it was all up to a mixture of science, chemistry, environment, and fate to determine if babies would be in our future or not.

When Mom and Dad returned from the doctor's office, she appeared very weak, so I did not frivolously bounce at her feet as I typically did. Dad got Mom settled in upstairs to endure a period of three days of bedrest. This was frustrating because I could not enjoy Mommom's company as often as I would like, because she was supposed to move as little as possible. As a result, Dad's attention was diverted between Mom and me. C'mon man, multi-task, buddy! Why can't you be in two places at once? Serve meals in bed to your bride *while* playing with your pup.

Mom followed the doctor's orders to a T by minimizing her effort, and remaining as still as she could without going stir crazy. She did not want to jostle her potential offspring, not one iota. I was often left to my own devices on the first floor, which was uncool. Don't get me wrong; Dad still fed me, let me out for potty breaks, took me for walks, and played with me. But, something was askew. It was draining to have a segmented household while Mom was trying to provide the right environment for her newly-injected eggs.

A week later, we received the news that would change our lives forever. Of the three egg cells that were implanted, guess how many survived to allow our little family to be pregnant? Drum roll please. Zero.

Mom walked through our front door carrying the overbearing weight of the worst imaginable news. Even from my vantage point in the kitchen, it was plain to see that Mommom was beyond distraught. My usual boxer wiggle to exit the crate came to a halt. After Mommom undid the latch to my crate, I slowly stepped out to offer my condolences as tears flowed freely from her soft green eyes into her grief-stricken hands. I licked Mom slowly and did not trouble her with my superfluous needs.

After our initial greeting, Mom wearily plodded upstairs to wish the world away. On this occasion, I thought it best not to tug on her pant legs. Instead, I matched her speed as we ascended the steps with Mommom in the lead, and me two steps behind. She made it as far as the bed where she curled into a ball and silently sobbed in despondent heartache. I looked on in horror as my mom spent countless minutes and hours trying to rid herself of the gut-wrenching anguish. I took this as a cue to lie down on the floor next to her side of the bed, and just take it easy. No hyper spastic episodes. No barking fits. No "in your face" demands of attention. No requests for treats. Mom's melancholy filled the room, and I was content to wallow in that dreary fog with her as long as she needed. In those moments, there was nothing more important to me than making sure Mom's day got no worse than it already was. I paid specific attention to my behavior, ensuring that I was not a source of discord.

Mommom gathered enough fortitude and strength to call Dad at work and shared the results. He offered to immediately come home to be with her. She, however, declined, stating that I was taking good care of her. Dad was astonished by her response, but was grateful for my demeanor and deference on this saddest of days. He assured her that he would be home soon.

The next several days, stretching into weeks, were rough. My parents had gone through so much pain, sacrifice, and even financial strain to make this happen. Here we were, still a family of three with no clear path forward to a family of four or five. I learned a profound lesson at a young age: family comes first. My parents surely would figure out something.

Our little family ... would it grow beyond this?

❖ MOMMOM WANTED TO get together with family to take her mind off the heartache she had been feeling. So, we decided to depart for a quick weekend getaway in the city of Williamsport, Pennsylvania. Most people know this as the home of the Little League World Series. While that is certainly true, we saw it as an approximate midpoint between Grandma Diane's and our residences so that we could meet up with Grandma and Uncle Adam.

Mom found a hotel that allowed dogs to stay, so that I could be co-located with my family. She also coordinated getting adjoining rooms so that we could share a wall with Grandma and Uncle Adam.

We enjoyed a low-key visit where we didn't do a whole lot of anything. My family sat around and visited for the most part, occasionally playing cards or watching the tube. The humans only left me on one occasion, to enjoy dinner at a restaurant. They didn't trust me enough to leave me alone in the hotel room; I had to be crated while they were out. I wouldn't have done anything wrong, I *promise*!

It didn't take me long to figure out the rules of the hotel. Still go potty outside, try to be reasonably quiet, and stay off the furniture ... well, as much as possible. That's not to say that I adhered to these guidelines at all times, but I at least understood what I should have done. I wasn't being purposely mischievous, just high spirited and fun loving.

Uncle Adam was willing to play with me pretty aggressively, although he tried to reinforce that silly "no jumping" rule, by stepping on my toes any time I tried to elevate. It was going to take a heck of a lot more than toe tapping for me to stay out of your face, buddy.

I was generally happy with my accommodations for the weekend. Although I would have preferred to have slept in the comfort of a big bed like my parents did, I only whimpered a few times about being crate-bound during my nightly slumber.

When we were preparing to leave on Sunday to head home, I was eager to get back into the car. As such, I paced to the door and was raring to go. Because my parents were occupied with packing, I decided to wander over to Grandma and Uncle Adam's room via the open adjoining door. To my astonishment and good fortune, their hotel room door was agape. I sprinted out the door and down the long corridor toward the lobby. That's when I heard Uncle Adam exclaim, "Pooch on the loose!" He and Dad called after me, "Newman? Come here, boy." "Buddy, come on back!" Eventually, I stopped and allowed the older, slower humans to catch up to me. I wasn't trying to run away; I was merely expediting our checkout process.

Mom and Dad seemed pleasantly surprised that I was well behaved for our weekend excursion. They needed to de-stress after such a woeful couple of weeks. It wouldn't be long before I would give them something new to worry about.

Down with Disease

I WAS EIGHT MONTHS OLD when Mom and Dad started noticing a handful of swatches of my fur thinning, the skin underneath reddening with irritation, and in some extreme cases, the fur altogether disappearing. Perhaps it was something temporary, perhaps not. Their initial thought was to see if I was in distress, and let that be the guide on whether a vet's appointment was necessary. I rarely itched or scratched, and truthfully never gave a thought to my fur abandoning me.

My mangy-ness at its worst.

So, a few days passed. My parents had hoped that this was a temporary situation. The patches of diminishing fur continued to erode to the point where you could see dime to quarter-sized areas along my sides where my fawn coat was gone. You could plainly see the dark gray, nearly black skin color in those spots. My neck was no longer gleaming white with the cute underlying grayish-black spots. It was pinkish-red and obviously irritated. The surface of my neck skin had become bumpy.

It had gotten to the point where family, friends, and even passers-by wondered what was wrong with me. My parents could not wait any longer. They called Dr. Keefe and got an appointment for me, to have the vet determine what was causing the abnormal skin condition.

After my usual behavioral histrionics in the lobby, we entered the small patient room. Mom and Dad described what should have been obvious to anyone: my fur was vanishing in some places. Dr. Keefe asked some questions to better assess the situation. How was my energy level? My family assured him that nothing was out of the ordinary there, as I was the same crazy boxer pup. What about itchiness of the patches? I had left them alone for the most part, but not entirely. Appetite? Same ravenous lunatic. Any agitated behavior? Goofy, fun loving, destructive. In other words, same old, same old. Dr. Keefe believed that he had an answer, although he wanted to do a little research before diagnosing and treating me. He took a quick cellular sample from one of the borders of an affected area to scrutinize under a microscope. While Mom and Dad agonized over the possible outcomes, I whined to get out of the smaller room to see the other pups in the waiting room. Could it be the dreaded "C" word? Did I have some form of skin cancer?

When Dr. Keefe and his assistant, Becky, returned, I

wanted only to play. Becky appeased my playing needs by allowing me to lick her face and bounce around in a frolicking fashion. She kept me preoccupied while the wonderful vet broke the news to my parents. He said that my immune system was being attacked by a disease called demodectic mange. This was caused by a mite that lives in hair follicles. He further explained that I did not contract this disease from poor living conditions. Rather, my immune system was somewhat deficient at fighting these Demodex canis mites. These mites live on the majority of adult dogs and even humans. Dr. Keefe explained that they resemble snapping alligators under a microscope. They typically do not cause any irritation except for those beings who cannot adequately defend themselves.

So, I can blame my birth mom for sharing these lovely creatures with me since they can only be transmitted via direct contact. I can also blame my sisters for crowding me out when it was feeding time as a puppy. In essence, they were keeping me away from obtaining abundant nutrients I should have received from my mother's milk to build my immune system into a juggernaut in those early stages of life. Thanks a lot, birth family! No bitterness there, none at all. I'm glad to be running with my new crew.

I wasn't a mangy mutt, but I looked as though I had been in a dogfight where someone got the better of me. Or, maybe I made the other guy look even worse.

Dr. Keefe prescribed antibiotics that would aggressively combat the nasty parasites. It was going to be a lengthy process to rid my system of these little punks. The good news was that I (and my fur) was expected to make a full recovery. Fortunately, demodectic mange was not a debilitating disease. Rather, it was a condition that could be eliminated with the proper pharmaceutical concoction and time. The mites may never fully leave the friendly confines of my hair follicles, but at least my immune system could battle them without a return of the mange condition.

Taking medication was always an interesting proposition. If you simply tried to force feed me a pill, I would instantaneously spit it out. Mom or Dad thought that burying the pill in my food dish would work. Come on people, I was smarter than that!

They resorted to one of two tactics that worked with varying degrees of success, albeit with extra effort that seemed over-the-top, if you ask me. One of my parents would bury a pill in a wad of cheese, and tried their best to ensure that the medication was hidden from my inquiring eyes. If this didn't work, then a more sure-fire approach was to slather the pill with a thick coat of peanut butter. Of course, you couldn't just let me lick the combination of peanut butter/pill off your finger. A second later, you would see a pill spewed onto the floor. The approach that begrudgingly worked the best was to give me a small taste of peanut butter followed by placing the rest of the "treat" deep into my mouth and hold my snout into the air to force me to ingest the pill. Needless to say, whoever administered the oral medication required a thorough cleansing of their hands afterwards.

It took several weeks for my fledgling fur to form. Once it began to grow, it still took forever for the patches to disappear. You could say that my fur growth was analogous to my maturity process: very slow to start and gradual throughout the process. Those brutal patches that strangers murmured about were finally becoming a thing of the past.

Smells Like Teen Spirit

THE ATTITUDE OF A PUPPY can best be described as energetic, unapologetic, and selfish. I liked to do what I wanted. Although days on the calendar continued to peel off, I was still a wild card, an untrusted soul who could only be counted on for creating chaos.

I was between seven and eight months old, in human years. As such, you might expect that I would have started to become a well-mannered dog with some common sense. Not so much. I followed basic commands rather well. Outside of that, I liked to enjoy myself and marched to the beat of my own drum.

Mom and Dad decided that it might be wise to give me a little bit more responsibility in hopes that I would mature more quickly. Instead of confining me to my crate while they worked, the parental units gave me a bit of freedom. I repeat, a bit. They were also hopeful that I would refrain from having any accidents while they were gone. I had not peed or pooped in the house since I was a very young puppy, and we were ready to take the next step: I had to develop a sense of self-control.

They left my crate set up in the kitchen. However, they left the door open and erected a baby gate across the entrance to the kitchen. This, in essence, gave me the run of the kitchen while they were gone. I had my dog bed, toys, and fresh water at my disposal. How much trouble could I create in only 120 square feet in a four-hour block of time? You have no idea.

It was going to be a learning process. Some days, I would go accident-free. Other days, I peed on the parquet floor. It was never malicious. I had hours to myself and simply couldn't wait for the responsible adult to return home to let me outside. The only tried and true aspect of this newfound freedom was that I never deuced in the house. I could always manage to avoid leaving a steamy pile on our floor. Potty issues were the tip of the iceberg in my reign of the kitchen.

One late afternoon, I got curious about the effort that it would take to remove one of the obstacles before me: the baby gate. It wasn't bolted into the wall or anything. How hard could it be? I only had to use a little exertion to topple the gate that was pressed into the wall with a latch arm. I hesitantly nudged the mesh surface directly in front of me a few times with my front paws. No movement whatsoever. I would have to break out the big guns. This took real courage on my part because I hated unexplained movement and I didn't really care for collisions either. With great reluctance, I lowered my head like a bull. I did not have horns, but rather, a very pointy ridge atop my skull. I rammed the gate and felt it start to give way. For good measure, I repeated the head-butt a second, a third, and a fourth time until the gate slid out of place and tumbled to the floor just ahead of my front paws. I panicked and skittered backwards to avoid the commotion.

Once I saw that the barrier was horizontal instead of vertical, I was satisfied with my work. I carefully tiptoed around the gate and moved through the dining room to the living room. I wanted to see what was going on in the neighborhood, so I parked my tush in front of the window, surveying the front yard. Within mere minutes, Mommom's little blue car was turning into the driveway. Wow, how cool was that? I got to greet her right at the door!

When she opened the door, I stuffed my face out into the gap between the door and the frame to welcome Mommom home, while also tasting the fresh air from outside. She seemed ready for me, and not a bit surprised. Mom grabbed my head and pushed her way into the house. Mom asked, "Newman, how did you get out? What are you doing out here?" I licked her hands enthusiastically and purposely avoided answering her pointed questions.

Again, this was only the beginning of my time spent alone in the kitchen; a puppy's brain needs to be occupied, otherwise we resort to … *our* interests. A few weeks later, it was a bright, pleasant spring day with buds forming on the bushes and leaves making their first appearance of the year. Mom and Dad left for work as per usual. They decided that they would barricade me in the kitchen for the morning, and see how it went to determine if I would deserve the same freedom after Dad's lunchtime visit.

To say that my morning was eventful is a vast understatement. I perused the room and was filled with an incredible sense of boredom. The toys weren't keeping my interest. I needed something to do, something to engage my brain. Oh crap, I had to pee. I squatted and doused a spot with a few ounces of urine below the kitchen window. A pang of guilt hit me. As quickly as the remorseful emotion arrived, it also receded.

I looked curiously at my dog bed. Hmm … could that be a toy? I playfully pawed at the bed, and watched it slide across the smooth surface of the floor. This was fun, although it was just an overgrown tug toy. I suspected that it wasn't being used to its full potential. There had to be another way to play with this bed that was more entertaining. I latched my teeth onto the foam rim of the oval bed and tossed it a few inches. I could toss the bed!! Each time I lobbed the bed, I got a bit more adventurous, either throwing it higher into the air or a greater lateral distance or both. What a fantastic way to pass the time.

After a few hurls, I pounced on the dog bed and picked it up for another romp. I picked up the fleece and foam cushion and shook it violently from side to side. The bed battered my head, shoulders, and sides as I thoroughly enjoyed myself. Now this was living! I again hoisted the bed, but only managed to grip onto the fleece covering before mischievously bobbing my head furiously. I heard a giant rrrrrrrrrrrrrrripppppp! My jaw instinctively relented and the bed plunged to the floor. I inspected my handiwork and detected a jagged three to four-inch tear in the exterior shaggy shell that was still covering my dog bed. That would soon change.

I buried my snout in the tear and felt the covering give way a bit more. I dug into the growing opening with wild abandon, soon cramming my entire face and mouth inside. It was nice and soft in there, so I yanked the spongy substance with my canine teeth and felt a fragment shred as I pulled backward with all of my weight. An uneven inch or two strand of foam was between my teeth. I bet that there are more foam toys in there for me. There's only one way to find out.

I spent the rest of the morning disintegrating the dog bed, both covering and foam, one piece at a time. The furry covering was gashed open wide enough that my entire body could have been comfortably obscured within the fleece. The contents that were once formed as a three foot wide, two foot long dog bed was nothing close to that anymore. My busy morning left a trail of evidence that very closely approximated the entire 10' x 12' area of the kitchen floor. I had destroyed the bed to the point that every square inch of the wooden flooring was littered by the innards of the former cushion.

Sometime later, I heard the front door and I peered between the mesh of the baby gate. Dad's mouth was agape far enough that you could guide a freight train down his throat.

He approached the gate dividing the dining room from the kitchen to get a full appreciation of my morning's efforts. For several seconds, he was silent. I backed up very deliberately, one paw at a time, to the kitchen table, very near to the aforementioned puddle of piss. I wanted to sit, but I could not find an appropriate spot because my behind would find foam or fleece wherever I decided to plop down.

Dad methodically crossed over the fence one leg at a time and I sheepishly approached with my nub slowly starting to wag. I looked into Dad's eyes and sensed a slow smolder that caused me to halt dead in my tracks. I heard the forthcoming words, but it was the decibels that blew me away, "What did you do? YOU ARE A BAD DOG!" Dad emphasized each of the words in the last sentence as he pointed his index finger angrily at me. I have never heard anything so loud in my life. I felt shame. I felt sadness. I felt scared. I felt ... oh shit ... I felt piss streaming out of me again onto the floor out of sheer terror. Dad barked at me, "Get the hell out of here!" He opened the exterior and storm doors to the backyard; I didn't need any further invitation. I Scooby-Dooed it outside to get away from the volcanic temper that I had just triggered to erupt.

I spent the entirety of Dad's lunchtime visit outside, not wanting to go near someone who was so incredibly angry with me. Meanwhile, Dad cleaned up the remnants of the dog bed and the puddles that I had left behind. He made multiple trips outside to the garbage can. Perhaps there was that much mess that required a few ventures outside; or more likely, he needed to pace to reduce his fuming. As the thirty-minute lunchtime break came to a close, Dad curtly commanded me to come back in the house. I obeyed while avoiding eye contact. He directed me into the crate for the afternoon. Since I had not yet eaten, he shoved my food bowl into my unpadded crate and departed without saying a word. My behavior after such an incident would only get better, right? Well ....

❖ MY TRUSTWORTHINESS WAS obviously a work in progress. Some days were far better, other days ... not so much. A few weeks later, I was about nine months old. Mom and Dad departed for church on a Sunday morning. They felt that I deserved the chance to prove myself (again). I was left to my own devices in the kitchen for approximately two hours. I decided to have some fun. The baby gate that blockaded me in the kitchen was no match for my pointy dome. I was out!! I had free reign over the entire house, and I was going to take advantage.

On the landing area between the first and second floors, we had a houseplant that was set in a deep, circular planter. I charged up the steps and perused the 18-inch-tall plant, wondering how it was standing so upright. With only the slightest delay, I latched my teeth near the base of the green leafless stalk and yanked. That was really solid in there! Not for long. I tugged again and felt the earth move under the plant. Whoa – there was a bunch of the plant that was hidden below the dirt. I sprinted back downstairs with it firmly planted between my teeth. Then I jumped on the love seat and flapped the stalk fiercely from side to side. Dirt sprayed absolutely everywhere with each cycle of shaking. I ran along the living room floor, then bounced back up on the love seat and stamped in the sprinkles of dirt as I played with my new toy. What a blast!

What else could I find that could serve as a toy? Oh yeah ... there was that odd-smelling thing on the bottom shelf of the sofa table. Let's take a closer gander now that I don't have to worry about being rebuked. I nudged the animal figurine and it toppled over onto the floor. Mmmm, new toy #2 of the day. I heard a light clink noise as the camel fell before my front paws.[4] That must have been the metal stirrup attached to the saddle. I nosed the humped animal and heard the stirrup jingle again. I delicately placed one of my canine teeth in the opening of the stirrup and it tore quite easily from the saddle. I rolled it around in my mouth and spit it out. I playfully pounced on the camel, but I still heard a little chiming noise. I flipped the figurine over and found the other stirrup, so I gave it the same treatment. Two stirrups detached. What else could I do to this thing?

I lay down in a nice little patch of sun that was streaming through the dining room windows and handled it much like a typical dog would do with a typical bone. I placed the camel between my front paws and relished my alone time by doing some quality gnawing. It turns out that the camel was made of plastic, cardboard, and metal. I never really ingested any of the materials, but I did indeed savor him from nose to tail. That is, until I heard another jingling. This was the telltale sign that Mom and Dad were using their keys to enter the house. Uh oh.

I moved with catlike quickness to the living room away from the camel. Maybe they wouldn't figure out who fawned over the figurine for the last hour or so. Maybe not. The look of astonishment on their faces was priceless, if it had not occurred to me that the consequences would likely match the crime.

Dad's ire was evident as the color in his face immediately turned beet red. Mom surveyed the new landscape

---

[4] Mommom's brother, Adam, served in a security role for the Marines in Jordan during one overseas deployment. He picked up a camel as a memento for our family. It had an earthy smell to it that never fully dissipated.

that was laid out before her. Her house plant was strewn on the floor in the living room with tiny dirt pebbles in a trail between its final resting place and its origin, some twenty feet away, with an obvious stop on the love seat where most of the dirt was ground into and buried between the cushions. What changed her mood from shock to sorrow was seeing the dismembered camel. She could make out the shape of the primary remnant, but there were little shards of cardboard and plastic scattered amongst the rubble. Mom and Dad quickly found the stirrups, as well. I was banished to the kitchen as tears flowed down Mommom's cheeks. Oh shit. Now I had done it.

Minutes transpired before they would even glance in my direction. They were considering multiple options: On the "concern" side, they recalled what the camel looked like originally to determine if it was possible that I had eaten anything sharp or toxic. Everything seemed to be accounted for, albeit a bit (actually, a lot) mangled. A short-term solution would be to crate me until I could mature enough to warrant their faith before trying to gradually give me more liberty. A future possibility would be to obtain a sturdier gate that would not succumb to my battering ram of a skull. A long-term solution that was being pondered was finding a new home for me. I was simply too destructive, too maniacal for their taste. Would I ever grow up? I was approaching a year old, and showed no regard for their possessions. It was all about me, and what I wanted.

They were both too furious to make any decisions in the moment, so they went about cleaning up the mess while I looked on from behind the kitchen gate. I wouldn't dare to step over the fallen baby gate between us after the reaction I just witnessed. So, I quietly plodded toward my kennel and proceeded to sulk.

❖ I ALSO HAD SOME behavior issues outside, too. The

flowers that I encountered (and loved to chew) were replaced in late spring with pre-cut strips of sod that were about four feet long by nine inches wide. Dad had laid three such strips on each side of our ground-level patio. He estimated that each chunk of sod weighed approximately thirty pounds. As the late spring warmth thawed the ground, Dad dutifully watered the sod each day for the better part of a week.

One day, Dad had to work some long hours, so Mommom was the first to arrive home and greet me. We went through the usual routine with the meet and greet after I was freed from the crate, followed by going outside to use the facilities. Mommom went into the house for just a minute. What she came out to was incredible, even to someone who has seen Newman-related carnage on a consistent basis.

She saw me with a full strip of sod dangling from my mouth as I sprinted across the yard. I must have stroooong jaws and teeth, if I could drag this weighty grass and earth as I ran through the lawn. Mom screamed at me to stop. I ignored her. She came out and yelled further while walking in my very pointed direction. I started to take another lap with the sod when she chased me down. Mommom forced me to drop my new toy and beckoned for me to go into the house.

I watched as she labored to heave the sod into its original position. No roots had begun to develop, which made it simple for me to tear off with in my mouth. This event caused my parents to keep a watchful eye on me each time I bounded out the back door to enjoy time outside. When Dad told his friends of my dalliance with the grass, a new nickname was coined for me: "sodmonster."

Mom and Dad were at a loss on how to correct my infantile behavior. One solution that they attempted was a

Grass is sooo delicious.

shock collar. I first had the collar placed around my neck in the backyard. Mom and Dad carefully monitored my activity to see if I would do anything that warranted some adjustment. The first trip came and went without any noticeable change.

    They kept an eye on me. As days went by, I got the same treatment of wearing the collar just to go into the backyard. I was minding my Ps and Qs to start, but this was getting ridiculous. I found some grass that was a little scraggly and needed a trim job, so I proceeded over toward the back fence and took a big bite of a few strands. All of a sudden, I heard this annoying beep that scared the living daylights out of me. I looked down and all around to assess the source of this annoyance. Nothing was obvious, so I went in for another bite. BEEP!!! What the ?!?! I moseyed off to a different area along the fence. The grass was calling my name. So, I bent down to taste the roughage. BZZZZZ on my neck. Holy shit, what was that?! I bolted away, ran a circle, and tried to figure out what that jolt was that started on my neck and the sensation that briefly tingled throughout my body. Mmmm, yummy grass. I revisited the scene of the crime. BZZZZ again. Damn it, damn it, son of a bitch! Meanwhile, a downpour of rain started to pelt me, so I was no longer interested in tasting the grass and came inside with an uncomprehending look on my face.

This shock collar experiment persisted for weeks. I could go several days or longer without hearing any beeps or feeling any buzzes. Then, without any provocation (or so I thought), I would be the recipient of the harsh tone or shock to my system. One such day occurred when I was having a glorious time on a sunny, crisp day. Mom and Dad had let me out to enjoy the day. I would typically announce my return to the back steps by either barking or pawing at the storm door. Then, one of the parental units would allow me back into the house.

Today was a break from the norm. The sun had reflected perfectly off the glass of the back door to cast a bright reflection onto the base of our back fence at the point where it touched the ground. This reflection captured my attention; not merely the usual interest that fades from my brain within moments, though. I was fixated on the gleaming image that diagonally crossed the fencepost and blended into the ground.

For the better part of an hour, I "worked" on the reflection in the yard. I tried to get it with all of my might. You may ask, "How did I get it?" By digging for it, of course! I heard that pesky beep again and refused to stop. Then, the nasty buzz jerked me from my current obsession. I peered over my shoulder and saw Dad glaring at me from inside the back door. I returned to digging furiously. I had to get at the reflection that refused to recede. The intensity of the buzz on my neck increased. I again halted, but only briefly. BUZZ!!! I barked because the sensation was maddening. I loped away from the freshly-made pit that was perhaps large enough in which to bury a football. About halfway across the yard, I glared at Dad with all the wickedness that I could muster. I knew that he was behind the noises and buzzes that afflicted my neck. To show dear old Dad who was boss, I bent down and took a bite of grass. I expectantly incurred another buzz as my eyes burned a hole into his.

Whether out of fury, frustration, or guilt, I never felt that collar on my neck again. My parents had to identify a better option to help me learn instead of merely punishing my many sins. It was ostensible that I had many months and perhaps years of remaining puppyhood. Houseplants, grass, reflections, and even camels could not be considered safe if I was left alone. I was in for a rude awakening.

Say It Ain't So

BEFORE I TURNED a year old, Mom and Dad sat me down to have a chat. They stated that we would be welcoming home a little girl in the next year. I cocked my head to contemplate this. Was Mommom pregnant? Did all the infertility issues get resolved and I just missed it? I was sure that I would have recognized the over-the-top elation that both parents would have displayed had they been pregnant. Why was it going to be a girl? A dog girl or a human girl? Why not a boy? Didn't I offer enough entertainment and responsibility opportunities for the two of them?

Within moments, my mind had moved on to something else yet they kept speaking about their plans to adopt a child from Russia. Unfortunately, both parents wanted to belabor the point. They suggested that the little girl would need help getting used to all of us, and I would have to work on my behavior so that she could have her own time and space.

To get me accustomed to the upcoming new addition, Mom brought a plastic baby doll downstairs in her arms. I nosed it aggressively and Mom gently turned her shoulder away to block my access to the doll. I was upset because Mommom would not let me satisfy my curiosity. She turned back to face me. After a minute or so, Mommom sat on the couch with the doll easily within snouting distance. I got right in that doll's face and nudged her again. This time, I backed away, slightly startled. The diminutive doll opened her eyes. What the ...? Out of frustration, I whined and started to bark. Dad beckoned me in a whisper to "Shhh, quiet Newman. The baby is sleeping." I refused to yield; my barks only grew louder and more incessant. Mom gently pressed on its stomach and what happened next took my breath away. It said in a high-pitched, robotic tone, "Mama." I tilted my dome and shut my mouth with my jowls dangling, no longer puffing with contempt. That thing didn't seem alive. But, was it? Its eyes moved and it *talked*. Mom delicately handed the doll to Dad. I eyed this new development with total bewilderment and horror. You're both going to hold that thing? What the hell for? No one holds me that way, not that I would enjoy it if someone did.

    The doll repeated the eye flutter and speaking while in Dad's arms. This was no good, no good at all. I began to bark because I was confounded. I could not discern with absolute certainly whether this plastic figurine was alive or not. Maybe this was the little girl that was coming to be with us. Mom and Dad seemed to be incredibly gentle and soft spoken with it. What did that mean for me? Was I being pushed into the background? No ... that could not be the case.

    My confusion was growing into frustration and anger. I felt obligated to share my feelings with the two people who introduced this nightmare into our household. Bark, bark, bark, whine, bark, bark, jowl flap of frustration, bark, bark. If you spoke "dog," this would be rather unpleasant language. Mom and Dad were growing annoyed at my reaction. They decided to take the doll away for the time being, but promised it would return so that I could get used to someone else being here with us. Awesome ....

❖ JUNE 6, 2005, was a date where the series of recent life-changing events kept on coming. I turned one year old: a whole revolution of our planet around the sun. Most of that time was spent coexisting with my parents and our relationship had grown significantly, but it was still far from perfect. I was absolutely still a puppy, but I was now armed with more knowledge to begin the process of maturing ... just not yet. There was still plenty of time for that.

After Mom and Dad returned home from work on my first birthday, they took me on a celebratory walk, which felt oddly similar to our normal everyday excursion. I did get a new stuffed animal to toss, along with a thick, green and white Nylabone to gnaw, plus some treats. After a typical dinner that somehow served as a birthday meal, I got one surprise that actually was unexpected.

Mom and Dad invited me to do something that I had never been permitted to do in my life. They both patted the couch cushion and said, "Come here, boy. You can come up." I looked at the couch questioningly with a subtle head tilt, wondering why this option had never been presented to me before now. With very little hesitation, I leapt onto the cushion and circled to pat down the cushion to get the position just right. After a few 360-degree turns, I found the ideal spot and lay down with my head and jowls resting quite comfortably on the armrest. I looked around as though I belonged up here, not feeling any trepidation whatsoever. Mom and Dad offered me a few back rubs, ear scratches, and initiated several one-sided conversations. I received them and ensured that this wasn't just a trick before dozing off in what must have been the best nap ever.

A few weeks following my first birthday celebration, Mom and Dad took me to the veterinarian's office to see how I was progressing. I was a frothing mess when I entered the building because there were other canines there that

I don't recall this picture being taken.

brought their humans with them. All I wanted was to play with the other pooches, but Dad kept me on a rather short leash, even with the Gentle Leader strapped securely from my snout to my collar, to limit such interaction. Wasn't the point of visiting this place for me to introduce myself to new dogs?

After a few minutes, one of the nurses and Dr. Keefe greeted me and took me into the private room. I could not control my enthusiasm. I wanted to lick both their faces so badly. The people who worked there were very friendly and welcoming. My heart was beating a mile a minute with the additional stimuli of humans other than my parents. I seemed to have forgotten what happened the last time I was here.

Mom and Dad were hopeful that my hyperactivity would have toned down at least moderately since being neutered. Well ... that hadn't happened. I was still quite the spitfire. The only difference between the pre-neutered and post-neutered versions of Newman was the significant reduction of humping.

Dad asked if a typical boxer would graduate from reckless and destructive puppyhood energy by age two. There was a noticeable moment of silence before our usual assistant, Becky, answered his question. She had a boxer of her own at home and didn't see her beloved dog calm down until somewhere between the ages of three and four. I looked on inquisitively as my tongue dangled from my panting mouth. Mom and Dad shared an uncomfortable glance. They were a little concerned about my exuberance, given that there would be another being in the house within the next several months. Becky stated to my parents that boxers are wonderful with children and that my disorderly nature should not be a cause for alarm. I had no idea how much would be changing once a little girl would be in our house to rule the roost.

Dr. Keefe proceeded to check me out and determined that I was a healthy, young boxer. I was 72 pounds and a lean, sleek, tan tornado of a dog. The vet was thrilled to see that my fur had mostly returned following my bout with Demodectic mange. He recommended that Mom and Dad monitor my weight to ensure that it leveled off. If I continued to pack on the pounds, my meals would have to be curtailed. Too much weight on my frame could result in premature arthritic conditions or perhaps hip dysplasia later in life. Dad was disappointed by this advice because he wanted me to become as big as a tank, but he willingly agreed to do what was in my best interests.

Visits to the vet took a little wind out of my sails in the

hours immediately following. I always got exceedingly riled up after seeing new people and unfamiliar dogs that captured my attention; although I still enjoyed my toys when I returned home, playtime was far more short-lived and subdued than usual.

❖ THE DOG DAYS of summer were upon us. It was another steamy season ... especially for those of us with fur. Sure, there are many areas of the country that are hotter, but South Jersey regularly had ninety-degree days. That was plenty hot for me. This year, I had the pleasure of enjoying my first 4th of July holiday with Mom and Dad. We celebrated by going to an outdoor park on Independence Day with Mommom's family in western New York.

I was kept at a distance from the party-goers because of the constant barrage of human food that went along with family get-togethers. So, I was stationed approximately fifty feet away under a shade tree where I had toys, food, and ample water. I got to play with so many relatives that I had never met. It was a leisurely, enjoyable day ... although I would certainly have preferred to have had the run of the park. There were some tasty treats that I would have devoured in the blink of an eye! By mid-afternoon, we packed up and made the six-hour journey back home because Mom and Dad both had that bothersome thing called work the next day.

We arrived in the late evening hours as the sun was setting. I was exhausted and ready for a quiet night at home with a nap before bedtime. I was lounging at Mom's and Dad's feet when I started to hear a whistling noise that lasted for a few seconds. My eyes opened in alarm and my ears were back, trying to figure out this new noise. All of a sudden, a BOOM sounded from not too far away. I hopped up and got in both Mom's and Dad's faces begging for an answer to the following question, "What in the bloody hell was that?" Within the next minute, the same whistle-boom sequence happened a few more times. I was so scared that I thought I was going to piss on the floor. Dad tried to hold me close, but I wanted no part of it. I needed to be mobile ... mostly so that I could shake and shudder out of fear. Was South Jersey being bombed? Did someone's car explode just behind our house?

The fireworks seemed awfully close. I was scared; Dad was infuriated. He stormed around the house looking out each window to locate the source. He started on the first floor, then moved upstairs and peered through the blinds. The prolonged whistles and booms continued. I was frantic in my fear. Mommom gently rubbed me to try and soothe me, but I was disconsolate. I heard Dad's footsteps thundering back down the stairs. He was seeing red. Dad said, "Newman, we're going for a walk." Huh ... out there with that noise?! I dim-wittingly agreed. Okay ... if you say so. Mom protested because Dad said nothing regarding his intent. He glared and said that he needed an excuse to go talk to some guys. Apparently, I was the excuse.

Much to my relief, the scary noises had ceased just as we left the house. Dad and I walked briskly about a hundred feet to the corner and made a sharp right turn onto one of the streets in our development. Before our eyes was a police car parked in someone's driveway with its bright headlights pointed directly into their open garage. Dad and I froze in our tracks. We watched as the policeman knocked on the front door repeatedly with no response. I don't know why we remained there so long. I was getting anxious to continue on our journey, but Dad insisted that we remain there for a few minutes more. We watched the policeman eventually back away from the residence and slowly leave the neighborhood. Within a minute, we saw four grown men appear from behind the garage after the coast was clear. When we returned home, Dad explained to Mom that these four morons were lighting off fireworks from their driveway. Their driveway! Our neighborhood was built to pack the houses together rather tightly, so much so that I could nearly aim one of my pee streams onto our neighbor's house from the property line.

The next day at lunchtime, I found something new to play with in the yard. Dad saw me carrying this object as I sprinted. He whistled to get my attention to assess what was in my mouth. After a good 45 seconds of keep away, Dad tugged the item out of my clamped teeth. It was pasteboard that came from, guess where? Fireworks. Dad was pissed off all over again. We scoured the backyard and found several chunks of shrapnel. Dad even found some fairly intact portions of two firework rockets atop the roof of our garage. I despised fireworks ... well, at least I loathed the noise that they made. If I could play with their remnants, that was a different story. Dad detested that these individuals shot off fireworks in a neighborhood where the homes were quite close in proximity. He deemed it dangerous, especially for novices like these boneheads. There was a suitable wide open field for their antics, just across the street from our housing development.

To put it politely, we had a few folks in the neighborhood who were a few cards short of a full deck. Another of our neighbors who lived behind the back fence was busily building a basement beneath their house. It had taken a few months for the walls and support beams to be erected, but we could discern steady progress on their construction.

I was scouting around the backyard and noticed my paws soaking in a milky liquid near the rear fence. It smelled earthy and left a faint, gray residue on my white socks. I trudged back into the house with sopping wet paws and was scolded for digging until it became evident that I had nary a speck of mud on me, just this wet film that could be seen only on the very tips of my paws. My parents dutifully cleaned off the mess and Dad inspected the yard, only to find that the back corner of our lot had an inch of cloudy fluid covering it. It looked like he had to go speak his mind (again) to another of our neighbors.

The middle-aged married couple explained to Dad that they were creating a wine cellar in their basement, and had just poured the foundation. They had run a pump and extended a line exiting their basement to remove excess water that had accumulated downstairs. This line was pointed directly into our yard! The water had combined with some of the unfinished cement and resulted in us being the unlucky recipients of the run-off. They graciously passed along one of their wine creations and promised Dad to re-route the line so that we were no longer the targets for their pollution. Like I said, not the brightest bulbs in the pack.

❖ AS I GOT A LITTLE OLDER and wiser, Mom and Dad decided that I could travel in the car without being confined to the crate. This was awesome! If the weather was nice, Dad would open the window next to me so that I could hang my head out the window and enjoy the fresh air. My jowls flapped in the breeze as I inhaled the cornucopia of assorted smells. If I got bored with the open air, I would sit perched on the back seat with my head extending far forward to rest my head on Dad's shoulder as he drove. *What can I say, I love the guy.*

I may have gotten smarter over the years, but there were sometimes conditions that you never outgrew. As a puppy, I chased things like flashing lights or I focused unnecessarily on reflections. When Dad needed a laugh, he would drive me to madness with this crap. I simply could not help myself because I likely had a case of obsessive compulsive disorder (OCD).

My vet noticed my obsessive behavior specifically related to lights and unusual sights. He recommended that my parents not feed into these obsessions because the fixations could become increasingly overwhelming for me. As such, Dad found different ways to torment me instead of following laser pointers or reflections from windows. I guess that he loves me, but he had a funny way of showing it.

Dazed and Confused

SOMETIMES I LEARNED lessons the easy way. Other times, I learned them the "Newman" way. One such occasion was finding myself in a dark, unfamiliar place because I was looking for my parents. We were all home, I was aware of that much. I didn't think that Mom or Dad was upstairs because I heard no noises coming from the second floor. The television was off and they weren't moving about. There was a noticeable absence of floorboard creaks. They weren't outside or anywhere that I could see downstairs.

I took it upon myself to investigate and checked in the one room where one of them could be that wasn't in plain sight: the downstairs powder room. I rammed the door open with my skull and walked into the three-foot by eight-foot area of the commode. The room was vacant and, although there were no lights illuminating the room, it was obvious that no one was in here. Before I could turn around to exit the bathroom, the door bounced off the doorstop and closed just as quickly as it had opened. There was one problem: I was inside, in the dark. I supposed it would take more than just a nudge of my bony head against the door to open it.

A few minutes later, I detected movement from upstairs. I heard Mom and Dad calling, "Newman, where are you?" I heard them, but did not respond. They looked in every area downstairs and I heard questions back and forth asking whether they had let me out into the backyard. Neither remembered doing so, but Dad offered to go check it out. He returned and said that I wasn't outside. The gate was latched, so I could not have escaped and had never shown a proclivity or interest in jumping the fence. I bided my time in silence behind the bathroom door. Mom took another look to ensure that I hadn't gone upstairs in full stealth mode.

Dad said that I never went into the downstairs bathroom, but that it was the only place that was left to look. The door opened and I bolted from darkness into light and scared the crap out of Mom and Dad. I showed my gratitude for being rescued by bouncing back and forth between my parents. They laughed loudly and could not figure out why I had sat there in silence while they were looking for me. Like I said, it's the Newman way. Note to self: never enter that trap of a bathroom again.

My thick-headedness was not limited to getting trapped in my own house. During the dog days of summer, Aunt Ally and Cody had taken me to spend some time near a small lake. I could be around some other high-energy dogs named Murray and Steady, who belonged to Cody's parents. They were playful, bigger dogs who were a few years my senior. Despite the age difference, they could handle my liveliness with their size and physicality. I saw them jump into the lake and swim. Boy, that looked like a ton of fun, especially since Aunt Ally was in the water, too.

I sprinted down the dock and vaulted into the water making a massive splash. Dog instincts were supposed to take over, right? I should have been able to swim like my new buddies, right? Well ... the body was willing, but my big, beautiful brain sort of forgot to do something. All four legs were moving appropriately to attempt the doggy paddle. It's really hard to swim, though, if you never think to pick up your head above the surface of the water. Dogs don't have gills. Aunt Ally quickly scurried over to me and had to forcibly lift my head so that I could take a breath.

She thought that she could relinquish control of my head and I would keep it above water now that I saw how it should be done. No one said I was the sharpest tool in the shed. After Aunt Ally let go of me, I once again dipped my head into the slightly murky water. I just couldn't get the hang of swimming by myself. Aunt Ally realized that I wasn't learning what should have been instinctual: to breathe. She was relegated to help me swim to shore to safeguard that I did not put myself into a dangerous situation.

❖ IT COULD GET STIFLINGLY hot where we lived in South Jersey with very few options for relief to beat the heat. We stayed inside, enjoying the air conditioning to avoid the thick, sometimes humid air that rolled over the hills of Pennsylvania before heading out to the Atlantic Ocean. If it was too hot, we would delay our walks until later in the evening, much to my dismay. I always was up for a walk, so waiting until dusk was the worst possible option.

We did not have an in-ground or above-ground pool. Neither did the overwhelming majority of our neighbors. Our yard would have barely accommodated the area for a pool. If my parents had opted for a pool, its' space would have significantly limited my fits of spastic energy that still brought on brief sprints in the yard.

Our family dealt with 90-plus-degree temperatures consistently during the summer months. Dad thought that it might be refreshing to have an inflatable pool for us to use to cool off. Yes, you read that correctly: a kiddie pool for two adults and a dog. Mom and Dad wanted me to enjoy playing in water without the threat of drowning since I could not ascertain how to breathe with my head above the surface of the water.

On a sunny and already oppressively hot, Saturday morning, I watched Dad take the plastic pool out of the box and inflate it by heaving long puffs of his own lungs into the valve. Mom was worried that he might pass out, but there was no need to worry: Dad is full of plenty of hot air. Within mere minutes, a pool appeared before my eyes. He ran the hose from the outdoor faucet and began filling up the plastic pool. The water was chilly, but took only about an hour to warm up enough for Dad to dip in his toe to determine that the water temperature was adequate.

Mom and Dad eased into the water and called me to come closer. I hovered near the edge of the pool, mildly curious about why they were lounging in the water. They both beckoned me to come into the water of my own volition. I looked at them uneasily and did not move an inch closer to doing as they asked. Predictably, Dad rolled his eyes in frustration.

He rose out of the knee-high water and I instinctively skedaddled toward the perimeter of the yard. Dad chased me for a bit. Mommom looked on at the comedy of a man chasing his puppy to try and get him to cool off in a kiddie pool. Were we white trash? No ... hopefully not, anyway.

Dad got his hands on me and carried my unwilling body to the pool. He gently placed me so that I stood up and got my paws and underside wet. He held me in place and slowly splashed water onto my back. I wasn't feeling the refreshment. This was more like an oversized bath without the running water. Dad took his hands off me for a moment and I tried to escape. The guy just wouldn't let me go! He wanted me to give it a minute, to give it a chance. He poured water softly over my hind legs and back, making sure not to get water on my head (which I hated!). Mom and Dad both pet me and attempted to put me at ease. This was ridiculous. Let me out! The next time there was an opening where Dad wasn't holding me against my will, I took it. I jumped out of the pool, shook violently to get rid of the water that was dampening my sleek coat of fur. I win, you lose, buddy. Neither Mom nor Dad made me get into the pool ever again.

I looked on with skepticism as Dad tried to use a toy to get me into the pool.

❖ LATER IN THE SUMMER, we journeyed from the Garden State to the northwestern corner of the Keystone State to visit Grandma and Grandpa, along with Aunt Chris and Uncle Toby. Up until this point, I had yet to meet either of Dad's sisters and their families. Aunt Chris and Uncle Toby were visiting for a class reunion. They needed to receive the full Newman treatment.

Lengthy car rides were becoming commonplace for us. I only needed a quick pit stop about halfway through the seven-hour trip. When we arrived, I saw a captive audience in the form of two new people to shower with affection. I was a lick-fest. I literally licked Aunt Chris from head to toe because I could tell she was definitely a dog person. She knew I was crazy, but didn't seem to mind. She called me a "hot mess," whatever that is. Mom thought I was loving on her a little too affectionately.

Uncle Toby was also fun, but I quickly discerned that he was a guy. I expected him to behave just like Dad. He should be playful, rough, and constantly focusing his attention on me. Right? I *refused* to leave him alone. All the adults were trying to distract me from focusing only on Uncle Toby. If he relaxed on the couch, I would nose his face or whine at him to get his attention. Come on, play with me! He would play with me in spurts but not nearly often enough for my taste. I relentlessly harassed him, much to my parents' embarrassment. I ended up being segregated from Uncle Toby for portions of the weekend because of my overenthusiasm for him.

Aside from meeting new family, the weekend offered another first for me, one that took me several minutes to fully comprehend. Grandma and Grandpa's house has three bedrooms in it. In my previous trips here, I had slept solo in my crate in one of the bedrooms.

This weekend, each of the three couples occupied the bedrooms. Where was I going to sleep? The crate was set up in its typical location. However, when it was bedtime, Dad turned out the lights in the bedroom where I was usually all by lonesome, and then climbed into bed with Mom. Did he just forget something? I was not asked to enter the crate. Wait ... what? I paced from one side of the bed to the other. I sniffed and licked the hands of each parent that

I found on either side of the bed. It seemed as though Mom and Dad were sleeping in the room with me.

I then entered the crate and exited just as quickly. No one was going to compel me to be confined? I meandered around the room trying to figure out what to do. After ten to fifteen minutes of looking for a spot to settle, both Mom and Dad urged me to lie down and go to sleep. Eventually, I did so after settling on a location just outside the crate on the floor. I got up a few times in the wee hours of the morning to explore my surroundings while I should have been fast asleep. I didn't need to go potty; I just enjoyed the ability to stretch my legs with this newfound freedom. I never had to sleep overnight in my crate ever again after that night.

When we got back to New Jersey, I got to stay up as late as my parents. I no longer had to be secured in my crate in the kitchen when it was bedtime. I slept contentedly on my dog bed on the floor near Dad's side of the bed.

One night, I was particularly tired, so I made the trek upstairs to turn in early while Mom and Dad remained downstairs watching a little television before joining me. I soundly slumbered until I could hear boisterous laughter coming from the first floor.

I stumbled toward the stairs and went down the first few steps to glare at the two noisy ones. With my eyes, I scolded them for the volume of their outburst. Once they recognized that they were being reprimanded and became silent, I trudged back upstairs to return to my sweet dreams. Geesh … some people! I needed my beauty sleep.

My rest allowed me to be bright-eyed and bushy-nubbed so that my gleaming personality could be unmistakable to all who encountered me. I had the good fortune of meeting Dad's sister, Carol, her husband Ponch, and their daughter Tori when they came for a visit. I viewed Aunt Carol and Tori much as I regarded the other females in my life. They were fun, sweet, and deserving of my affection. I could immediately sense that they were dog lovers, which was always a gold star in my book. We may have lived more than a thousand miles apart, but how they treated me was tremendous. It was like I was one of their own. They loved on me, catered to my wishes, and we played together comfortably.

Then there was the male of this faction of my family, Uncle Ponch. As with all guys, he needed to adhere to my set of expectations for males. I would whine at Uncle Ponch; he would pet me and scratch my ears. I'd get a little toothy and he would just smile. I wanted to play, ya know, roughhouse. "Bark!" He would laugh because I treated him so differently. You're missing my drift, big guy. Let's try this again. "Double woof!" I followed this was a snout in his face. Certainly no teeth, merely an eager invitation to play more vigorously. Come on, buddy, give me something. He patted my sides and did his best to appease me. He wasn't playing like Dad, though. After a while, I gave up on my spirited attempts. He became the recipient of disparaging looks. Uncle Ponch had never met a dog with such personality before. He could always tell that I was eyeing him, and it almost always left him chuckling. Well ... I did aim to please.

Gotta Get Away

WARM, SUMMER DAYS were absolutely the best. Mom and Dad occasionally dragged out the pool and I avoided it like the plague. I did, however, enjoy lounging in the yard, feeling the hot sun beating down on me. I liked to roll around in the yard, sunning all of my parts: back, belly, and legs. Mom and Dad exerted caution with the amount of time that I spent outside, because boxers are inclined to contract skin cancer and other dermatological ailments.

One rather sweltering Saturday afternoon, Dad had filled the pool, running the hose from the side of the house under the gate to the backyard and into the inflatable pool. He concluded filling the pool and returned the hose to its rightful place, looped around the outdoor faucet. However, Dad failed to realize that he did not latch the gate closed after returning from his short jaunt to take care of the hose. This is a fact that I quickly identified and I capitalized on the opportunity.

While Mommom was in the house, Dad and I were baking in the mid-afternoon heat in our predominantly shadeless backyard. He was preoccupied with trimming some of the grass along the back side of our garage. I took it upon myself to nose open the unlatched gate and I was FREE! I jogged over to our next door neighbor, Tom's, house. I found that it was quite similar to our yard, aside from the oversized fountain in the front yard and the recently manicured landscaping.

Although it was brutally hot, I sprinted in short fits in Tom's yard with my collar and identification tag jingling with each stride. That's when I noticed a problem: Dad had discovered that I had escaped. He dashed toward me. I took off in a large circle that encompassed four different yards, portions of our (luckily) traffic-free street. He was right on my nub with each pace. Dad could move more quickly than I had anticipated. As such, I was forced to loop back to avoid being captured. I traveled over the same circuitous path in reverse. Dad could not maintain the sprinting speed that was required to keep up with my strong, youthful legs.

As I came to a halt to incite further hounding on Dad's part, he resumed his pursuit with renewed spirit. He ran hard and closed in on me. More important, he had started this portion of the chase in Tom's yard and started working me back toward our lawn. Dad finally cornered me into a spot between Mom's car parked in our driveway and our house, where I had three choices: enter the unlatched gate to the backyard, make a break for the porch by our front door, or try to escape out to the front yard once more where the chase would continue. Two of these choices would ultimately yield in my capture, and likely punishment. I made up my mind.

Dad pretended to take a step forward. I lowered to the ground in response, primed and ready for the next round. I loved playing chase!! Both of us were panting heavily, but unwilling to give in to the other, for that would be admitting defeat.

He faked two steps forward to chase me toward the backyard and wheeled around the back bumper of the car. I had already made my choice of paths: I chose freedom by way of the front yard. Dad was out of sight and I was galloping toward what I thought would be more fun and games. However, Dad mustered all of his strength and a surprising amount of speed to take the other path to the rear of Mommom's car. He beat me to the spot just before I would have had plenty of room to exit into the front yard. This unexpected result caused me to panic. I could have given in and allowed Dad to apprehend me. Not a chance. Dad may have cut off my path to the front yard; however, in my mind, my remaining exit path was the front porch, and I was going for it.

There was one significant problem with this impromptu path selection. I jumped up the two steps onto the porch and looked for options. The porch was enclosed by vertical wooden slats about every eight inches that rose up approximately three feet from the ground. I was trapped. I turned back around to contemplate a quick escape. Dad had blocked the entrance to the porch, so our chase session was done. He grabbed my collar and guided my overheated body through the front door. Both of us were exhausted, although Dad's tongue did not hang out of his mouth quite as far as mine did.

To my shock, I did not get punished for breaking out of the backyard. I sloppily drank a few quarts of water and napped on the cool, comfortable carpet in the air conditioned climate for the rest of the afternoon. The fun was not over for the day ... far from it.

It was late evening when I announced that I had to go to the bathroom, likely from the vast water intake from earlier in the day. I scurried about the backyard without a collar around my neck. I eyeballed the side of the house. The gate was still wide open! It had never been shut from earlier in this afternoon.

I sauntered out toward the front yard into the dark of

the night. I stealthily began walking down our development's sidewalk. I made no noise, thanks to being collarless. It was a beautiful night out and I passed two older ladies who were out walking as I started to get further away from home. Oddly enough, they seemed to pay no mind to the canine (with no human) that was freely walking past them. I was two houses away, three houses, four, now five. That must have been about the time that my absence had been noted at the homestead.

I heard hard, heavy hoofing coming from behind me, but paid it no mind. I had reached a point about 300 feet from home when I heard an out-of-breath voice state sharply, "Newman." My footsteps came to an instantaneous halt. I did a 180-degree turn sheepishly and looked to match the sight with the sound of the familiar tone of my dad. Sure enough, there he was, standing about fifteen feet directly in front of me on the sidewalk. The two older ladies were still walking away from us in the distance. Neither a walking dog, nor a dashing man had caused either woman to even hesitate for a moment.

Dad bent down and got on one knee and sweetly coerced, "Come here, Newman. Come on buddy." He placed both of his hands in front of him, with open palms facing me, and then made it look like he was repeatedly squeezing something imaginary with each hand. I knew what this meant: it was Dad's signal to me that he was going to scratch my sides. My nub instinctively began to wag and I took a few steps in Dad's direction. I was a sucker for a good scratch on my ears, neck, and sides. Then I paused, as we were about five feet apart now. Do I want to play some more chase? Hmmm ....

Dad did not give me the opportunity to consider this option for very long. He quickly closed the gap between us and got his paws on me, scratching behind my ears and giving me a good rubdown.

With no collar or leash on hand, Dad picked me up and carried me with my head on his shoulder as we started the return trip to the house. He whispered in my ear, "Thank you for not running on me." Mommom met us halfway. She had brought peanut butter in the event that it was needed to persuade me to return home. Our tight, little family walked back home. Dad deposited me in the living room with Mommom. He then did something that had eluded him all day: he latched the gate.

❖ I HAVE MENTIONED before that Dad is a huge Steelers fan. I came along at a time (in 2004) when his team rarely lost, but yet they had not won a Super Bowl in over two decades. They had 15 regular season wins in 2004 and 11 more in 2005, yet no one gave them much of a chance when the 2005 playoffs began because they narrowly squeaked into the playoffs as a wild card team. Following a road victory over the Cincinnati Bengals, the Black and Gold took an impressive 21-3 lead into the fourth quarter against the AFC #1 seed, the Indianapolis Colts. Dad watched the game with growing intensity as his hope for victory actually turned into belief that the Steelers could win.

As you may recall, I don't care one iota about football, so the details of the game were meaningless to me. The contest started to tighten as Peyton Manning and the Colts mounted a furious fourth quarter comeback to narrow the lead to 21-18. I snoozed on the love seat with Mom and Grandma. Dad was far more animated on the couch amid rising concern that his team would lose a painful defeat. That's when Pittsburgh forced a turnover on downs with less than two minutes remaining. All the Steelers had to do was run the ball, maintain possession, and victory was theirs. Not so fast. That's when the unthinkable happened:

eventual Hall of Famer, Jerome Bettis, fumbled on first down at the 2-yard line. Dad leapt off the couch and stood, screaming at the TV, "No, NO, NOOOOOOOOOOOOOO!!!!" I was so startled by this uproar that I also jumped off my soft perch to figure out what was happening.

Thankfully (for Dad), Colts defensive back Nick Harper could not elude Ben Roethlisberger's crouching tackle as Harper returned Bettis' fumble in the opposite direction. Big Ben's tackle forced Indianapolis to face either driving at least 25-30 yards to attempt a game-tying field goal, or worse yet, moving the ball 58 yards for a game-winning touchdown. Dad slumped back onto the couch and looked on in horror.

First down—22-yard completion. Dad buried his head in his hands, not wanting to watch, but unable to look away. I felt as though Dad needed comfort. As he looked to the floor, I nudged my face between his knees and he faintly rubbed my head mindlessly. First down again—8-yard completion followed by a time out. The Colts were already in field goal range. Tears started to fill Dad's eyes. I licked his face to make him feel better. Second down—incompletion that scarcely grazed off Reggie Wayne's fingertips in the end zone. Dad thought that was the nail in the coffin right there. He said that Bettis' fumble likely would have been the last play of his career and the saddest sports memory ever. Third down—incompletion. With fourth down looming, Dad said that Pittsburgh would lose in overtime because Indy had too much momentum. Pittsburgh coach, Bill Cowher, tried to ice the Colts place kicker, Mike Vanderjagt, with a time out. The most accurate field goal kicker in history, at the time, lined up for a 46-yarder that would almost assuredly result in overtime, especially considering that the game was played inside a dome where wind or precipitation could not alter the field goal attempt.

The kick was up and ... wide right, WAY right. Vanderjagt missed the uprights by a country mile.

Dad did not jump up, did not hoot or holler. He grabbed my head and thanked me for consoling him. I still don't like football, but he's my Dad. If something hurts him, it hurts me. Those last minutes were my favorite football memory, not because the Steelers won, but because our bond had strengthened. I think I helped Mommom a lot more during our family's struggles with infertility, but this was Dad's turn to need a little something extra and I was glad I could be there to help.

Oh ... I guess I should note that three weeks later, Dad got to see his team hoist the Lombardi Trophy for the first time in his memory after the Steelers defeated the Seahawks, 21-10, in Super Bowl XL. Bettis was able to retire as a champion, not a goat.

Dad's celebration involved adorning me with this silly shirt. I was not amused.

❖ MOMMOM POINTED OUT how cute I looked when I was sleeping comfortably. I sometimes twitched while having delightful puppy dreams. My eyes would roll back in my head when experiencing rapid-eye-movement sleep. Best of all, we boxers are among the top snoring breeds. At times, it would be a soft, wispy breath of a snore. Other times, it sounded like a battle sequence between two heavily fortified armies. And, with all this, Mom was suggesting that it would be a terrific idea to have me join my parents to sleep in the big bed. Dad, as he was oft to do, rolled his eyes in disagreement and mild protest.

When late evening rolled around, I asked permission to hop up on the bed by placing my chin on the edge of the bed and stamping my paws repeatedly with a soft, sweet look in my eyes. Dad rebuffed my requests for weeks. Mom suggested that it would be great for us to be close at night. Dad tried to stay strong, but his stance weakened and he eventually relented.

One night, he huffed and realized that he had lost this round. Mom and Dad both patted the bed and beckoned me to come up with them. I excitedly jumped onto the queen bed from Dad's side to give Mom and Dad some kisses as appreciation. Dad directed me to calm down as he regretfully told Mom that this was a bad idea. I circled to find the right spot in the very center of the bed and curled up for my first of thousands of good nights' sleep with my parents.

❖ MOM AND DAD WERE preparing for a nearly month-long trip to Russia to bring home my new sister. I was told that her name was going to be Hanna, and I watched as they erected a crib in one of the upstairs bedrooms. After seeing that annoying doll that blinked and talked, I guessed that it would be unpleasant to have a little girl around here. The blessed event had not yet occurred, but seeing all the preparations let me know that changes were imminent.

It was an unseasonably nice February day in 2006 when Mom and Dad packed all of my earthly possessions. They told me that I was going to stay with Aunt Ally and Cody while they were gone. Mom and Dad met up with my surrogate parents so that they could take me and all my stuff to their home.

Mom and Dad both shed a tear or two when they said their goodbyes. I was all jacked up, and ready to hop into the pickup truck, so I could not concern myself with their somber feelings. Aunt Ally promised that they would take extra special care of Mom and Dad's firstborn, and bring me home as soon as they could, once Hanna was home.

Once I realized that I was departing in the pickup without my parents, I became a little misty about being apart from Mom and Dad. Aunt Ally opened the sliding glass on the pickup truck's rear window and I poked my head out to watch as the distance between my parents and me grew. It made me sad to see them drifting away from me, but I knew that I was in good hands.

Where we lived in South Jersey sometimes gets cold weather in winter, occasionally receives snowfall, but rarely gets hammered with a significant accumulation of snow. I had sensed the displeasure of dealing with snow earlier that winter, but it had never been brutally cold or snowy. For that, I was thankful.

I had the excellent fortune of departing for Aunt Ally and Cody's only a few days in advance of a nasty nor'easter that dropped nearly two feet of snow on my home. Haha ... suckers. But, the joke was on me. The next time I saw my home, we were a family of four. Yikes.

Back in the USSR

I HAD A FANTASTIC TIME staying with Aunt Ally and Cody while Mom and Dad were AWOL. There had been times when I enjoyed visiting my deputy parents, but it was usually for a day or two. More and more days passed, and I began to wonder if I would ever see Mom or Dad again. Nevertheless, I was still happy-go-lucky Newman. Days turned into weeks, and weeks turned into nearly a month. Where the hell were Mom and Dad? I have to admit that I did miss them, despite being so comfortable and content with my current caregivers. And I certainly preferred the milder winters of South Jersey as opposed to the colder, snowier climate of western New York.

Then, it happened. I saw Aunt Ally and Cody loading up all of my gear. I was going on a trip. Woo hoo! I eagerly jumped into the car, after giving Cody some licks to say, "so long for now." Aunt Ally and I snuggled as she drove us to our destination. Nearly six hours later, it was pitch black, but that did not prevent me from seeing that we had turned onto a very recognizable residential road with extremely familiar-looking houses. I was home!!

Aunt Ally could barely contain my enthusiastic efforts to break down the front door to get inside my house. Mom and Dad opened the door to us. They were beyond excited to see me. Without paying much attention to either Mom or Dad, I scampered through each of the downstairs rooms, reacquainting myself with the area.

In that moment, it dawned on me that my parents had given me away for more than thirty days, and for what? I didn't understand why I could not have stayed with Mom and Dad for the past several weeks. A trip to Russia could not have been *that* big a deal. So, what did I do in response? I gave them both a very cold shoulder. It was a rather chilly reunion because I was aggravated. They wanted to fawn all of their fondness upon me. I wanted no part of this pathetic endeavor to make up for their little disappearing act.

Aunt Ally asked whether Hanna was sleeping. Mom responded that she has been asleep for a few hours, but Ally could go up and see her as long as the noise was kept to a minimum. I gave a half-cocked look asking whether I could join Aunt Ally. Mom and Dad didn't tell me to stay, so I accompanied Aunt Ally on the trip upstairs to see what all the fuss was about.

We slowly opened the bedroom door and I could immediately smell that something was *very* different in this room. I began inhaling vigorously as the aroma of baby powder and perhaps a little urine filled my nostrils. I tried to peer into the crib and was alarmed to learn that a (human) toddler was peacefully sleeping in our house. I had been prepped for this to occur, but the reality of the moment was overwhelming.

I had long since forgotten that we were adopting a little girl, frankly because we dogs can't hold a thought for longer than a few moments. From my vantage point, I had just spent the last month of my life with Aunt Ally and Cody in snowy and cold western New York. Now, I was back home and more than mildly miffed at my parents for ditching me for so long. To put the cherry on top, a young girl was here ... now ... in MY house. Does she always sleep?

Could she walk? Could she talk? What does she eat? Was she a third parent? Was she my toy? Was I her toy? So many questions, so little focus.

As Aunt Ally's focus remained on Hanna, I continued to snout around the room to try and become a little more acquainted with this new situation. The three adults were speaking in hushed whispers about "Hanna this and Hanna that." After carefully considering the contents of the room, everything looked much as it did before today; there was the same dresser, bed, closet, diaper container, mirror on the wall, with one rather significant exception: Hanna. With my inspection complete, I failed to see the purpose of being in the room any longer, so I began to whine. At that moment, Dad rapidly guided me out of the room for some strange reason.

The next morning, Mom, Dad, Aunt Ally, and I awoke to the sound of something bouncing in the bedroom where the little girl slept the prior night. We had varying levels of urgency to locate the source of the noise. The adults methodically moved toward the bedroom, whereas I jetted off the bed and was ready to break down the door to find out what was causing the racket.

When the door opened, I bounded through the door to find a little girl jumping up and down in her crib. She had very short, sandy colored hair, although she looked as though she were predominantly bald. I guessed that if she were at ground level, our eye levels would be pretty close in height. Mom and Dad announced us each by name: "Hanna, this is your dog Newman." "Newman, this is your new sister, Hanna." I took a deep bow with my front shoulders pressed near to the floor. This wasn't a sign of deference. No, not in the least. As is typical of boxers, I was merely stretching so that I was properly loosened up and fully limber.

I was prepping to approach her until she took one wide-eyed look at me and shrieked at the top of her lungs for several seconds. I reactively took a step or two backwards, while Mom and Dad looked at one another with trepidation. That was quite a way for her to introduce herself to me. They tried to reassure Hanna that it was okay, and that I was a nice doggie. Why weren't they reassuring *me*? She was the one who woke up the neighborhood with an octave and decibel level that should never, ever go together.

When Mom lifted Hanna out of the crib, I attempted to sniff Hanna's dangling feet to get to know her better. She instinctively retracted each limb to avoid me, and put forth a few more sharp, shrill, short chirps to let Mom know that she disapproved of my attempted interaction. Hanna made that ridiculous doll that monotonously said "Mama" seem like pizza, hamburgers, treats, ear scratches, or anything else that was remotely positive. Dad decided that he and I should go downstairs and get breakfast to de-stress the situation. We ate while the girls stayed upstairs for quite a while.

When they came down, my inquisitive nature compelled me to check out Hanna again. She did not scream this time. No, now Hanna was crying because of me. *Great*. Mom and Dad wanted us to get acquainted. Meanwhile, big crocodile tears were streaming down Hanna's cheeks.

For the first several hours after our initial greeting, I was instructed to keep my distance from Hanna. It was exceptionally difficult to do so! She was a new person with new smells that alternated among baby powder, leftover food, boogers, and shit. All were interesting in their own way. Hanna was in *my* house, she was an easy target because she was smaller and relatively helpless, and apparently, she was my sister! With my eyes, I asked Dad when she was going home because I couldn't continue to be yelled at all day long. No response.

By the time Hanna's afternoon nap rolled around, I was exhausted and needed a break, too. I could not be subjected to such vehement rebukes. I dozed off as all three adults consoled me. Aunt Ally decided that it was in all of our best interests that she should head back home. She was extremely busy with work this time of year, and thought it was best for our family to have time to begin figuring out the new family dynamic. I could not disagree more. When Aunt Ally said goodbye, I really didn't want her to leave. She and Cody have always had a special place in my heart, and I wished that we could spend all of our time together.

❖ WHEN THE NOISE of bouncing from upstairs stirred me from my own afternoon siesta, I realized that I had heard that exact sound earlier. Evidently, this was Hanna's way of telling Mom and Dad that she was awake and ready to get out of her crib. We all went upstairs to greet her following her slumber. She was once again far less than enthused about seeing me. Her eyes were focused on me, like a hawk. Hanna cringed when she saw my face looking at hers. Once I had turned away with my back to her, I felt a sensation that was quite unexpected: the touch of tiny, delicate fingers on my back. Hanna had touched me! The instant I wheeled around to face her, she locked her eyes on mine and began to scowl and writhe around in Mom's arms as though I had injured her. You're the one who touched me!

Mom and Dad developed a theory based on Hanna's reaction to not only me, but stuffed animals and dolls that were presented to her. She did not like anything with a face unless it was a person. Wonderful. Last time I checked, I had one of those face things. Oh, and I wasn't a person. That could potentially explain why Hanna was willing to touch my back and she exhibited increased curiosity about me as I faced away from her. But, if my deep brown eyes met her grayish-blue eyes, bring on the four horsemen.

The apocalypse was underway.

At mealtime, she was perched in her highchair while the humans sat around the kitchen table. My goodness, Hanna was a speedy eater! By the time the adults tasted their first few bites of food, Hanna had inhaled everything in front of her. Hanna was also a bit sloppy when devouring her food. I suppose that is to be expected when you're barely a year old. I considered the crumbs that either fell into her lap or onto the floor as my domain. As such, I hurriedly gobbled up the morsels that I could. The ones on the floor did not pose a problem. The others that I attempted to gently pick off Hanna's legs or at the base of the highchair were a bit more of an issue. She repeatedly tried to kick me to keep my face away from of her body parts. Hanna was not crying, but was obviously irritated by my insistence to retrieve the human food that she had discarded. I received multiple thumps heaped upon my dome, but the tasty human food was well worth the minimal physical pain that was being inflicted upon me. There may be some things that I will have to get used to about you, little girl. But, one thing is for sure: you need to understand that I would risk almost anything to eat your unwanted human food.

I saw a small bin of toys set up in the living room that looked interesting. Every once in a while, Hanna pulled out one of the toys to enjoy. I desperately wanted to see if she had anything better than what I had, but I was afraid that I would get berated or pelted, so I left her stuff alone. It didn't mean that I wouldn't keep both eyes affixed to her every move.

I descended from my position on the couch to get a drink, when I surprisingly felt a small hand rub the entire length of my back. It caused me to shudder slightly, but I knew that Hanna was once again touching the fur of my body. Maybe we were making some progress after all. Well, aside from, you know, the small issue that I could not look at her without hearing a yelp or seeing clear body language that she was not yet a big fan of the Newman.

    I felt like that was enough headway that I had a surprise of my own in store for little Miss Hanna. When I returned from my glugging down a few ounces of water, I meandered over and gave her a big, sloppy kiss right on the mouth. After the first lick or two hit their intended mark, Hanna furrowed her brow and forcefully pushed my face away from her. I then lowered my aim to lick each of her hands as she tried to swat me away. Mommom and Dad let this happen for a few seconds because Hanna and I were both asserting ourselves, and doing no harm to one another. When my licking persisted too long (as was often the case), Dad pulled me back to beyond arm's reach of my sister. Hanna's reaction was not a scream, nor was it tears. Rather, she glared at me with a scowl of contempt. Another positive: she was looking at me.

    Our first day was a rocky one. We had a lot of work to do to find common ground, but I certainly wasn't going to maul Hanna. She had far too much potential as a playmate. I may try to lick her to death!

    Because of the day's events, I had long since forgotten about the grudge I wanted to hold over my parents' heads for them leaving me. I could barely focus on one thing, so keeping any secondary thoughts in the back of my mind was a losing proposition.

    I tentatively approached Hanna the following morning and she slapped my head, but I think it was done playfully. So, I cringed, squinted my eyes, and let her swat away. After several seconds of receiving a light beating, I exacted a bit of spirited revenge by placing my nose in her face and snouting her. We toyed with each other in a fun-filled way for the better part of a minute. Mom and Dad were ecstatic that Hanna was not verbally accosting me. Who knew that a sister could be fun? I intended to spend the rest of my life finding out.

❖ AS HANNA BECAME adapted more to life in our house, the hierarchy of the family made more and more sense. Mom and Dad still liked to think that they were the bosses, but in actuality, it was the youngest one who called the shots. She had a very hot temper for being so small, often making her intentions crystal clear. Even though she did not have a full grasp of the English language, she could make her feelings quite well understood with her lungs. When she didn't like something, we all knew about it, as did our neighbors, those in bordering townships, and maybe even ships in the Atlantic Ocean more than sixty miles away.

Hanna's personality started to grow on me, and I would defer to her needs being met first before mine. One game that she especially enjoyed playing was giving kisses to everyone in the house, including me. Hanna would get a kiss from Mom, then get a kiss from me, and share her slobber with Dad. This was especially enjoyable when someone like Grandma Diane was visiting. She was not the biggest fan of kissing Hanna following my sister's acceptance of a slobbery, wet kiss from yours truly.

I came to understand that we each had our bin of toys. Mine remained rather small, while Hanna's seemed to grow exponentially. Although I was quite curious about Hanna's playthings, I would only sniff them extensively for a minute or two to determine if they were any fun for me. Once I gave one of Hanna's toys an initial inspection, I was done with it. Mom and Dad were amazed that I was able to constrain myself from gnawing on Hanna's toys. The way I looked at it was that they were boring. Dolls, building blocks, a toy drum, teddy bears. Yuck! If she ever gets something interesting like a fake newspaper or a rawhide bone, then she might be in trouble.

Hanna's drum ... yawn. You got any squeaky toys on you?

One of the best aspects of having a little sister was that Mommom was now a primarily stay-at-home mom. I could be left alone for hours, but Hanna evidently could not do the same. Why not? I think she and I would take good care of each other. The house might be destroyed, but that's not our problem.

Any time Hanna was around, at least one of my parents was there, too. It was a welcome change to now spend the overwhelming majority of my days with Mom and Hanna. Not only did I get to be with my girls, but equally as important, I was rarely in my crate. Thanks for coming along, Hanna. You changed my life for the better!

❖ BECAUSE WE LIVED IN New Jersey and our backyard

did not offer all that much room to roam, Mom and Dad started taking Hanna and me to Laurel Acres Park, a local park that had some softball fields, a hiking trail, a picturesque pond, but most important, included a dog park. This dog park offered owners a chain link enclosure that measured about 60 feet by 120 feet where dogs could run, play, and interact with other canines and owners. We met all different kinds of dogs. Thankfully, most of the owners were laid back and did not mind the freneticism that I brought with me to the dog park (I think that every pooch I met was just like me—a bundle of irrepressible energy).

One spring morning, after a massive rainstorm had dumped an inch or two of rain on us the night before, I had the entire area to myself. That's when I noticed a young woman running along the path just outside the confinement. She was running!! I thought I might join in the fun, so I sprinted along the front edge of the fence closest to her for several yards. I realized that I had failed to account for the results of last night's downpour; a puddle, which could be better categorized as a small pond, was directly in front of me. It was about twenty feet long by five feet wide. There was no avoiding it, no way, no how. My best option was to leap and see if I could get to the other side. I did my best Bob Beamon impersonation and tried to long jump the full length of the water.

Despite a rather heroic effort, I managed to jump about 10 - 11 feet of the required 20. I landed in the low-lying area, spraying water in a circular pattern around me. Uggh! I was absolutely waterlogged and now ready to go home. Dad observed the whole thing and had a good laugh at my expense. He made me stay in the dog park for a few minutes to dry out a bit before getting into the car all soaking wet. The good news was that this was my last trip to the dog park at Laurel Acres. Not because I got drenched or misbehaved. We were moving!

New York State of Mind

ONCE HANNA HAD BECOME part of the family, Mommom had talked to Dad about moving closer to the majority of the family. Both she and Dad desired to raise us "kids" where we could have a bigger house and more expansive yard. We had a very nice, yet simple home in New Jersey. Moving closer to where both Mom and Dad grew up would afford us the opportunity to potentially upgrade, because the cost of living was substantially lower in western New York than it was in South Jersey.

Fortunately for us, it only took Dad a matter of months to accept an employment offer in suburban Rochester, New York. We were headed north! I had the good fortune of moving prematurely with Hanna to stay with family for a few days while Mom and Dad packed up all of our belongings. I bid adieu to New Jersey and never stepped paw in the Garden State again. We created a lot of great memories in our first house together, but now it was time to move onward, upward, and northward. As I crossed the Delaware River for the last time, I did not hurl as I did two years ago when I had first entered South Jersey.

Once my parents rejoined Hanna and I in western New York, I was given some exciting news: we were temporarily moving in with Aunt Ally and Cody! They had enough space to accommodate two more adults, one child, and one tremendous dog at their place until we had a home of our own. It certainly didn't take me long at all to get settled into my new environment. I'd been here before on extended stays, so the adjustment period for me was minimal, perhaps just a few minutes to mark my territory in the half-acre backyard that was enclosed by a chain link fence.

I had more room to roam in my new backyard.

Everyone had their own room and it was a comfortable, very dog-friendly environment. Each night, I cuddled with Mom and Dad on their bed, often lying in a dead horse position across one of their legs. Because of their work schedules, Aunt Ally and Cody arose an hour earlier in the morning than my parents. When I heard footsteps coming from their downstairs bedroom, I jumped down from my perch atop Mom or Dad to begin my day. I was always greeted by Aunt Ally and Cody with such vigor and love that, in response, my nub wagged enthusiastically. I might possibly achieve liftoff. What a fantastic way to get rid of the typical morning doldrums! I went outside, did my business, had some breakfast, and played with my housemates for a bit. When they left for work, I could go back upstairs and nap with my parents until it was time for Dad to prepare for his usual workday. I loved the new routine where I got a turn with everyone as they awoke. After Dad took his turn to get ready and leave for work, I relished watching Mom get Hanna out of her crib, my two girls. It was like a series of new adventures each time another member of the household awakened.

I loved having so many people in the house who were willing to devote their attention to me. We all ate dinner together. More often than not, multiple people wanted to go for a walk with me, or even toss some of my toys inside the house. I had four people to harass for treats, and for potty trips outside (Hanna wasn't quite ready to be a caregiver, but she sure was growing!). We had started to get so familiar with one another that I nearly considered Aunt Ally and Cody as equals to Mom and Dad.

My parents were actively looking for a house, but were very particular about what they wanted, especially considering our house in New Jersey had not yet sold after a few months on the market. Aunt Ally and Cody told us that we could stay for as long as we needed, which made the transition to Rochester an easy one.

Autumn 2006 was huge for our family. We had already moved, and then Hanna had her first birthday celebration with us at age two. A day later, Cody was getting a new title; he was officially becoming my uncle! Yep, that's right. Two of my housemates were tying the knot.

Just about everyone from the family was attending the

wedding; except for me, that is. I guess it's one of those special "people only" events where lovable dogs are excluded from the festivities. Dining, dancing, and drinks. Come on people, that's right up my alley! You should see my dance moves.

My usual dogsitters—grandmas, grandpas, aunts, uncles, parents—all got invitations to the wedding and reception. But, even though I was their housemate, I still was snubbed from being part of the guest list. Instead of being an invitee to the blessed event, I traveled to Grandma and Grandpa's house to stay in their basement, which was not my ideal way to spend a Saturday night.

Since my first trip to their house, I had gotten used to spending time in the basement. It certainly wasn't my first preference. For regular weekend visits, I had stopped trying to dig my way to freedom. However, I still whined if I felt starved for company, knowing that my humans were close in proximity.

A friend of the family graciously offered to take care of me for my food and facility needs in the afternoon and evening of the wedding. I was rather well behaved for my dogsitter. She and I made two trips out to the yard without incident, going potty as needed. She noted that I refused to eat, which was not uncommon when I was away from my comfortable home. I was just more "on edge" when our typical routine was abandoned.

She guided me into the kennel in the late evening hours so that my time in the basement would be minimized as much as possible. I willingly followed the orders, but looked on questioningly as she departed. When would she be back? Would I see my family again that night? My anxiety started to build and build until I could no longer take it.

I barked and moaned, wishing that someone would come to keep me company. Please, please help me. Hours passed and the only noise I heard was my own voice. Not knowing that Mom or Dad would return the next morning, I began to go stir crazy. I needed to get out of the eight foot by ten foot kennel NOW.

I could not leap over the fence because it was nearly five feet tall, and I feared that I would somehow injure myself. I had not yet figured out how to unlatch the gate, so I couldn't exactly just let myself out. The best solution I could come up with was to revert to clawing at the floor. I furiously tried to create a crater large enough to slide underneath the bottom edge of the kennel. The poured cement floor was a pretty stout barrier and did not yield as readily as I had hoped. I was only able to loosen a tiny portion of the top layer of flooring into a small pile. After significantly wearing down my front toenails over the course of countless minutes, it was evident that I wasn't going to get out this way.

I was fuming MAD. So, I persisted by making noise throughout the night. The frustration boiled in me so hot that I leaped and shook the sides of the chain link fence that was encasing me. I pushed hard enough with my front paws that I knocked over onto the cement a nearby halogen lamp that was a few inches outside my kennel; glass shattered into about a hundred tiny pieces. The only good news was that no shards found their way into my kennel, so I didn't end up injuring myself.

As the light of the morning came through the basement window, my long night of solitude was coming to a close. Mom and Dad finally opened the exterior basement door to see me. I had never wanted to see someone so badly in all of my life. Unfortunately, when they viewed me, they focused more on the piles of crumbled cement, broken glass, and toppled lamp.

Dad's temper rose instantaneously. I knew I was in deep

trouble by the way that he abrasively placed the collar around my neck and attached the leash. Neither he nor Mom greeted me with their typical baby talk when we have been apart for a period of time. It was silence, only broken up Dad's grumbling commands of, "Newman. Outside. Now." Ooooh ... he was pissed. I needed to find a way to get back into their good graces, and fast.

I went potty, drank water, and ate breakfast without prompting either parent for anything else. I think that I was on the receiving end of a fury that was roughly equivalent to how I had felt when I was neutered. Maybe I just needed to lie low for a while.

It was a pretty dark mood for the next day or so. I gradually worked up the courage to ask for playtime, treats, and the like. I had to win them over and show that I had some redeeming qualities. Time eventually healed this massive wound that I had triggered with my conduct as Aunt Ally and Uncle Cody had wedded.

Man in the Box

THROUGHOUT OUR FIRST FALL and winter in suburban Rochester, Mom and Dad spent several evenings and weekends out with a woman whose professional title was called a realtor. My parents entrusted Hanna and me to the care of our live-in babysitters while they were out looking for a house. I didn't understand why we couldn't just continue to live here with Aunt Ally and Uncle Cody; but, as usual, no one asked me for input on this decision.

After weeks of visiting houses, my parents finally found the place that the four of us would call "home." Once all the paperwork was finished and the house was officially ours, we were able to move some of our furniture, home appliances, valuables, and other possessions into the new house. It was in an area that was suburban, bordering on the rural side of things. When we first got inside and took a look around, I had to investigate each of the spacious rooms to assess if they were Newman-worthy. Mommom kept snapping photos in each room. Despite my reluctance to be the subject of photographs, I thought this was a worthy occasion for Mom to see what a good-looking dog would look like in each of the rooms that were not yet fully furnished.

The new house had so much more room than our previous digs in New Jersey, both inside and out. The downstairs had a very open floor plan, which allowed me to have ample room to maneuver. I could no longer be segregated in a room, like the kitchen, with only a baby gate. It would require a heck of a lot more ingenuity to isolate me anywhere in the house, aside from putting up a barrier at the foot of the stairs.

    I bounded upstairs to snoop around the second-floor living quarters. There were four bedrooms, two bathrooms, and an airy bonus room that were all connected by a common hallway. I could sprint the 25 yards from Mom and Dad's bedroom to the bonus room window in a straight line, allowing me to get from one end of the house to the other in a flash. This allowed my nosey behavior to investigate both the goings on inside the house as well as outside our four walls. The bonus room offered a great vantage point from which to look over the neighborhood from the second floor. I could see our driveway, the next door neighbor's house, along with an extended view along the street of our new residence. If someone was out exercising or walking their canine, I would see it all. This would also prove to be valuable to see who was coming to our house. Once I scoped out whether it was family or a visitor arriving, I might even have enough time to sprint down the hall, bound down the steps, and get to the garage door to provide a proper greeting to whoever it was. I needed to test that out. The bonus room "perch" felt like a kingly throne, with my lowly subjects appearing on the street far beneath me.

    I had quickly figured out that there are three ways to get in and out of the house from the first floor: the garage, front door, and back door. Visitors tended to approach our domicile from the front door while we family members typically came and went via the garage door. The sliding glass door that led to the backyard opened onto an elevated wooden deck with a set of ten steps that led down to the lawn. This became the most important door for me, as it was my preferred route to relieve myself. After moving in, we had one significant problem: our yard was not fenced. As such, each time I had to go outside, I was attached to the leash and collar with a parent in tow. It was ridiculous that I had to urinate or defecate with Mom or Dad a few feet away at the other end of the leash. We had to come up with a different solution, and fast!

My parents researched several options. I was accustomed to being contained by visible barriers that surrounded less than a quarter of an acre. One option was to erect a traditional fence around some portion of the nearly two acres that we owned. Even if we only fenced the area between a half-acre and a full acre that enclosed our back and side yards, it would come at a hefty price.

Another potential solution was an invisible fence, where a wire would be interred in the ground to set the perimeter. In this case, I would wear a collar that emitted a warning tone if I were approaching the border where the wire was buried. If I continued closer to the line, I would receive a low dosage static correction that was meant to deter me from proceeding any further and keep me safely within my own yard.

It was quite the conundrum considering that Mom and Dad were unsure how I would respond to an invisible barrier. I was always an "out of sight, out of mind" kind of pup. But, they didn't want to segment their yard with an unsightly fence and shoulder a significant cost in doing so. After receiving a quote of several thousand dollars for a vinyl fence, Mom and Dad met with the Invisible Fence folks. My parents were apprehensive that my hyperactivity and craziness in general would not lend itself to securely staying within the confines of the established perimeter of the invisible fence. The trainer mentioned that a pet drifting outside the fence line was obviously the most common concern of the invisible fence among pet owners. If Mom and Dad decided to pursue this route, a trainer would come to the house to work with me on understanding the boundary and ingraining it in me so that I got it through my thick gourd where I could go and where I couldn't.

They reluctantly signed the dotted line to have the invisible fence installed at our house. Mom and Dad had to first determine exactly where they wanted to have the wire installed. After significant deliberation, the entire backyard, entire side yard, and about one-third of the front yard would be included. Mommom felt that my menacing appearance could intimidate guests if I were given access to the entire front yard. This would allow walkers, vehicles, and pets to traverse our quiet lane without fear of being jumped by this boxer pup.

Once the installation was complete, a series of short, white flags were displayed every few feet, dotting where the wire had been laid. These flags were meant to act as a temporary visible barrier around which I could wrap my mind. A trainer came to the house to educate me on the area that was available to me. He put a new collar on me with two prongs that gently protruded into my neck. It didn't hurt, not one bit. The young man put me on a leash and walked me to various areas inside the flagged area of the yard. As we approached any of the flags signaling that we were nearing the perimeter of the invisible fence, he would yell, "Back!" and we would take a few sprinting steps back toward the house. This seemed like a fun game! We kept doing it, over and over, until we had completed a 360-degree lap around the house.

The next time, he allowed me to get a bit closer to the flags. The first time I heard the tone, I cocked my head and immediately headed for the house. That startled me! I was considerably more reluctant to approach the flags now that I knew that they made noise. Yikes! We picked a different spot in the side yard to approach a flag, and I sensed the same sound. This time, instead of being allowed to bolt for home, the trainer led me a few inches closer to the flags. I felt this wave go through me, starting at my neck. I yelped and instinctively ran away from the problem. Damn, that really shocked me! I didn't want to go toward the flag if that was going to happen.

While we were back in the safe area of the yard, the young man petted me and reassured me that I was a good boy. If I was so good, then why in the world was I hearing noises and succumbing to jolts of whatever that was? After a minute of positive reinforcement (affection and treats), we again neared a set of flags. As we got within five feet or so, I bucked backward with my body so violently that the trainer could not get me to go anywhere near the flags. I really despised that sensation, and never wanted to feel it again. He paraded me around the yard to give me confidence in where I could go. Then, the unexpected happened: he dropped the leash.

I walked around the yard nervously, afraid to go anywhere. I wondered if I would be zapped at any given moment. I tentatively put one paw in front of the other to see where I could go. Right now, I felt as though our yard had shrunk. The backyard was always my favorite, so I sniffed around back there, hoping to avoid any sudden noises. All the areas I had used to make deposits seemed to be accessible without any incident. After a few minutes of exploration, the trainer said that it was probably overwhelming for me to have this sudden change. So, we all returned inside the house. He thought that the initial training session went extremely well, and that I honored the boundaries flawlessly. Perhaps I gave them a little too much respect, but it was better for me to err on the side of caution.

Over the course of the next two or three days, Mom and Dad continued to work on improving my comfort with the yard. Someone always accompanied me outside. Often, they coerced me to expand the territory I could enjoy. If I was tentative about being zapped, I would put my nose to the ground as a sign that I didn't want to take another step forward.

I could only do portions of the yard at a time because I never felt confident about taking the full lap around the house. Dad worked on this with me by appealing to my compulsion to burn energy. We lined up in the front yard and he stood next to me, exclaiming, "Ready, set, GO!!" He was off in a flash (well, as flashy as 30ish-year-old white guys can run), sprinting across the yard. What choice did I have but to follow? He left a blur as he approached the side yard, but I was gaining on him. Dad drifted far into the side yard and dashed toward the back side of the house. I was even with him as we hit the blacktop driveway and completed the full 100- to 150-yard circuit right back to where we started. Dad slowed to a stop and congratulated me with lots of head rubs and playful slaps to my sides. Huh, what did I do to deserve that? I just ran, what's the big deal?

Dad got down next to me and asked if I wanted to go for another run. You know I'm game, old man. He and I took off together this time and I easily took the lead. Ha ha, ya old slow fart. By the time we hit the backyard, I looked back and jogged in a taunting way to allow someone's slow two legs the opportunity to catch up to me. We finished another lap. This leashless freedom was fantastic!

Dad steadied me for a minute, and yelled, "Ready, set, GO!" one more time. Only he didn't join me. I bolted as fast as my legs would carry me. When I got to the lawn behind the house, I saw Dad standing in the driveway, beckoning me to run faster. He pointed for me to continue running, so I immediately took another lap with eyes wide, jowls flapping, and drool flying. It was simply glorious.

Mom and Dad had made the right choice with the fence. I loved the ability to circumnavigate the house to spy all the comings and goings of our quaint neighborhood. After that night of running, my days with a leash in the yard were a thing of the past. Over the next few weeks, I saw the number of white flags marking the invisible fence perimeter diminish in number from 100 to 50 to 25, until they completely disappeared from our yard. I maintained a healthy respect for the tone and the zap that I would receive at a certain distance from the house where the flags used to be. Believe me, that distance was etched permanently into my brain. I knew that I never wanted to experience that sensation again. Mom and Dad still watched me intently, but allowed me the liberty to enjoy my yard to its fullest.

❖ AS I WAS EXITING the terrible twos and about to be of legal age to drink, my conduct had actually begun to stabilize.[5] There were no longer any destructive outbursts. I could even be trusted to stay in the house (in short stints anyway) all by my lonesome without ruining any of our belongings. I used to be the problem child, the loose cannon whose expected behavior was the unexpected. Now, I was a big brother. I had a little girl who needed a lot more assistance than I. I also got the sense that we were settling into a home where we would stay forever.

Hanna was a goofy, fun-loving girl at the age of two. She liked to bounce around and danced quite often. One night, while she was dancing in the living room, I had a short dose of pent-up energy that I needed to expend. So,

---

[5] Nowhere is it documented that dogs can legally drink, but I was nearly three years old. A dog's age is roughly seven years for every human year: 3 x 7 = 21, just sayin'.

I started sprinting laps inside the house. I jetted from the living room through the house to tap my toes atop the treacherously slippery tile of the kitchen to the dining room. There, I liked to take a side excursion that included at least one circuit around the dining room table at full speed. You could hear my "cornering" as I dug my claws into the Berber carpet at each corner of the table to maintain as much velocity as possible. I needed to maintain a high rate of speed as I ventured onto the tiled entry area and returned to the living room.

Once back in the living room, I would take a tight turn to loop around the couch and begin the lap all over again. I think that I was on lap number two or three when I returned back to the living room and was passing within a foot or two of my little sis, who was bopping along to some music. She promptly plopped to the floor on her back side. I slammed on the brakes with my paws skidding to an immediate halt. I slowly turned around and nosed Hanna gently. "Did I hurt you? Are you okay?" She wasn't crying and I don't recall touching her while sprinting my laps, or even coming all that close. I placed my snout in her face and looked at her more intently just to be sure. I gave her a lick on the cheek, then off I went for the start of another lap.

❖ HANNA DEFINITELY RULED the roost at home. I felt as though I had to cater to her because she was the youngest and smallest member of the family. Once her initial disgust with me subsided, I think that she viewed me as a playmate. She was a very "monkey see, monkey do" sort of girl.

Mommom was busy showering one morning, so Hanna replicated something she had seen occur on a regular basis since coming home to us ... only she used *me* as a guinea pig. When Mom came out of the shower, she took one look at me and burst out laughing. Hanna had used the roll-on deodorant to keep me smelling extra fresh. She had picked up each of my front paws and rolled on the deodorant in each of my "armpits." Not only that, she had gotten out the Vaseline to lotion my head. These are products that never had any business touching a canine, but I begrudgingly sat still and accommodated Hanna's desire to have my fur looking extra clear and my pits being protected from sweat (that we dogs never secrete from under our front shoulders).

I would also succumb to other playful endeavors of the little one. Hanna enjoyed doing girly things, which is perfectly understandable; except that I'm a *male* dog. She often would pretend to paint fingernails and toenails, only she chose to extend this privilege to me more than once. I would willingly submit to allowing her to do this, but only with pretend nail polish. Mom and Dad ensured that I never actually had painted toenails. After all, what parent would allow a two-year-old who can't color within the lines to have access to actual nail polish? Not my folks, thank God.

It takes a masculine male dog to sit for a pedicure.

Now that Hanna was around, my parents were homebodies more often than in the past. There still were times that they ventured out without the two of us, but it was infrequent. On such occasions, they would often get a grandparent or two to take care of the "kids." Even though I was very comfortable with other family members, I still felt the obligation to watch out for my little sister. I deemed that the babysitter needed to be babysat. If one of the grandmas or grandpas was playing with Hanna on the floor, I tended to be inches from Hanna to ensure that there was no funny business. I had taken it upon myself to add "watchdog" to my list of responsibilities. It's not that my caretakers were untrustworthy. It was more so that I was overly protective of Hanna. What can I say, she had grown on me.

❖ AFTER WE HAD FULLY furnished the house, I habitually watched from the fringe of the living room carpet while the family ate at the dinner table, which was a mere three feet away. But, in other people's homes (like Aunt Ally and Uncle Cody's, or Dad's parents), I would worm my way beneath the table where the meal was being served because I loved being around my people. Perhaps of equal or greater importance, I might find an occasional morsel or two of food that dropped down to me if I happened to be in the correct position. I could much more easily beg for scraps from this location, with a simple whimper or a nose to someone's hand. I didn't always receive them, but I thought my chances were greatly improved.

Mom and Dad wondered why I had chosen to lie on the carpet of the living room floor, as opposed to the smooth tile under the kitchen table during meals. When they ordered a rug to be placed beneath the kitchen table, the answer became obvious: I preferred the comfort of carpet under my delicate body, as opposed to the hard tile surface.

The first time that my family had a meal with the brown

area rug covering the tile under the area where they dined, I immediately found a spot to lie where my family could touch me with their toes. I enjoyed mealtime a lot more now that I could be closer to my crew.

On my third birthday, Dad had the brilliant idea to present me with something very different to imbibe. He had poured a few ounces of a new liquid from a brown-colored bottle into my water dish. At first I had paid zero attention because, after all, it was my birthday. I was preoccupied with receiving extra attention, treats, presents, or maybe even playing with one of my new toys. Dad had to beckon me over to my food/water dish by the kitchen table. He pointed to the water dish. I bent down, smelling that it was different than the odorless water that always quenched my thirst. Sniff, sniff, sniff. Hmm ... let's try that. I took down a few gulps' worth, and then looked over my shoulder at Dad. This was delicious! I chugged down the ounces of beer even though I wasn't even all that thirsty. I licked the bowl clean to get every last drop of the Yuengling lager. After giving the water dish a thorough cleansing, I also licked my jowls repeatedly to savor the taste. Using only my eyes, I begged Dad for more beer, but he refused to comply. He was afraid that too much alcohol would be bad for me. Can you imagine how uncoordinated a *drunk* boxer dog could be? A scary thought indeed.

The Pretender

ONCE A DOG EXITS the puppy stage, you probably think that there won't be too many more surprises about being a dog owner. You may have survived the reckless energy, chewing, destructive nature, potty training, and even humping. I had grown up to the point where I didn't even require a Gentle Leader. I could be walked with the freedom to roam nearly twenty feet on a retractable leash.

Having said that, I will confirm that every now and then, life throws you a curveball. You think a ball is crossing over the heart of the plate allowing you to lace a single between the third basemen and shortstop. Instead, the ball breaks several inches and you nearly get plunked because the baseball breaks eight inches inside. As my parents arose on a weekday morning for work, I provided them with a pitch that broke the *opposite* way, much like a Fernando Valenzuela screwball.

They noticed several long shit streaks upstairs just outside our bedroom. There weren't piles of crap, just three separate 8 to 12-inch-long, narrow brown smudges that lined the carpet without much substance. There were a few other spots on the carpet that were primarily clear, but had a tinge of brown to them. Many questions sprang to their minds. Did I have a one-time accident and try to dispose of the evidence? That didn't make a lot of sense because I *never* went potty in the house since my first week with my forever family.

What surprised them more than anything was the odor. Yes, it smelled awful, but there was a stench that was altogether different than dog crap, which combined to make the bouquet unbearably putrid. Dad got right down next to one of the streaks and made the mistake of taking a big sniff. The acrid odor was so noxious that he recoiled and nearly gagged. He asked Mom to do likewise, but he sold it so well that she declined.

Would I tell them the truth if I spoke human? Nah ... probably not. It was a gross bodily function that I did not understand. I just knew that stuff had leaked out of my ass, but it was not poop. I scooted my back side along the carpet to try and get this foulness out of me a few times. As the juices were flowing out of me, I also took to licking my own rear to "clean" myself. That explains the dirty streaks and wet spots.

When my parents called the vet, everything became crystal clear on what had happened. Dogs have anal glands that occasionally fill. When this occurs, the glands need to be "expressed." In essence, the glands spewed out a smelly liquid. Dogs often respond just as I had done. Mom and Dad asked the vet's office if this was likely to happen again. In short, the answer was yes. It may happen periodically, but should not be a common occurrence. Ah ... the joys of being Newman's parents are endless!

❖ ON A BEAUTIFUL SPRING evening, Mom, Dad, Hanna, and I took a drive to go see Aunt Ally and Uncle Cody. We often visited with them and Aunt Lindsay now that all of us lived in suburban Rochester. This get-together proved to be far different than the typical dinner; it also served as an introduction to a new family member.

When we arrived, I heard loud barking coming from inside their house. My eyes darted to the source of the noise, where I saw a lean, young canine. I needed to investigate IMMEDIATELY. Uncle Cody led this new dog away from the front door, through the house, and out to the backyard so that we could greet each other in open space. He felt that it was the safest option with Hanna around, in case any melee ensued. In case.

I bolted through the front door with bulging eyes, trying to locate him or her, but Uncle Cody and the dog had already departed to the lawn. Dad escorted me to the back door, where I couldn't get through it quickly enough. When the door opened, I sprinted outside, across the deck, and onto the lawn to meet Bailey. He was a bit shorter than me with coarse yellowish brown fur, a long wagging tail, and a lengthy, rail-thin body. I chased Bailey throughout the yard to familiarize myself with him. We scoped each other out as we took turns being the aggressor and the submissive beast. Each of us sniffed and growled and tried to discern more about each other while trying to establish our position as more of the alpha male.

I had a few pounds on him, but, at barely one year of age, Bailey was younger and spryer. Suffice it to say that we did not exactly see eye to eye. I could not fathom why he was there. Was he a visitor? Where did he come from? Was he staying? Aunt Ally and Uncle Cody served as my surrogate parents on multiple occasions, so I considered them MY humans. I took offense that Bailey was invading my territory. Bailey was only defending himself, and he clearly viewed me as the outsider.

We each were protecting what we deemed as our personal territory. I understood all the background leading up to this moment. I could not make sense of the here and now. Correspondingly, Bailey had no previous perspective, but he felt as though he was top dog right now at MY aunt and uncle's house.

We chased each other throughout the yard, stopping and starting to smell each other, and pouncing on one another's backs. It was playfully ferocious. Our energy was boundless. We did not want to hurt the other dog, but we wanted to stake our claim to being the big dog on campus. Both Dad and Uncle Cody broke us up a few times when we got too rough. The humans comprehended something that we canines did not: we had to become more accustomed to each other so that we could coexist.

After forty-five minutes of the initial "how do you do" romp in the yard, we were guided into the house to eat dinner. The humans gave us food and water in segregated areas of the kitchen while they prepared their own meals. We downed our food and investigated each other's water. Despite coming from the same source, we both drank out of our own, as well as our adversary's, water dishes. We began to settle down as our humans dined, perhaps because of fatigue. We both lay under the dining room table without any significant incident for the majority of dinnertime.

Before the meal concluded, Bailey and I suddenly roused and played a game of chase in the house. We growled and carried on a bit too much. Aunt Ally was particularly concerned about us potentially injuring ourselves while traversing up and down the stairs. We made such a cacophony of sound as we ran through the house, took tight corners, and did countless flights of steps, that our behavior led to the adoption of a new rule: if we were going to act crazy, we had to go outside. Uncle Cody opened the door and allowed us to resume our introductions while the adults and child had dessert.

It was more of the same from before dinner: pouncing, snarling, and sprinting. It could be viewed as "play fighting."

We did not want to hurt each other. It was more a matter of showing who was more athletic, and best dog. We didn't care what the humans thought of our agility. It was a contest of pride between the two of us.

When we left, and Bailey remained with Aunt Ally and Uncle Cody, the realization began to sink in that they had their own dog now, and it wasn't yours truly. I loved them to death, and always would. My initial thought on Bailey was that he was an imposter, and I wanted to expose him as a fraud; he didn't belong here.

We saw Bailey a handful of times over the course of the next several weeks, and he had become a fixture of their household. It became readily apparent that I was the primary dog only of my own household. Each time we visited and romped together, our relationship became less contentious. Bailey and I still liked exerting ourselves to the max, but there was gradually a decrease in the hostility to our encounters. I was softening to the idea that Bailey's

Bailey and I weren't best buds right away.

place in Aunt Ally's and Uncle Cody's life was like a bland rice cake. It was acceptable, although not palatable.

Heavy rolls must have been in the wind because I already had a new cousin with four paws and a long tail. I had to get used to the idea of tolerating this change. There was another adjustment to the family structure that was going to hit, one that was considerably closer to home. This one had two hands, two feet, and he would come from a far off land. Here we go again ....

He Ain't Heavy, He's My Brother

ANOTHER ONE? Really? Why? You already had a young male that deserved a ton of attention: ME!! Without asking me for input on this monumental family decision, Mom and Dad had started the process of adopting another child from Russia. This time, it was going to be a little boy of a similar age as Hanna was when she came to her forever home. Oh dear. Did that mean that he would hate me at first, too? Would he scream and yell because of my face?

Things were now great between Hanna and me. Would she forget about me when the boy came to our home simply because he was a human and I was a dog? Would she only want to play with him? We moved into a new house shortly after Hanna arrived. Would we have to move again?

Mercifully, neither parent chose to break out a doll to get me adapted to life with a little boy. I guess they figured that I had gotten used to a little girl for the past two years. So, another child wouldn't be that different, right?

This adoption process proved to be dissimilar from Hanna's homecoming. Mom and Dad took two week-long trips overseas and returned home with no boy ... yet. While they were gone, Hanna and I were able to stay in the customary confines of our own home with our grandparents for the majority of the time. Aunt Ally and Uncle Cody took me in for a few days ... just because they kind of liked me. Plus, it allowed Bailey and me the opportunity to become more familiar with each other. We continued to roughhouse together, wearing each other out. I don't want to admit it, but I was often lethargic the day following play time with Bailey. He had a bit more youthfulness on his side. My lengthier recovery was likely attributed to excessive exertion of muscles that rarely got used quite in that way. Sure, Dad and I wrestled together from time to time, but frolicking with a fellow canine was considerably different.

Between the world travelers' (aka, Mom and Dad) voyages to Europe, I began to see signs around the house that we were getting closer to bringing my future brother home. The crib was brought up from the basement and reassembled in one of the bedrooms. The rocking chair and dresser were situated in the same bedroom to accommodate all the toddler's needs. His closet was filled with a trove of clothing for boys. I smelled the vaguely familiar scent of baby powder as a load of diapers were purchased and ready for the little guy's arrival. That fragrance, which I considered more of an odor, conjured up memories of my own bath time. Gross. So, he was going to be a pooping machine, too? Great. I was potty trained within one week and I don't even speak human. Why couldn't any child learn right away, too?

The third week-long trip to St. Petersburg, Russia, proved to be the game changer. The grandmas and grandpas split the child care duties again for the week. I kept my usual laser focus on those pesky grandparents as they took care of Hanna. If they stepped out of line, I would be sure to report back to Mom or Dad about it. But, they toed the line reasonably well. I guess I could give them a passing grade for their babysitting acumen.

Dad's parents took Hanna to the airport to meet her little brother. Again, poor Newman gets excluded from the festivities because of this silly "humans only" rule at airports.

A few hours later, I heard the entourage of vehicles entering our driveway to signal the return of the family. I blitzed upstairs to the bonus room to see who was here. I witnessed six or seven cars flood the driveway. Who all was here? Did they get 15 kids? I carefully observed who was exiting each vehicle. There were about twenty people in all, including grandmas, grandpas, aunts, uncles, cousins, and a great grandma; then I honed in on the newcomer. Mom was holding the little guy with curly, brown hair as she approached the house. He looked so tiny! I suppose that I was used to Hanna's size, who was two years his senior. I guess the day-to-day growth of Hanna was imperceptible, but two years' worth was quite a bit. Before the guests entered the house, I had to hustle downstairs to perform the duties of the official welcoming committee.

The garage door opened and the throng of people entered. I stood back to get a glimpse of everyone. Aunts, uncles—you're always fun, but not now. Grandmas, grandpas—nice of you to come. Cousins, Great-Grandma—it's been a while, good to see you, too. Dad—I missed you, buddy, but there's someone I'm waiting to meet. Then, Hanna walked in with Mom, who was holding my baby brother, Rudy. Oooh ... he was different than I had pictured. The little guy had looong curly hair, was rail thin aside from chubby cheeks, and he had a unique look and vibe to him. He was extremely meek and introverted, not offering much in the way of a response to any stimulus. Was he a mute? Was he overwhelmed?

Should I take it as a good sign that he didn't try to beat the crap out of me when I put my nose in his face? He didn't seem to care at all. Rudy seemed to just take it all in without reacting in any form or fashion. This was quite dissimilar to my first meeting with Hanna. I sniffed Rudy from his long locks of hair down to his teeny toes without hearing so much as a peep from the little guy. Hmm ... he must have seen dogs before.[6]

After I thoroughly familiarized myself with Rudy's scent, I properly greeted the rest of the crew. Everyone was busy chatting throughout the house, so I had to make my rounds to see everyone. Anyone who was enjoying a snack got special attention. That's when I heard an outlandish scream. I shuddered, and turned my body to find the source of the noise. It was Rudy. He was expressing disdain for Grandma Diane trying to hold him. Rudy reached his arms for someone else to hold him. He willingly accepted a pass-off to Mommom's Uncle Roy's arms. The boy *did* have some personality.

Throughout the evening, all the women in the family tried to hold Rudy to no avail. He would only permit the males and Mommom any contact. He barely even wanted anything to do with Hanna. Heck, he seemed to prefer my presence more than the ladies who were not Mom. Hanna's initial pecking order for favorites was: females, males, dog. Rudy's was: males, dog, females. The good news was that we had all the time in the world to foster our relationships together so that Rudy would feel comfortable with all of us, like Hanna already did. I hoped that I could be both Hanna's and Rudy's playmate. It would maybe have to wait for a few months, at least until Rudy got steadier on his feet. He could walk, albeit very wobbly. Rather, Rudy desired to have someone carry him. He preferred others to do for him instead of trying out things himself.

Rudy definitely had a different vibe to him than Hanna did at this age. His personality had yet to fully emerge,

---

[6] Rudy's orphanage had an outdoor dog, and rabbits, that the children saw on a regular basis.

whereas Hanna was far from shy in her first days with us, expressing herself quite emphatically. Rudy seemed as though he was shy about exploring his new surroundings. So, I opted to bring the surroundings to him. I wanted to see what kind of growing pains I could expect with Rudy. He allowed me to get close to him, and willingly touched me without hesitation. Rudy evidently enjoyed the texture of my sleek fur because he often rubbed my back and sides, going with the grain of my fur.

The one thing that he objected to was excessive face licking. For that, I received a few thumps on the head and high-pitched screams that announced his aversion. Got it. *Try* not to lick the boy in the face too much. Well, unless I desired to agitate Rudy; but sweet Newman would *never* do that.

Considering that I didn't know what to do with a plastic doll, I think I was adapting pretty well to having two actual

Getting used to my little brother was going to be a piece of cake compared to Hanna.

children who would always be my siblings. Was there going to be a third?

❖ LATELY, I'D BEEN inhaling my food so rapidly that I didn't even taste it. I think that I was swallowing equal parts food and air. At each meal, I was famished and I blitzed through the small kernels of lamb and rice so quickly that it had an adverse effect on my digestive system. Unfortunately, after it went down the hatch, there were some occasions when it came right back out. I had been spewing undigested chunks of dog food sporadically over the past few months. Mom and Dad worried that I was eating too quickly, so they called up my new local vet, Dr. Bryce. He proposed a few options. One was to insert something solid as an obstacle into my food dish to force me to eat around this object and work a bit harder to obtain all contents of my meal. Another alternative that Dr. Bryce suggested was to divide each of my meals into two portions. This would force me to take a short break to allow the food to actually progress toward my tummy before resuming the food inhalation process.

My parents tried the latter option. I gobbled up what was placed into my food dish, but I felt as though something was missing. As such, I keenly looked at Dad as I awaited more food. I paced between my bowl and him. After the better part of a minute, my cheeks puffed and a belch escaped my jowls. My parents chuckled and took this as a promising sign that I was ready for round #2 of my meal. Dad poured it into the dish and I wolfed it down rapidly. To be on the safe side, Mom and Dad continued this eating ritual on a permanent basis. As a result, we never again had an issue with barfing after eating too quickly.

Everything about me was fast. I ate fast, I thought fast, and I especially moved fast. My siblings enjoyed watching my intense bursts of energy play out in the form of sprinting laps in the house. They liked to wait until I was approaching before leaping (or, in Rudy's case, quickly scrambling) onto the couch or love seat to avoid a collision, giggling all the while. I always knew that they would get out of the way because, after all, I was the windshield and they were the proverbial bugs.

We loved playing together like brothers and sisters. Both of the kids liked to toss my toys for me to fetch. Despite his diminutive dimensions, Rudy was enthusiastic about playing tug with me, using whatever toy was my current favorite. He would hold on, yanking it from side to side, trying to pry the toy away from my clamped teeth. I'll just say that we each won some battles; we were both relentless. Even if one of us temporarily lost grip on the object of our mutual desire, we each always allowed the other one to grab hold for a follow-on round of fun. The little guy had all sorts of hyperactivity, which happily coincided with my fits of energetic play.

Ants Marching

WHEN I WAS FOUR YEARS OLD, there was yet another massive change in the household dynamic. Dad was leaving. He deserted us because he needed to accept a short-term work contract away from home. Dad was going to be employed on Long Island for a few months. The guy who walked me every day, gone. My playmate who allowed me to exert endless energy by playing with me when no one else would, gone. My best friend, sadly, gone. Dad promised that he would come back as often as he could when he wasn't working. Who was going to roughhouse with me? Who was going to take me for a walk, especially on those bitterly cold days? Mommom *despised* the cold temperatures that we often suffered in the late fall and winter months in western New York.

When Dad departed, none of us knew what to expect. Mom had to shoulder the lion's share of, well, everything: cooking, cleaning, child care, dog care, transportation. It was all on her. Usually, Mom and Dad had an equal partnership to divide and conquer the adult duties.

The first few days were strange. We all sort of anticipated Dad would appear each late afternoon. The kids looked to the garage door, hoping that we would hear his car engine come to a halt, followed by his keys unlocking the door after a full day of work. After dinner, I took to staring out the dining room windows for long periods of time, waiting for a certain someone's red Escape to enter our driveway. No such luck. Minutes and hours transpired and I felt very sorry for myself. Reality started to settle in that days and maybe weeks would pass without the patriarch returning.

Dad called home each and every day to talk to us. Mom even put the phone up to my ear so that I could hear his voice. It didn't mean much to me because I did not comprehend why there was the sound of a familiar voice coming from an object that was a few inches in length. My ears twitched and flipped up and down as a sign of my confusion. Dad couldn't possibly be inside the telephone, although his voice sure was.

The family learned of a technological advancement that allowed them to video chat via Skype from Dad's laptop on Long Island to Mommom's laptop near Rochester. These Skype sessions took over as the preferred method of communication. If he wasn't working long hours, Dad called us each evening so that we could see one another. Mom and the kids got a lot out of it, having a daily conversation with the guy that belonged here at home. Me? I saw the laptop for what it was: a 15-inch screen that projected images of objects in two dimensions. Last time I checked, Dad was a three-dimensional being who was a heck of a lot bigger than fifteen inches tall. Dad tried calling my name, imploring me to respond to his image on the screen. I never took any notice of the audio or visual communications from Dad. Instead, I would often curl up and lie down on the couch next to Mom or the kids while they chatted. I still wanted to be by my people, but if I couldn't touch them or recognize their three-dimensional likeness, it was as if they weren't there.[7]

---

[7] There were some two-dimensional events that captured my attention. It wasn't Dad, it wasn't still photos of our family or anyone recognizable to me, nor was it movies about fellow canines. I found myself absolutely transfixed by men's gymnastics and men's ballet. Lord knows why, but flairs being done on a pommel horse or the successful execution of a pas de bourrée were must-see TV for yours truly. Make of that what you will.

I couldn't be bothered with Dad's image and voice. A quick snooze was far more important.

Dad managed to return to our home every other weekend despite the six-hour car ride from the easternmost extent of the Empire State. It was wonderful to welcome him home a few times each month, but bittersweet to bid adieu to my best buddy when he inevitably had to go back to work. We tried to cram in a lot of quality family time in a tight timeframe. This included playing in the snow, building snowmen, sledding, having meals together, going to plays (well, not me), and most important, lots of walks with four-legged friends.

While Dad was gone, I took it upon myself to be the alpha male of the house. God knows that little Rudy wasn't remotely ready for that role yet. Not to discount Hanna either, but she was a little girl. Mommom is a woman, so she needed someone to act as a caretaker while Dad was temporarily away on his contract work assignment.

If something stirred, I immediately alerted Mommom and sounded like the biggest, meanest, most vicious dog ever. She was grateful for my presence, and my demeanor.

I tried to be outwardly scarier, and inwardly less of a fraidy-cat. I felt as though she needed me to serve as the family's protector. The only issue was that sometimes I heard things that were of no consequence, which needlessly put Mom on heightened alert.

One of many things that Dad could not do from Long Island was to clear the driveway of that awful white stuff when it snowed a couple of inches or more. Mommom decided to contract that task to a local residential snow removal company. Sure enough, early December rolled around and we had our first significant snowfall of the season. The snowplow truck dutifully took several swipes to push the snow off the driveway. I went upstairs to bark at the snowplow from the bonus room so that I could get a full view of what was being done on *my* property. I felt unsatisfied that my frustration was not being completely conveyed, as it was muffled by the noise of the plow's diesel engine. So, I bolted downstairs to continue my ongoing and quite one-sided conversation from the dining room window as well. Each time I barked, I glared intently at the truck making its forward and retreat trips up and down the driveway. Eventually, he had pushed all the snow beyond the garage past the back edge of our driveway, leaving a massive mound of snow about four feet high.

As he reversed down the driveway for the final time that day, Mommom finally gave in to my persistent requests to head outside so that I could "communicate" with him, even though he was done with his deed for the day. I stood atop the new snow pile as the conquering hero and showed him who was boss. I was the big, tough dog that was overlooking *MY* kingdom. I looked directly at the snowplow truck as he was leaving. I gave him a better idea what I thought of his work. I puffed my cheeks and dropped a big ol' deuce right on top of his freshly made snow pile. One pile deserves another. What's the saying? "Don't eat yellow snow." Well, I would recommend that you stay away from brown snow, too! This is *MY* driveway. *MY* human does this work, not you, buddy. Just keep that in mind if you intend to come back and clear the driveway again. I think that Dad would have been proud.

As winter began to subside, Dad shared some good news with all of us. He was moving back home! At the end of March, he was hired at a company that would allow him to live with us at home and have a somewhat lengthy, yet reasonable commute to work. No more extended absences. The biweekly visits would become a thing of the past. Mommom could share some of the parental duties with Dad. Our family had its man of the house back. Who was the happiest dog on the planet? ME!

Touch of Grey

I WAS FIRMLY ENTRENCHED in a regular routine, and my conduct had become exceptional. Yes, it's really true! Of course there were bouts of boisterousness where I barked to announce my distaste for something or another. But, you knew what you were getting there. I was never shy to share my feelings about a topic. I had an expressiveness that I exuded from my eyes. I was eternally optimistic, always hoping for the best of things: the best food, a bevy of treats, a great walk, and the most affection from my humans and their extended family. Truth be told, I usually received whatever I wanted. My family treated me tremendously well.

I wanted to be with my crew constantly. When Mom meandered toward the kitchen, I would *always* find my favorite spot, which was immediately behind one of Mommom's knees so that I could keep ultra-close tabs on what she was doing. I needed to know her each and every move. Of course a primary reason that I accompanied her almost everywhere was her willingness to fork over treats for no reason at all. My mere presence was enough to warrant a reward. When she did household chores, I would always be in tow. Upstairs to vacuum, check. Back on the ground floor for a load of laundry, guess who? Preparing meals? Heeeere's your sous-chef, Le Newmain. You get the picture.

I was very particular about my desires. It stood to reason that I had become ridiculously territorial. If someone were in "my" spot, I would stare at them in hopes that they were willing to move to accommodate my wishes. Often, Mom or Dad would be the recipient of this knowing look that told them to shimmy their rumps out of my desired position. Once they slid over, I could immediately assume my throne. Although I had a favorite position, it tended to rotate depending upon who I wanted to be near, along with my desired point of view. Did I want to look out the front windows, or was I content to doze off without a care in the world? Did I want the ability to gander at the door leading to the garage if I was expecting company? These options had to be carefully considered before requesting one of my people to move.

Couch positioning was a crucial part of my day. When I was visiting with family, I tried to impose my will on others, too. It worked some of the time, but not always. Dad's mom and I enjoyed some spirited disagreements about who would win the battle for supremacy of the couch. One time, Grandma wanted to sit in a particular spot on her couch under the light so that she could read. I begged for her to move. She resisted. I whined and whimpered, and she chose not to move. Our stubbornness met like two rams smacking horns to show who was sheriff in these here parts. Neither of us gave an inch.

She didn't move, so I clambered up onto the couch and wedged my way into a position squeezed into about eighteen inches of spaces between Grandma and the armrest. Aside from the general lack of room, there was the additional obstacle that she had a blanket in this spot. I had burrowed my head and shoulders under the blanket and refused to yield any room. I remained in this position for hours to show that I was more than willing to live with a little bit of discomfort to get *my* spot. Grandma and Grandpa laughed and laughed at my obstinate behavior.

While not fighting for couch positioning, I was enthralled by scratching my back while lounging on the floor, rotating from side to side with paws flailing up in the air. I tried to hit all the good spots that I couldn't quite reach with my toenails. Another favorite pastime was trying to steal desirable human food. If we had food up on the counter, I felt obligated to check it out. Sniffing the aroma of the food was one thing, but obtaining a bird's eye view would help me figure out if the human food was worth pursuing. I jumped on my hind legs and rested my front paws on the counter so that I could see the object of my affection.

If it was something that I deemed tasty, say perhaps cheese or meat, I would use one of my front paws like an arm and try to sweep the food closer to my mouth. If I could get at least a toenail on food, it would be mine. There was more than one occasion when I ingested some goodies. Mom and Dad habitually remembered to keep the food out of paw's reach, but I always needed to ensure that I wasn't missing out on an opportunity to vary my diet.

There were several occasions when one of my parents caught me wolfing down delectable cuisine. They had tried in vain to keep me from counter-surfing. In my opinion, it was always worth the consequence. Always. The verbal attacks, stepping on paws, and threatening glares never amounted to a punishment that would prevent me from seeing up close and personal what was cooking on a given night.

There was a time when Hanna had eaten and gotten ready for school in a blur. Lunch was packed, her backpack was adorned, and she raced to the end of the driveway to catch the bus. Normally, I would head out with Mom and Hanna. On this day, I had an ulterior motive for remaining in the house. A certain someone (I'm not mentioning names, but she's the shortest female in the family) did not finish drinking her milk, and serendipitously left her glass on the sofa table behind the couch.

    I knew that I had to act quickly, so I placed my hind paws on the couch cushion and my front paws on the couch back so that I could reach something of interest on the sofa table. I protruded my tongue down to the bottom of the cup to sloppily slurp up the calcium-enriched goodness. Mmmm ... this was so much tastier than the typical H_2O that I enjoyed. I was lapping the milk down my throat when the garage door opened and Mommom returned from taking Hanna down the driveway to catch the bus. I froze still, with my tongue extended into the cup, dipped slightly into the milk. As she and I locked eyes, I could not move. Then, Mom started to approach me and I retreated onto the living room floor, licking my lips in an effort to dispose of any evidence of wrongdoing. It was too cute to punish, right? Yes, yes it was.

    I don't know which was better: milk or beer. Both were delicious in their own way. I would always be on the lookout to see if someone had left their unfinished beverage within tongue's reach.

    On regular workdays, Dad returned home to a greeting committee of children. The kids both scampered quickly when they saw or heard the garage door open before dinnertime because our guy was home for the night. I waited as patiently as I could while the four- and two-year-olds took their turns in getting hugs from Dad. When Hanna and Rudy had gotten their fill, I showed Dad how excited I was to have him back home by giving him a Boxer "U."

Before he touched me, my anticipation was such that my body would bend just below my ribcage causing my body to arc in the shape of the letter U. Dad was always appreciative of the showering of affection when he returned home. I was just glad to have him back with us.

❖ APPARENTLY, THINGS CHANGE as you approach middle age. Routines may have been like clockwork, but some physical changes started to present themselves. The whole family was outside when the kids and I were goofing around playing. Mom thought it was a good idea to snap a few pictures, one of my least favorite activities of all-time. When we got a closer look at the resulting photographs, Dad pointed out that a few gray flecks of hair had crept their way into my mask. Mommom denied it, but the truth was out there. I started being called "Old Man" from time to time. Thanks a lot, Dad.

You aren't getting any younger either, buddy. One day, Dad returned home and sat down on the couch. He beckoned me to come sit in front of him. He grabbed two clear windows that had thin black and metallic frames that held the clear glass together. Dad placed them in front of his eyes as they rested neatly on his nose. What the hell is that? I nosed Dad in the face because he looked very different with this crap on his face. It's like he was hiding behind those windows even though they were clear. I really disliked this change in Dad's appearance. Fortunately, he was not required to wear his glasses at all times. I needed at least a few days to come to grips with Dad's different look. Any time he adorned them, I glowered at him to show my annoyance. Over time, my contempt for Dad's new appearance diminished. I just didn't get why he wanted to wear those stupid things.

The aging process has allowed me some perceived additional freedoms, too. When Hanna and Rudy were younger,

I believed that anyone not named Mom or Dad needed "help" in babysitting. I have come to the realization that my babysitting duties (of the babysitter, not the kids) were no longer required. Up until now, I had felt as though I needed to be very close to the kids to ensure that they weren't in a precarious situation with a babysitter. It's a combination of factors that has allowed me to yield to the trusted adult in these situations.

1. I had gained some experience with whoever was selected as the babysitter, and I supposed that I could have confidence in someone that Mom and Dad trusted. Hanna and Rudy appeared to be comfortable with those who were routinely given the role of babysitter. 2. The kids were now five and three years old. While they were not self-sufficient, they weren't exactly crapping their pants either. 3. To quote Danny Glover, "I'm getting too old for this shit." If the kids hadn't burned down the house or killed each other by this age, I imagined that they would be fine without my constant supervision. I still checked in every once in a while, but my perch on the couch was a comfier place to enjoy the festivities.

However, if someone was visiting the house in anything other than a babysitting capacity, I deemed that they were present merely for a social interaction. As such, what is more social than a nosey, gregarious, fun-loving boxer? When one of Mom's relatives had arrived and "social hour" was underway, I wanted to be part of the conversation. Wherever the participants went in the house, I would follow. If their discussion lasted more than a few minutes, I barked at them. "Hey, talk to me! Stop yammering on about that boring human stuff. I'm more important. Don't forget about me." Mom and Grandma were the worst offenders. They had the gall to get annoyed when I wanted in on their chat. It got so contentious that I was often given treats as bribes. I knew what they were: "hush treats." I may have kept quiet about as long as it took for the biscuit to enter my throat, but after that, bring back the barks. I don't think that social hour was fun for anyone.

Despite advancing into middle age, I was as spry as ever. When Hanna and Rudy went outside, I loved being part of their activities. In summer, soccer was fun to watch. I also took great pleasure in acting as the last line of defense when Dad and Rudy took shots at the hockey net in the driveway. Fortunately, neither of them had a wicked slapshot. I just liked to be part of the action, even in winter.

One snowy day, Grandma Diane took the kids outside to build a snowman with them. They spent a lot of time mounding the snow and getting the snowman to be proportionally correct. They had searched the yard for something appropriate to use for the overgrown iceball's arms. When Grandma guided the kids to attach the sticks to the torso, I took it upon myself to amputate the arms. After all, those were much better suited as dog toys than jammed into a four-foot-tall blob of snow.

An arm to some. To me? It's just a yummy stick.

❖ I STILL LOVED to sprint into our bonus room on the second floor to get a bird's eye view of my realm. It was the best place to know who was approaching or departing our home. One day, I had heard a tinny, rather loud noise from beyond our property. Neither being outside in the yard nor looking out the dining room windows offered me an adequate view of the persistent clamor. I decided that the bonus room would offer the best chance at identifying the source of the commotion. I skipped several steps on the way up, galloped down the upstairs hallway, and then lowered my pointed skull to pop open the partially closed door to investigate matters more meticulously.

As I neared the large window, I quickly honed in on a vehicle that was exiting our next door neighbor's driveway. I directed all of my attention to watch the hatchback depart. When it left, I strolled toward the entrance to the room. Wait a minute. Why couldn't I get out? In my haste to enter the room, I must have inadvertently rammed the door so powerfully that the door kicked back off the doorstop to completely shut. I was trapped in the bonus room. Ugh! I allowed my shoulders to slump. Then, I waited and waited and waited until at least a half hour had elapsed. I never made a peep, preferring to wait in silence rather than vociferously requesting help. Finally, I heard Mommom's soft paces advancing toward the closed bonus room door. When she opened the door, I simply looked her over before exiting my unintended, yet self-imposed prison. It was reminiscent of getting enclosed in the tiny, dark bathroom of our old house in New Jersey. Thank God I had more room ... and light!

❖ I STARTED TO become more sensitive to how people interacted with one another. When I was younger, it was all about me: what I was doing, where I was going, and who was going to help me do what I wanted. Now that I had become this mature, seasoned veteran of life, I tended to let the game come to me more often. I picked up on body language cues beyond those that pertained to me. Sure, I knew when it was time to eat, go for a walk, sleep, go for a car ride, etc., etc. There were other nonverbal communications that started to make sense.

One such behavior started to annoy me. By this stage in my life, I felt as though I had become Mommom's protector. She didn't need the help and could assuredly take care of herself. However, she was my best girl, so I had to be on the lookout for her, including watching for external and even internal potential threats to her safety. I'm talking about the ever-present menace that goes by the name of Dad. You see, Mom and Dad hugged on occasion. That was unequivocally, certifiably unacceptable in my rule book. When I caught wind of any sign of affection between the two of them transpiring, I would approach the happily married couple and glare at the male with all the contempt that I could offer. Depending upon my mood, I might bark while staring at my father or just whine. One thing was for certain: he needed to stop holding Mom like that. As soon as he relinquished her from his embrace, my raucous objections would cease. Was that really necessary, Dad?

I tended to punish Dad for all those times that I felt unjustly wronged. If Mommom wouldn't let me outside when I wanted to eat grass, bark at Dad. If Hanna did not give me the right kind or an inadequate amount of treats, get in Dad's face and let him know that his poor, sweet Newman was treated unfairly. When Rudy closed the pantry door as I was trying to steal some candy, it was time to trudge over to Dad to tell him a thing or two. If we had relatives over who didn't pay abundant attention to me, Dad would justifiably be on the receiving end of an earful. You should always register any and all complaints upward in the chain of command, never laterally or downward. There was no question who I thought was number one in the house.

You may think that I treated Dad harshly. Perhaps. I had the sense that he had been given a bit of a free pass for acting immaturely around me. How many grown men chased their dogs around the house? Do guys usually annoy their four-legged friends while we're trying to sleep? What kind of person desires to antagonize a dog for no apparent reason? Yeah ... I think we were even.

I expressed my agitation often in very verbose tones. Other times, I offered a more understated, subdued set of clues to announce my annoyance. If I was mad, I would always, without fail, yell at Dad. When I was forced to calm down and relax after a bout of perceived misbehavior, I would resort to gnawing on one of my harder toys to work out some of my aggression. I selected the object of my chewing based on who had upset me. If it was Mommom, I would dig through my overflowing toy bin to find the hard, eight-inch-long pink bone. After all, she was a female. For Dad? Simple choice: the oversized green and white Nylabone. Plus, he might accidentally step on the bone, which would probably annoy him. I'm not vindictive, I'm pure sweetness.

Brown Sugar

ONE THING THAT I HAVE learned in my life is that there is nothing better than feeling comfortable. I loved relaxing, especially when I could be right next to one of my people and oversee the family's day-to-day events. I have come to understand that there would be times when everyone in the house would have to depart, and leave their favorite dog to watch over the house for a matter of minutes or hours. By now you know that this wasn't my first choice, but I understood it.

If they were going to leave me on my own, I wanted to be comfortable. Mom and Dad understood this fact all too well. Thus, if I had to live a life of solitude, my parents would often offer me an awfully cozy position from which to perch. During daylight hours, they would open the horizontal blinds to allow the direct sunlight to stream into Rudy's bedroom. They knew how I loved to lie down in sun patches in the house. On top of that, Mom usually placed Rudy's fuzzy orange blanket atop his bed to provide me with a cushy place to partake a view of our street. I wasn't spoiled ... no, not at all. Mom got a kick out of returning home to find an indent of my body on Rudy's bed.

Comfort does not only extend to how I recline; it also pertains to the types of food that I enjoy. No, not dog food ...

human food. I was of an age where a little human food every now and then could not hurt. Quite frankly, I looked forward to at least a morsel or two of human food on a daily basis. My parents knew that certain food-related stimuli could result in various forms of begging from me.

The family typically ate pizza on Sunday evenings. Without fail, I received a portion of someone's crust. It got to the point where I would begin to whine for the cheesy, doughy goodness five to ten minutes after their meal had begun. My family always managed to accommodate my desires.

Cheese seemed to be a common theme among my comfort foods. When I heard the rustling of aluminum foil as a bag of Doritos opened, it elicited a response from me unlike any other. Obviously, I would get as close as possible to the source of my desire. I even sat silently and waited to receive my reward for being such a good boy. My begging included an involuntary, Pavlovian reaction that showed how much I coveted the nacho cheesy goodness. The drool formed at the lowest hanging edge of my jowls. It wasn't one or two drops. The saliva was free-flowing and spilling out of my jowls and congealing on the floor in a puddle. Mom or Dad had to give me at least a couple of Doritos to stop the salivation. Eating this tasty treat was *always* followed by a paper towel scrubbing my jowls and a cleansing of the floor.

I relished the prospect of trying new human foods even if it posed a danger to me. On a beautiful and hot summer evening, the family picked up some corn on the cob for dinner from a local farm. It seemed to be a summertime favorite of my crew. The kids thoroughly enjoyed eating it off the cob. Shh … don't tell them that it's a vegetable.

As the crew was cleaning up after a satisfying meal of steak with corn, Dad was disposing of what most people would classify as garbage. I saw an opportunity. While the old man was focused on getting dishes into the sink, I did a little dumpster diving. I pulled out one of the bare corn cobs and bolted for some privacy to enjoy it. Dad caught wind of my activity rather quickly and screamed, "No, Newman!!" and was on my nub in no time. I had to act fast. So, I tried to inhale the entire nine-inch cob lengthwise down my throat. He yelled louder. At this point, Mommom joined Dad in his efforts to take away my nourishment (oh, and save my life). He shoved his hand into my mouth and started extricating the cob that was wedged into my throat, on the verge of extending further down my digestive tract. Mom held my mouth open as he yanked the cob out of me. I coughed and licked my lips as they took away my healthy human food. Pfft ... parents.

One night, Mom, Hanna, Rudy, and I had gone to sleep while Dad remained downstairs watching TV. I was passed out, cuddled up to Mommom and had figured on sleeping until morning. A subtle sound from downstairs startled me. I swore that I heard plastic peeling apart to signify that a cheese stick was being opened, but it was incredibly faint. There was only one thing to do. I shot out of bed, scurried downstairs, and looked for the genesis of the noise. Dad wasn't in the living room, dining room, kitchen, or the bathroom. I noticed that the laundry room door was closed, so I plopped my rump down outside the door. He must have heard me coming because the door opened. There was Dad, holding the evidence that proved his guilt. He was evidently trying to hide that he was eating a mozzarella cheese stick by doing it behind closed doors. What he failed to account for was my superb (selective) hearing, along with my sheer willingness to do anything for cheese. He handed me an inch-long chunk of cheese. I thanked him and promptly trudged back to bed.

There was an occasion where I stayed the night with Aunt Lindsay and Mike because my crew was out of town. My aunt and soon-to-be uncle decided to have some friends over to their place. I liked to think that it was because everyone wanted to see me.

What would a gathering of people be without snacks? Lame. So, Aunt Lindsay and Mike put out a spread of goodies for everyone: cheese, crackers, pepperoni, veggies and dip, among others. Any time someone had one of the "good" snacks, I was their best friend. I sat still, was the best-behaved pooch you'd ever want to meet, in hopes that I would be the recipient of a savory scrap of food. The guests very quickly learned that the goodies needed to be positioned out of my snout's reach, or I would consider them mine. There was one platter of snacks that I deemed wholly unnecessary. You guessed it: the vegetables. The tray could be placed on the coffee table—at perfect height to be inhaled by a boxer— and I would pay it no mind. I walked by the raw carrots, cauliflower, broccoli, and cucumbers many times throughout the evening with barely a sniff. Gross. Who eats that crap, besides bunny rabbits?

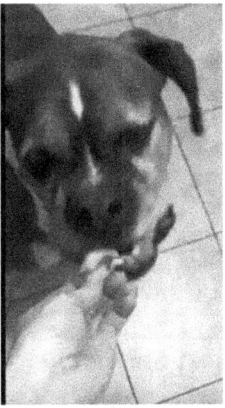

How did this get in the book? I refuse to admit eating cooked cauliflower like a treat. Please don't visit **http://tinyurl.com/IAMNEWMAN-video** *for proof.*

I certainly preferred comfort food like bread, cheese, and (if given an opportunity) sweets. Mom and Dad strictly prohibited candy and chocolate, but the sugary smell was absolutely intoxicating and worth my effort to beg, just to see if my cuteness could alter anyone's attitude.

You would think that a dog like me with a ravenous appetite would have no issue keeping up a healthy weight. For most of my life, that was absolutely the case. However, at age six, my parents were shocked to learn that I had unexpectedly dropped eight pounds over the course of several months. My eating regimen had not changed and my activity level remained fairly steady. This set off all sorts of alarms at the vet's office. What could possibly have changed to cause the precipitous decline in weight?

Dr. Bryce was concerned enough to send me to a different facility to have an ultrasound performed on me. My vet wanted to rule out some things: any blockages in my digestive tract, abnormalities in the shape of my internal organs, or any masses that would have otherwise gone undetected.

Mommom had the good fortune of taking me for this doctor's visit. Or, perhaps I should say that I was in luck to have her with me. After all, her profession is an ultrasound tech, although her scanning was solely focused on humans. As we entered the exam room, the technician said that I may need to be shaved to better see the images resulting from the scans. Wait, what? Dad shaved his face. Why do I need to be shaved, too? I liked my furry face and black mask. The technician examined my chest and belly with his hands and realized that I had very little fur that covered my underside. He called out to the doctor, "Naked boxer in Exam Room 3. No need to shave!" I guess this was one instance where I should have been grateful for experiencing the effects of demodectic mange, for my fur had not returned to its prior thickness on my undercarriage.

The ultrasound tech and Mommom placed me on a table to be examined. What I did not expect was that I needed to lie on my back to allow the procedure to be performed. When the technician flipped me over from being comfortably upright so that instead I was on my back, I flailed my paws about wildly. I despised being forced into this supine position, a position of complete submission. Mom looked into my eyes and rubbed my face and chest. She said many soothing words, none of which I heard. I was experiencing sensory overload. I felt hands all over me that were trying to keep me still. I looked around and saw nothing familiar, aside from Mommom's sweet face. My heart was beating at an astronomically high rate in response to the stress I felt while lying flat on my back. The young man ran his gel-covered transducer across my barrel chest and lower abdomen. He examined my esophagus, stomach, and internal bowel in search of any irregularities. The feeling of being dominated was too much to bear. I *needed* this examination to be done. Fortunately, my feelings of panic were put to rest within fifteen minutes as the ultrasound procedure was completed as efficiently as possible.

There was good news and bad news. On the plus side, there were no abnormalities detected. That was simultaneously a negative. We could pinpoint nothing that caused my weight loss.

When the results were conveyed to Dr. Bryce, he recommended that I eat some high-calorie dog food in order to try and pack on a few pounds for a period of a few weeks. Thankfully, the weight that had magically disappeared came back very quickly. A scare had been averted, and my weight was now something that would be vigilantly monitored as time moved forward.

❖ MOMMOM DISCOVERED THAT I possessed an unusual healing capacity: to remove the itchiness from pesky bug bites. You see, I was a very affectionate dog. As such, I liked to lick. During the summer months, my people occasionally found themselves the target of mosquitos' lust for blood. I noticed Mom's attention focused on scratching to relieve some of that terrible sensation. I sniffed to see what the big deal was. I found a bug bite on her shoulder and proceeded to lick the affected area. Mommom sat there and felt immediate relief from itchiness. It was a great partnership; licking was one of my favorite pastimes, and this made my beloved Mommom feel better. Definitely a win-win. Dad jokingly suggested that my awful dog breath may have killed all the surrounding cells.

My mouth was perpetually active. When I wasn't licking someone's bug bites, I was eating, licking myself (in theory to clean), along with barking or whining to share my opinion on matters. I loved talking to my humans and letting them know how I felt. It's the whole feedback loop thing. Even when I wasn't the one making noise, I often had a voice. Mom often called me her "Newman baby" or "fur baby." I thought it was cute, although Dad began speaking on my behalf to say, "I'm not little. I'm a big dog. I'm a big boy." I was indeed a big dog, but I loved being babied by my Mommom.

Walk This Way

WE LIVE IN A HOUSE that is on a corner lot of a cul-de-sac road that can only be entered via State Route 64. Our street is only a quarter-mile in length. Despite living on a rather quiet lane, our neighborhood sees its fair share of vehicle traffic on adjacent routes, including many diesel

I loved taking walks on my road with my BFF.

engine trucks and motorcycles that get my full attention. When I looked out the front door, all I could see was yard, trees, and the cars zooming up and down the slight grade of the hill that Route 64 traverses. I had lots of room to roam in my yard where I could absorb the fragrances and get a good view of things. There were a few other dogs in the neighborhood, but our house is at the entrance to our lane, so I consider all vehicles, pedestrians, and animals who use the thoroughfare to be *my* guest.

I have a sixth sense when it comes to other critters' presence on my road. I could be dead asleep looking in the opposite direction of our street. If a person and dog were taking a walk, I would rouse in a flash and go to one of my favorite perches at one of the "Newman" windows to try and communicate with them (yes, that means barking at them).

We occasionally saw deer, which look a lot like me aside from the long legs, of course.[8] Deer and I had an interesting relationship. In the wintertime, they occasionally came right up to the house to try to eat some of the greenery of our bushes. I was intrigued by their presence because they were so scared of everything. If I saw them up close, I may have hazarded a low growl so that they knew I was present. Barking at them seemed unnecessary unless they were at a distance and didn't pay me any mind.

We've seen many deer on our walks, especially at dusk. One autumn, we regularly saw a family of four deer including a mom and three fawns. The herd was extraordinarily tentative when they saw us approaching. If we got within a few hundred feet, that would set off the momma's internal alarm. We were too close for her comfort, and she would lead her youngsters into the woods.

One evening, we saw one of the fawns all by his lonesome. Given a little latitude without his momma present,

---

[8] Mommom told me that boxers are the offspring of a female deer and male pig. Talk about the perfect blend of graceful elegance and grimy squalor. How is it possible that more people don't have boxers?

he proved to be awfully curious about me. Let me tell you, the feeling was mutual. Once I recognized that he was less shy than usual, I cautiously attempted to approach him. He froze and I thought he was going to bolt. Instead, he took his right front hoof and pounded the ground a few times, showing his playful side. I whimpered until Dad allowed me to extend the leash a bit to allow me to approach him more closely. He repeated the stomping as I got within a mere fifteen feet. We stared at each other. I just wanted to play. I think he did, too. Regrettably, the fawn's instincts that were instilled in him to be hyper-shy took over and he bounded off, likely to find his family, before we could become closer friends.

At the far end of our street, we have a small pond that is tucked just behind the tree line in the woods. This marshy area served as a home to several geese from spring through fall. They were loud, obnoxious, annoying, and disgusting. I was glad that we lived at the opposite terminus of the lane. We saw these prima donnas soaking up the sun's rays in our neighbors' lawns and driveways. They lounged around and desecrated our neighbor's yards constantly. They ate the grass, they crapped everywhere. Before you ask, I absolutely did the same thing. But, I ate grass and crapped in MY yard. I was quite certain that our friends didn't have 10-20 geese as their pets. Go live in the pond, and leave the yards alone!

They honked and squawked as they seemed to be arguing with one another. Nobody liked them. Then they would procreate, which just meant a bigger problem.

If one or more of them was within 20-30 feet of the road, Dad gave me the green light to do what I was born to do: chase. He would prep me. "Boy, are you ready?" My ears perked up knowing the sequence that was to come.

Then, he would hold me in place for a moment while

he loosened the retractable leash to its maximum length. "Get set." Ohhhh, I'm set, Dad. Never been readier.

"GO!!" With that one syllable, I galloped with every fiber of my being and Dad would indulge me by sprinting alongside for me to chase the fowl (and foul) creatures. Of course I never got one, but scaring them to take flight and return to the water or vacate the neighborhood temporarily was good enough for us.

I once spotted a three-foot-long garter snake slithering among our Rose of Sharon trees behind our garage. This creature was sliding along the mulch, which caught my eye. It moved so differently than anything else I had ever seen. I first pawed at the snake, and then tried to pounce on it with my front paws, but it managed to avoid me.

One thing you should know about Mommom is her excessive and irrational fear of snakes. She saw me trying to box the snake into submission and immediately started screaming louder than I had ever heard her in my entire life. At the time, Rudy was swinging on the kids' playground. Mom yelled for Rudy to get off the swing and go up on the deck. When he obediently darted up the steps, Mommom quickly joined him. That may have been the only occasion on which I had ever seen her actually run rapidly. From the deck, she yelled at me to come. It was a shriek that was full of fear. I wanted to further inspect the beast, but Mommom's anxiety and secondary screams eventually won out. I bounded up the steps to join her and Rudy on the elevated deck.

We saw the snake around the house a few times in the following few days. Mommom prohibited any of us "kids" (Hanna, Rudy, or myself) from going in the yard while it was visible. She was afraid that it would bite one of us. Mommom presumed that my curiosity would have gotten the better of me to conduct a thorough investigation. Dad had the good fortune of having to "take care" of the snake to mitigate Mom's misgivings and thwart any additional recon efforts on my part.

Some months later, Dad was mowing the grass and stopped to get the kids to see something. He claimed that there was an animal that they had to see. I gave him the "Oh boy Dad, can I go, too?" eyes and stance. Of course the answer was yes. We all walked toward the road and saw nothing but an eight- or nine-inch dark, oval rock in the middle of the lawn. The kids thought it was really cool. I thought that they were out of their minds. Then the rock *moved*. I barked out of confusion when the rock appeared to grow four short limbs and a head. What the hell was that? I whimpered and stomped my front paws. I was astounded and tried to swat what I thought was a rock, but turned out to be a turtle. I sniffed it, but not too closely because Dad did not want me to scare it. The turtle trudged along very slowly in no particular direction. I still could not believe my eyes. I think I'll be a bit more careful around all rocks in case they try and move on me. As we walked back toward the house, I wanted to probe the turtle a bit more to try and understand. Dad said that the turtle had places to go and things to do, so we needed to leave it alone.

❖ I ADORED OUR household's daily routine in the neighborhood. Mom and Dad woke up, showered, and got the family going in the morning. The kids came to life and got ready for school. Whoever went downstairs first was usually accompanied side by side on our coated wooden steps by yours truly. I loved to see what the new day would bring: warm or cool weather, sun or precipitation, wind or calm. Would we divert from the typical routine or not? About 99 percent of the time, I would eagerly bound down the deck steps to take care of business, then made the return trip into the house to voraciously devour my food.

Hanna and Rudy would head off to school on the big yellow school bus. It would not be a school day if I didn't join them outside in anticipation of the arriving bus. Of course, I would stay within the confines of the invisible fence perimeter. While waiting for the kids to depart, I felt it was as good a time as any to use the landscaping as a worthy butt scratcher. Doesn't everybody like to scratch themselves in the morning? I would maneuver my body into position to use the bushes in front of the garage to get those places that I can't quite reach with paws, tongue, or teeth. The kids always found this humorous to watch me halfway buried in the bushes to have my itches satisfied as they were whisked away to school.

On many Sundays, I could look forward to another favorite pastime: riding in the car. Dad often took the kids to Sunday School. It was a brief 10-minute ride to St. John's Lutheran Church in the nearby town of Victor. The jaunt was long enough to enjoy the sights along the route. If the weather was pleasant, Dad would open the passenger window for me to enjoy some fresh air. Even at 30 to 50 miles per hour, my canine sense of smell could pick up many of the varying aromas that were in the vicinity. You humans might smell the pretty flowers. My squarish snout identified not only the flowers, but small oil spills on the two-lane road and the dreadful stench of an active runner's body odor after mile #5. Ooh ... there was dog crap back there, Dad. Can we stop, PLEASE? I wanted to cover that scent with some of my own. Dad and I would return home before the parental units departed for church, leaving me to my own devices at home. I knew that I could count on seeing them return in the next two hours. I may not have worn a watch or had access to a sundial, but I could tell how long each event would take after seeing it happen enough times.

Even if it was for a short errand, I loved sitting in the front passenger seat acting as the co-pilot. I felt like I had put in enough time to earn that distinction. Heck, sometimes Mom would sit in the back of either vehicle with the kids on longer trips to permit me to assume my perch in the passenger seat. Gotta love the Mommom.

Mom or Dad would gladly take me with them to pick up the kids from school or from one of their many extracurricular activities. When the parent left the car, I would hop over the center console and get in the driver's seat. People would look at me, smile, point, and sometimes even chuckle. I just sat there and took it all in ... loving the ride, loving to be outside, and loving to see new people, new dogs, and new places.

Mom started a running joke with Hanna and Rudy that she let *me* drive to pick up the kids. It made sense, given that I always appeared in the driver's seat when the kids came out to the car. For some reason, neither of my siblings immediately dismissed the idea. This only allowed the notion of me driving to gain further traction and exaggeration from both parents. Can you imagine?! My front paws manipulating the steering wheel with my back paws dangling and expertly operating the pedals for accelerating and braking? I could potentially even honk the horn at others with a quick head butt or a two-pawed pounce. I'm sure that people would understand if a turn signal was missed or if the headlights were not illuminated, right? I had no opposable thumbs after all!

When the kids asked why I didn't drive them home, Mom said it was for their own safety because I wasn't quite as good a driver as Mom or Dad. Still to this day, I don't think that the kids ever fully rejected the notion that dogs can drive.

One of our errands took us to the mall to have family

pictures taken (I didn't drive). We entered the building through the food court and the smells were overwhelming to my overactive snout. Dad attempted to guide me quickly and quietly on the smooth tiles to the photo store within the mall. There was so much to take in: people, smells, and a series of rooms and backdrops at the studio. We had our own private area to snap a few pictures.

I despised having my picture taken by anyone. Combine that with being worked up over the new situation and I was a panting, unfocused mess. The photographer tried to grab my attention—while taking pictures with the kids, with Mom and Dad, and of me by myself—to little avail. She shot a significant volume of pictures to pump out a few meaningful pictures. I was so overheated that my tongue was quite prominent in most of the photos. As my interest in the photo store started to wane, so did my ability to sit even reasonably still for poses. I wanted to explore beyond the confined area. The food court seemed like a place that was worthy of my attention. Burger King, Sbarro, Arby's, Subway all sounded delicious. Maybe we should go back there. Dad blocked the entrance of the private area to prevent such an event from occurring. Always two steps ahead of me ....

❖ DESPITE OUR ROAD only having nine houses on it, you might be surprised at how many vehicles use our thoroughfare during the day. Of course we regularly saw the folks who live on our street. We also observed lawn-mowing services, snowplows, and delivery trucks coming and going. If any of these vehicles even thought of slowing down at our driveway or our next door neighbor's, I would be sure to properly proclaim their presence for the whole world to know. If at all possible, Mom and Dad kept me inside on such occasions. I suppose that I may have been just a hair too loud or "in your face" for these folks to handle.

If a delivery guy had to make a stop at our residence, I simply couldn't control my exuberant, loud barking. The individual usually dropped the package on the porch and quickly returned to his or her vehicle for the remainder of his deliveries. One time, I was outside as the UPS man entered our driveway. I waited for him along our sidewalk. When the stocky man was halfway into our yard, our eyes met and he froze dead still in his tracks. He did not move for the better part of a minute. When I vociferously announced his arrival, Mom came to rescue him by leading me back inside the house. I would have preferred to see how he would have completed the delivery of the package, but Mom did not give him (or me) the opportunity. I suppose that the delivery man did not realize that we have an Invisible Fence that prevented me from mauling ... er, I mean, licking him to death. I know fear; there was sheer terror in his eyes. Honestly, I was surprised that I didn't see a wet spot cascading downward from his midsection. After the ever-gracious Mommom "saved" him from me, the poor guy quickly approached the porch, dropped off the package, then scurried across the lawn to get back into his truck. What can brown do for you, buddy?

The delivery folks don't need to be frightened of me. I simply wanted them to know that they needed to take care of their business then promptly move along. The same is true for a guest that I saw six days a week: the mail carrier. I'm quite certain that the regular mail lady was not too fond of my predictable fits of boisterousness. But, she would continue to hear them on a daily basis until one of us no longer patrolled this lane.

We have had a handful of repairmen come to the house. I can tell (and smell) a dog person within moments. Let me smell you, see what you're about. If you show me a little affection, you can move about freely and I will only look for a pet on the head or scratch behind the ears. However, if you come to our house and show apprehension towards me, I pick up on those things. Why are you worried about me? I'm Newman. I want to be everybody's friend. You have to give me a chance. If you don't, I will keep an eye on you; actually, I will penetrate your very soul with an intense stare from *both* eyes.

We have had two guys pay us a visit who fell into this boat. The first was a handyman named Shawn. He did a few outdoor projects for us, including the replacement of our front porch. The instant we laid eyes on each other, I could sense some misgivings from him. I was trying to be friendly. He wanted no part of me. Shawn was grateful to be doing most of his work outside. I liked to perch in the dining room and stare a probing gaze in his direction. I got the sense that this really freaked him out. Good. You're a grown man, and I'm the furthest thing from a vicious dog. If he wanted to come into the house to speak with Mommom, she would do her best to usher me outside so that Shawn could be at ease. Unbelievable. Please just be friends and everything will be cool. Hopefully you'll figure that out the next time you visit a house with another sweet pooch like me.

The second was a cable repairman named Larry. Yes, you read that correctly – Larry the Cable Guy. He did not, however, wear a shredded tank top or a camouflage cap. Larry also did not speak "Git 'er done!" with a southern drawl. Rather, he was a burly African American man. When I introduced myself to him, the guy did not even want to pet me. I gave him a few inquisitive looks as he walked to and fro in our house. I didn't understand what he was doing nor did I really care. I was still inquisitive about him, so I would often look at him and occasionally attempt to see why he kept going upstairs, downstairs, and outside. Eventually, Larry the Cable Guy asked Mom to be separated from me. Mommom had to use one of the baby gates to keep us apart. What a fraidycat! Mom chuckled and was grateful that I could provide an intimidating presence so that she felt safe if Dad was not around while we had visitors.

State of Love and Trust

THE SUMMER MONTHS always proved to be the hottest ... obviously. The kids and I liked to come and go out of the house, using the sliding glass door and darting down the deck steps to the backyard to play. So, Mommom got the idea to have a screen door that had an opening running the full vertical length of the mesh screen. This would, in theory, provide easier access for each of us. Mom, Dad, and the kids slipped through the opening effortlessly to show me the way. I could not make sense of it. All I saw was a giant barrier. The screen door opening was not readily apparent to me, even when someone opened the gap for me. I was pushed through the door a few times, but verrry reluctantly. Within weeks, this experiment was mercifully abandoned. The normal screen door was reinstalled and opened or shut when I needed it.

Ever since the invisible fence was installed, I could readily inspect each part of the yard, along with a portion of the driveway inside the boundary. I was scampering happily along the driveway, and cornered when I reached the garage to bounce along the front walk, when I felt my toenails lose their traction. I managed to make the turn, but one of my right rear middle toenails did not escape unscathed. It bent at a sharp angle, but did not break entirely. There were drips and drabs of blood that oozed from the wound. This stupid injury really smarted.

I wanted to lie down and lick it back to health. Although my saliva had mystical healing powers, the toenail remained at an unnatural and awkward position, making it burdensome for me to walk comfortably. One of my toepads also started to swell from being chafed on the driveway. My parents felt obligated to call the vet (yet again) to determine the appropriate remedy. After seeing the injured area, it was determined that I would undergo some minor surgery to cut off a portion of my toenail and cauterize it. The toenail would need to be confined within a protective boot to allow the nail to heal before exposing it to the elements (and me).

Surgery was far from my favorite thing on the planet, but my parents were advised to have the procedure done to prevent infection from attacking this open wound. My nemesis, anesthesia, was administered, and I lost track of a few hours. When I awoke, I did not have free access to my right rear paw. It was wrapped tightly in a pink bandage. Really, pink? I am a *male* dog. Save the pretty rainbows and pink bandages for the females. Pick green, blue, brown, black, or even red, all of which complimented my fawn coat quite nicely. Anything but pink. Good grief.

I vigorously chomped away at the bandage with absolutely zero success in loosening even a strand. How did the doctors know my tricks? Not fair, not fair at all. When my parents arrived to take me home was the moment that I realized my gait was forced to be considerably different. Instead of the typical Newman slight side gait that resembled a smooth glide, I was forced to pick up and put down my injured wing in a more emphasized way. Think of it as a staccato note in music, a bold dot on a letter I, an extended follow-through on a basketball jump shot. That's what I had to endure each time my right rear tire struck the ground for the foreseeable future. Ugh.

Even worse, if it were the least bit damp or raining while I desired to be outside, Mom and Dad heaped an additional layer of humiliation beyond the pink boot. They would take time to adorn a flexible plastic wrap to serve as a bootie to cover my sweet-looking pinkness. The extra layer also added to my pronounced stepping motion. Presumably, this was not a punitive measure. It was likely done to keep my bandaging clean, as I would be required to wear it for a week or two.

The days trudged on painfully slowly. Every time I looked down hoping to clean my paw, there was the boot. When I scampered through the house, I could hear Mr. Pink on every fourth pitter-patter. If I was sleeping on the bed and I thudded my paw up against Mom or Dad, it wasn't my bare paw doing so; it was this awful bandaged contraption. I could not wait until things got back to normal.

Two long weeks of waiting later, I returned to have my wound checked out. I was excited to see that my bandage was being removed within moments of arriving! I didn't need to be knocked out or anything. I watched as my little pink friend was cut, peeled, and fully dispatched.

My paw felt like a foreign object. I dropped to the ground and scrutinized my appendage. My one toenail was considerably shorter, but it was certainly still mine. My paw held the aroma of the bandage, which had become slightly soiled. I don't know how that was possible because I was such an immaculately clean dog. The entire car ride home was spent licking my rediscovered friend; I had to rid my paw of the strange smell and replace it with something much more suitable: my saliva, which of course smelled tremendous to me. I'm grateful that this dilemma was now behind us.

❖ THERE WAS AN EVENING in December 2012 when I zipped down the deck steps and found four to six inches of fresh snow. Winter ... again? I took several steps into the yard, calmly looked around, took a few sniffs of the crisp, winter air and looked up into the dark night sky. I sharply exclaimed a single, solitary syllable. It may have sounded like a bark to Dad, but there should be no confusion as to the true meaning of my utterance.

To provide some perspective, when I bark, I persist until the recipient acknowledges me or the offending party moves out of sight. This was different. My cursing exclamation was the only possible word to publicly broadcast my exasperation that I was enduring yet another snow-filled season. I was not cursing at anyone or anything; that is, unless Mother Nature is a tangible being. I never said that word ever again; not because I felt guilty, but because I never had the reason to do so.

I have always recognized that I need to go to the bathroom outside, no problem. However, I hate the fact that I have to head outside in the winter chill and freeze my paws, deal with the biting wind, and squat with my barely-covered-by-fur cheeks hovering just above snow level to take care of business. I sincerely wish that there were another alternative; but I knew that I would continue to trudge through the snow to make deposits in the yard instead of inside the house. That would be gross. Mom or Dad should have potty-trained me on the toilet.

I really enjoyed our daily walks ... even in winter. Dad religiously took me down the road as far as I cared to go. When our road got icy or was coated with a significant snowfall, I preferred to cut our route short to return to our warm abode to thaw. There have been a handful of times that I overestimated my paws' ability to complete our walk. When this happened, I raised my most wounded paw into the air and fruitlessly tried to lick the cold off the paw to revive enough life in it to resume our amble down Friends Lane. My temporary solution might have provided enough comfort for a few more paces, but never solved the problem. In such times, Dad tried to coerce me to run to hasten our return and minimize the number of steps we had to take. Sometimes, that would help for a bit, but who wants to run in the snow? Really. There have been several occasions when our neighbors saw Dad and me walking westward, only to see him carry me for portions of the eastward return journey. I loved Dad for trying to keep me safe and pain-free.

Of course, Mom tried to outfit me with a coat and wanted to give me booties, but I detested wearing anything. If Dad put on my coat, I'd wear it ... initially. However, I would shake my body vigorously after a handful of paces to cause the Velcro to forcibly detach, causing the coat to loosen considerably. Rinse, lather, repeat. I would continue doing this until Dad would concede defeat and take the coat off me, exposing me to the elements.

Throughout the winter, I heard a new dog barking next door. I was extremely curious and interested to learn all about the new pooch. It wasn't until springtime that I officially met Reba, because neither of us was outside much during the winter months. She was a similarly aged mutt with a thick coat of predominantly black fur.

On our initial meeting, I wasn't a big fan. I am nothing if not territorial. I like MY yard, MY driveway, and feel as though people should ask ME permission to come onto MY property. Reba felt as though she could come and go as she pleased. Not cool. As we tried to feel each other out, both of us barked and snarled a bit, but not too seriously. We certainly had some issues to work out about understanding our boundaries.

Within the first week of our spring meet and greet, I saw Reba pissing in MY yard. Not cool. From inside the house, I barked vociferously to try and get her to vacate the premises. She just kept on at it. This is NOT your yard. Mom and Dad were miffed that Reba was left to her own devices with no boundaries to follow.

Reba started to make a habit of marking her territory ON MY TERRITORY, which only served to further sour Reba's and my relationship. As this began a regular pattern, Mom and Dad tried many different methods to enforce boundaries from our side. Mom attempted to guide Reba calmly into her own yard. Reba saw how sweet and nice Mommom was, and tried to exert her dominance by baring her teeth to show who was top dog. That freaked out Mommom to the point where she did not want to encounter Reba anymore.

So ... it was Dad's turn. If he heard or even sensed that Reba was out, he approached the property line like he was a freshly deputized border patrol guard. If Reba thought she was going to venture into the Stroup's yard, she was sorely mistaken. If she made it into our yard, Dad forcefully commanded Reba to return home. She regularly complied because she felt that she had to submit to him. Who's top dog now? Dad wanted me to feel as though my yard was my yard. So, he kept up this routine of getting Reba out of our yard asap before she could make herself at home.

When he felt as though Reba knew not to enter our yard, Dad would allow me to be out while she was in her yard. He did not want a confrontation because we really like our next door neighbors. They are truly a wonderful family. Dad wanted both dogs to be safe and get along. At a bare minimum, we needed to respect each other's space.

I was still reluctant to trust Reba. If she was out in her yard and she did not notice me, I assumed a "stealth mode" stance because I felt that it made me invisible. I would drop to the ground and stay low, remaining as still as possible, just lying in wait, awaiting Reba to screw up and make one wrong move. I could do this in the yard, although the contrast between green grass and brown dog did not seem very effective for hiding. The deck offered a better camouflage. I was elevated and the deck was stained a deep brown color, so I definitely blended in better ... or so I thought.

Dad called this my "crouching tiger, hidden Newman" pose.

Reba eventually grew to understand that the yard that I inhabited was not meant for her. Unfortunately, she was still a bit of a roamer and did not stay within the confines of her yard. She often wandered leashlessly the entire length of our quiet street, including our property across the road, an area beyond my invisible fence boundaries. Reba's meandering dismayed Dad because he would find her poop in areas that he had to mow. However, it was far better to deal with her excrement than to worry about a confrontation between two canines.

Crazy Train

I'D LIKE TO THINK that I'm a pretty good dog now. Sure, I can exhibit bad manners from time to time, but with a little maturity and seasoning (and years of aging), I've grown into a dog that most folks would consider fun, friendly, loving, and considerate.

We were living the good life. I had a family that took excellent care of me. We had our fun during the day. The constant activity in which each of us partook on a daily basis wore me out as I got older. When Mommom and Dad put the kids to bed each evening, I was ready for a late evening nap ... just in time for a full night of sleep.

I would nuzzle up next to one of my parents and slumber. I would lie adjacent to Mom more often than not. As I slept, occasionally I would awaken to a smell. It was gas, and it was absolutely appalling. I would attempt to find the perpetrator of the crime. Almost without fail, I would look over my shoulder at Mommom with utter disgust in my eyes. I couldn't believe that she could possibly do something so foul. If the smell was too intense, I would clamber down to the floor and allow my gaze of contempt to remain on Mom. She was incredulous and could not fathom that I was blaming her for the odor. Meanwhile, Dad was laughing hysterically, evidently thinking that this was the funniest thing that he had ever witnessed.

If the same situation occurred except I was lying next to Dad, I would still awaken and look at Mom with disdain. How could she reek so badly that I smelled it from several feet away? My goodness, how awful. Dad's laughter in these instances was borderline uncontrollable, and I didn't find anything humorous about stinky farts at all.

❖ WHEN I WAS SEVEN of your human years old, I noticed that Aunt Ally's belly had started to gradually grow. It didn't prevent me from wanting to jump up and play with her. It had become noticeable that she greeted me more at my level than she used to do in the past. We had always had more of a rambunctious way of saying "Hello" to one another. I still skittered spiritedly around her feet, but she now prevented me from gaining much elevation to appropriately greet her. Yep, you guessed it. She was pregnant with hers and Uncle Cody's first child. Many factions of the family were eagerly anticipating the arrival of the baby boy. All I knew was that my aunt's belly continued to swell for months. I didn't really detect anything different, but my family had never gone through this process. In early February, we got "the call" to announce that my new cousin, Emerson, had been born. Maybe now I could go back to jumping on Aunt Ally without repercussion.

When Emerson and I met for the first time, I couldn't get over how tiny the little guy was. Something that small was a person? He was so much more helpless compared to Hanna and Rudy when they first came home. I suppose it makes sense that children grow quite a bit over the first year of life. I had never been exposed to babies that young, so I didn't know what to expect. He moved very little and actually did very little as a young pup, so I pretty much left him alone. He didn't really respond even when I got a closer glimpse and tried to smell that unique baby smell, so our interactions were minimal in his youngest days. As we all know, that baby smell could be very sweet and angelic like baby powder, which reminded me of my shampoo. Yuck! Emerson's aroma could go from benign (although disgusting to me) to something quite the opposite. When he grows up, I'm sure that we'll be buds. Bailey will be there to watch out for him and show him the ropes of growing up in this family.

❖ SHORTLY AFTER I turned eight, a puppy was brought into our home for the better part of a week. This puppy was part of our family because Aunt Lindsay and Mike had just gotten the little guy a week previously. Because I have been blessed with so many family members who were willing to take me in when Mom, Dad, and the kids went out of town, we (well, Mom and Dad anyway) thought it was only fair to return the favor by welcoming others' pooches into our home. Thus, we were introduced to Mosby, the three-month-old pug puppy.

When that snack-sized dog bolted through the door with his big eyes and tiny paws pitter-pattering promptly across the tile, I could tell right away that we had very different energies. At age eight, I had short bursts of sustained energy. At age nothing, Mosby was ... what's the word? Cray-cray.

He immediately came to introduce himself and meet me. I wanted to sniff Mosby and figure him out. He wanted to bounce around and instigate. Was I ever like this? I've been assured that the answer is "Yes." Mosby liked to bark and get me to chase him. I love a good chase, but Mosby was so little that I was afraid to be even remotely aggressive. I would wave my paw at him instead of offering him a full swat, which would assuredly have seen Mosby take flight.

Instigation was only the tip of the iceberg. Mosby's most irritating habit was his desire to hump me. Picture an eight-

or nine-pound dog that stands about one-third of my height trying to wedge his unit into me. He tried to put his paws up on my hips, but he was nowhere near being on target. It was not a pretty picture. He tried to get inventive by attacking my side to grind on one of my hind legs. Aaaargh! This was demeaning and ridiculous. I often delivered a close-mouthed growl to announce my displeasure. Mosby was not comprehending any of the auditory or body language cues I was expressing to inform him that I was incredibly opposed to this action. So, I would lightly snap at him without making any contact, which was in essence only mouthing off with no intent to injure. Mosby would retreat, but only momentarily. He would give me a vacant look, which told me that within seconds, I would again be the recipient of one or more of his unwarranted behaviors.

    I wasn't the only one who was on the receiving end of undesirable actions from our diminutive guest. No, he didn't hump anyone else in the family. Rather, he had fits of barking during which he would stare at Mommom and just bark at her. It went on and on. I couldn't stand it any longer, so I slapped the little guy on the shoulder to say, "Leave her alone!" Mosby glanced at me to ask why I would do such a thing. Come on, buddy. Give my mom a break.

    Apparently, Aunt Lindsay and Mike knew that Mosby required some solitude to calm down. For the week, we were the temporary owners of a hard plastic gate that could be set up as an octagon on the floor to segregate the puppy from the rest of the household. When I could no longer tolerate Mosby's shenanigans, Mom, Dad, and/or one of the kids would go through the effort of cornering the elusive pug to place him inside the octagon gate to give Mosby a bit of a time out. I could relax, knowing that I was not going to be violated. The area within the octagon gave Mosby about 20-25 square feet to operate with the two-foot high gate preventing an aerial escape.

Mosby was a pretty quick study on potty training. When we went outside, I did my deeds and Mosby often accompanied me. Mosby was also learning on the Invisible Fence at his home, so he accompanied me to try and understand the boundaries here. If he had followed me around consistently, he would have been in good shape. Mosby, however, liked to explore (and what dog doesn't?) and found the barrier the hard way more than once. I could tell this by the noise from his collar and his yapping reaction that ensued shortly thereafter. He picked up on the size of our explorable yard pretty quickly.

We all tried to keep in mind that Mosby was just a puppy. We gave him a fair chance, but time and time again, he took the metaphoric rope and hung himself. The problem was that Mosby was obsessed with me ... and all of my parts, if you catch my drift. In an effort to not be crude, he would try to lick portions of my underside ... even as I was trying to relieve myself! Mosby obliviously was the recipient of more than one golden shower despite my parents' best efforts to keep him clear of my urine flow.

Yikes ... this little guy needed to dial it down a notch, or twelve notches. This was day one with Mosby. We had five more to go. At least I displayed a fair amount of tolerance; otherwise, I may have had a heart attack from the constant frenetic attention that Mosby gave to me. When I climbed up onto the couch to take a snooze, Mosby would jump to join me, thinking that this was simply a continuation of the fun and games. I just needed a rest ... you'll understand someday, buddy. I couldn't imagine having that kind of liveliness now.

Mosby wasn't all bad. He and I actually could coexist at times when he respected my space. This didn't occur all that often, but we played occasionally without incident.

Heck, we even napped together a time or two. I was trying to show him the ropes. He deserved the opportunity to learn and I was as patient as possible.

Mosby could be calm, just not very often as a little guy.

Things improved steadily as our week together progressed. If Mosby went outside, I felt obligated to join him to ensure that he didn't create any mischief. Maybe there was some hope for him. We'd have to see how much he grew up in the next year or two. Hopefully, he would control himself a little better in the future to become a lovable little guy.

When Aunt Lindsay came to pick up Mosby, he was very excited to see his mom. Perhaps he learned a little something during his stay here with us. I think tai chi is the next step for him to relax.

We all slept and napped better over the few days that

followed Mosby's departure. I hadn't realized how much energy puppies require. Whew ... I'm glad that Mom and Dad never got another dog. That likely would have sent me to an early grave.

Uncomfortably Numb

I WAS EIGHT YEARS OLD and the picture of good health. Don't tell anyone, but I've always been a little on the lazy side, so it's not surprising for me to lounge for approximately 80% of the day. I would rouse for mealtime, daily walks, and to expend my sporadic spurts of energy that I never seemed to outgrow. Let's not forget that someone in the house needs to be on the receiving end of my regular dose of harassment to announce my displeasure about anything that was bugging me. I still needed to bark to make sure that the mail truck and other unwanted guests were required to steer clear of my house or the next door neighbor's, for that matter. Having said that, I was still very lazy.

One night after dinner, I hurled. I did that on occasion when I ate too quickly, so my parents chalked it up to that.[9] But, then I vomited again in the late evening, which was very unusual. I felt physically uncomfortable. My routine was to spend most evenings resting on the couch. This turned out to be no normal night. I paced, lay on the floor, and did everything except rest.

When bedtime came, I was eager to make the climb "north" to go to sleep. But, it was a fitful night to say the

---

[9] I liked to barf on carpet and have some privacy while doing it. I felt like I would be in less trouble if I was in hiding, and who wants an audience when their insides are being emptied? I didn't get why Mom and Dad tried to usher me to the smooth tile surface when I didn't feel right. It made a lot more sense to me to have a plush, carpeted surface to catch vomit.

least. About an hour into my usual slumber, I quietly trudged from our bedroom to our bonus room at the opposite end of the upstairs hallway for some privacy. To do what? You guessed it: puke. After a few minutes, I wearily returned and settled in to sleep.

A bit later, my belly was in absolute upheaval, so I wanted some space. I ventured into the hallway and sprawled at the top of the stairs all by myself. It killed me to feel so ill, but I did not want any company. However, my uneasiness must have eaten at Dad to the point where he lay down next to me to try and comfort me in my misery. I appreciated it, but I couldn't think of anything besides my abdominal pain. My exhaustion level had never been higher. It was the middle of the night and my stomach was churning uncontrollably.

We eventually returned to bed to sleep for an hour or so. My guttural disturbance persisted, so I once again rose, leaped off the bed, and dragged myself down the hall to the bonus room. Round #4 of vomit was underway. Dad could hear me retching down the hall. Based on the foamy consistency of the vomit, I was digesting food to some extent. However, it was obvious that everything was coming back up. Again, I plopped down in the dark room, exhausted. Dad tried his best to soothe me ... petting my back, scratching my ears, lightly rubbing my belly, talking to me. I slumped there with my eyes open, unable to rest or sleep. An hour or so passed before Dad unsuccessfully tried to convince me to return to the bedroom. I was miserable.

As Dad hoofed back to the bedroom to try and catch some Zs, nasty thoughts started to creep into my brain. I stared at the ceiling, watching the ceiling fan spin, thanks to the nightlight casting light from the hallway into the bonus room. Similarly, I felt my mind spinning out of control. What is wrong with me? Was this a lifetime of grass-eating catching up with me? I was racking my brain to remember whether I ate any foreign objects. Nope ... nothing came to mind. Could this be *the end*? The house was deafeningly quiet. I ached in sheer agony. I knew that I had too much life in me for something to be seriously wrong, right?

I heard Dad's alarm clock, which rudely signaled the end of an awful night. When he arose, I wearily plodded down the hall towards him. He looked at me with thankful, tear-filled eyes. I was upright, although very weak.

As night turned to day, we proceeded through our normal morning ritual of potty, food, and drink, but I wasn't my usual self. I had no energy, none, totally sapped. I lay around all day, trying to catch up on the sleep that had eluded me the prior night. This was a rude awakening that I wasn't a puppy, or even remotely youthful anymore. I was actually mortal. That stinks. I wanted to live forever with my family. I hoped that at least we had a lot of time remaining together.

As I aged, Mommom and Dad saw a few skin growths, which is common for us boxers because of our susceptibility to skin cancer. Each time, we had my favorite veterinarian visually inspect the three well-defined lumps on me. They were located on my right front shoulder, near my right rear hip, and along my left side. Although they had been present for a few years, Dr. Bryce looked at them with a bit more scrutiny than previously. He believed that they might now be mast cells, which is a form of the dreaded "c" word: cancer. After a thorough checkout, he felt that their locations were advantageous to have them excised. Dr. Bryce suggested to Dad that googling mast cells was a bad idea (so, of course, Mom promptly nearly shit her pants after doing so). I felt no different after this visit than I had on previous ventures to my favorite vet. All I knew was that a follow-up visit was in my immediate future.

Within the week, I was jostled out of my restful sleep and thrown off my beloved routine. I went downstairs and dutifully went outside and peed, coming back in with the expectation of the usual: a treat, food, and water. Not only did I not receive a treat, but my food and water dishes were conspicuously absent. Dad tried to divert my attention away from this anomaly by offering to take me in the car for a ride. Ok ... sure! But, I'm HUNGRY!! I recognized that we were on our way back to the vet and settled in for the enjoyable outing.

Usually, Dad stays with me at the vet's office. But, after a quick check-in process, I was escorted to the back room among a few other pooches and I didn't see Dad again until much later in the day.

When I awoke, I felt very weak and could barely stand up on all four paws. I loathed medication, especially one that makes me lose track of hours. If my stomach were not so upset, I would be clamoring for sustenance. But, I was whooped. And my fur felt different. I remembered it being a really warm, nice day outside. In here, I sensed an extra breeze on a few joints on my right side and the left side of my belly felt open, too.

Dad was waiting for me in one of the exam rooms. He looked me over in a concerned way with penetrating eyes, but I was too mad at him and too drowsy to return his glance. We have to stop making these trips to the vet where I lose track of time and feel awful.

Dr. Bryce explained that the three lumps had been removed. Because of the locations of the cells, he was extra cautious and took more skin to reduce the risk of any cancer remaining in any of the margins. Dad asked how long it would be before the diagnosis could be confirmed. The affable vet responded by saying that the growths would be examined in the next seven to ten days. He also noted that the fur would begin growing back within weeks, and be full length within a few months. Dad was visibly surprised that it would take my short coat so long to return to normal.

Dr. Bryce confidently proclaimed that the growths were fully removed, but asked Dad to carefully monitor the healing of my scars to ensure that the skin grew together without puckering before the stitches were removed. Stitches? Had I become a piñata that is sewn together with little goodies stuffed inside of me? After further thought, Dad requested a soft cone for me. I wish it had been a cone of the ice cream variety, but that's not how it turned out. When the nurse brought out the soft cone, I couldn't believe that this hideous contraption was for me. It was a dark blue (not that I can see that particular hue) circle that fitted around my head, with a white trim. The insane part about this "helpful tool" was its size. From my neck to its outermost fringe, the cone had a radius of approximately 20 inches. As such, it dragged on the ground as I wearily moved forward. I looked like a goddamned flower with blue petals. How embarrassing?

Its purpose was to help keep me from more closely investigating (i.e., licking or gnawing) at least one or perhaps multiple affected areas. With my burgeoning curiosity and adept flexibility, would I do that? Yes. So ... once again, father knows best. I was ready to collapse from exhaustion and Dad quickly stopped at the counter to settle up and we plodded to the car.

Dad took me home and tried to take me for a walk with my soft cone, which was a losing proposition. I was weak and the temperature was pushing 90 degrees, never mind the blasted soft cone that I tripped on every few steps. We turned around after a few hundred feet and Dad graciously filled my food and water dishes to restore some of my beleaguered strength. As I was chowing, he called Mom to forewarn the family of my appearance and condition. The term "patchwork quilt" was bandied about. Dad alluded to bare fur patches of skin that were about six inches by six inches. Of course, this was hard to picture without seeing it for yourself.

A few minutes later, the crew returned home. I was anxious to say hello to everyone to ensure that we could return a sense of normalcy to this chaotic day. As I peered into the garage, I could hear wailing from the minivan. My ears perked up and I honed in on the noise. It was Hanna. She was sad and confused. Dad rudely closed the door in my face so that he could go out and explain and console. Hanna was sobbing. While I didn't like my situation, it really wasn't *that* bad. I paced at the door while waiting for my humans to come in and greet me.

They finally entered the house with Mommom putting on a brave face to greet me. I licked her feverishly to assuage her anxiety. Hanna's tears started anew as she got a full glimpse of me. Did I really look that bad? I tried to help her get over the shock of my appearance by licking her. It didn't help much, if any. Rudy seemed ambivalent. Maybe it was Dad's explanation, maybe he had better things on which to ruminate, but he was handling my lack of fur and my additional apparatus without the facade of alarm.

It was clear that the soft cone was inordinately cumbersome, so Mommom gradually worked to convince Dad that I did not require the soft cone at all times. Within the first day following my surgery, the soft cone was cast aside during meal time, sleep/naps, walks, and being outside in general.

Mom and Dad were already reluctant to let me stay outside for long periods of time because of my breed's predisposition to skin cancer. Now, I was temporarily at further risk from sun exposure on areas without fur. If it was sunny, I was not permitted to remain outdoors for more than a stretch of a few minutes. As usual, I was restricted, but it was for my own well-being. Mom and Dad jointly decided to take the soft cone off full time after a few days. I was grateful to be back to normal and avoided the stitches as much as I possibly could. But, that new skin and fur growth was reaaalllly itchy at times.

Mom and Dad tried to reassure Hanna that I was the same old Newman. The fur would eventually grow back, but it might take some time. The God-forsaken soft cone had already been abandoned, so we were on the road to recovery. As days passed, Hanna became used to my predicament and could actually look at me without tearing up or seeming depressed.

My fur grew at a painfully slow rate. The upside was that I returned to the vet to have my stitches removed after ten days. This amount of time had allowed the skin to grow together satisfactorily. Once the stitches were out, three nasty-looking scars remained. The skin puckered a tiny bit at each juncture, but it would eventually smooth out. Boy, were the scars uncomfortable now! All I wanted to do was lick. My tongue is the ultimate healing device.

After doing some light touching and prodding on each of my scars, Dad discovered that the scar tissue on my left side was extremely sensitive to the touch and caused me to involuntarily respond by kinking my neck and twitching involuntarily. The other scars didn't bother me nearly as much.

We saw some factions of our family pretty often. This included Aunt Ally, Uncle Cody, Emerson, and Bailey. On occasion, Mom would watch Emerson because Aunt Ally and Uncle Cody had work or something silly that got in the way of living. One day, Mommom was watching Emerson.

He was about sixteen months old at the time, so he was mobile, active, and reminded me of me as a youth. He was into *every*thing. Drum set, upstairs, downstairs. Check, check, check. He secretly liked to grab my nub with a mischievous glint in his eye. That part of watching the little guy was frustrating. The other part was his reluctance to nap for his Aunt Laura, my Mommom. When he didn't nap, I didn't get to nap. And I *love* daytime naps when the house is quiet. Mom was exhausted from chasing Emerson here and there and everywhere. It was late afternoon and I had given up trying to help. I lay down in our bonus room, hoping to catch a few winks.

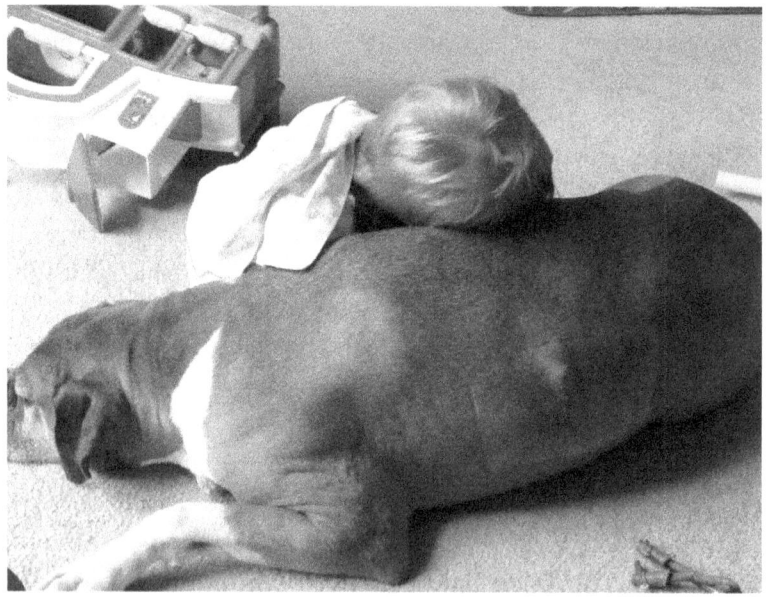

Everyone should enjoy a good nap from time to time.

As I closed my eyes and began my siesta, I felt a gentle thud on my back. My eyes sluggishly rolled forward and opened to see Emerson resting his head on my side. The little dude decided to join me for slumber. I don't mind being your pillow, buddy. Go for it. Sleep—good; chaos—bad. I closed my eyes and went right back to sleep. Mommom got his cloth that he slept with and allowed him to begin dozing on me until she was convinced that she could put him down for a nap in a pack-and-play, as opposed to the canine bed. Thank goodness. One thing I have learned as I've matured is that naps are a good thing. Enjoy them!

Over time, the itchiness of the scars disappeared, aside from times when my left side was inadvertently touched. That area remained sensitive for quite some time. It took about four months, but my fur was finally all back in place. No more breezy feeling on my patches. No more nickname of "Quilt" or "Patches." The scars remained, but chicks dig scars, right? I could say that I got into a scrap with another dog and you should see how he looks!

❖ I LOVED GETTING INTO the bed with Mom and Dad when it was time to sleep. I could select my location, which often was somewhere in the middle of the mattress. Often, I would perch my head on one of their limbs and cuddle closely to ensure that I would be alerted to any activity if one of my cuddle buddies were to arise.

Dad came up with the idea to place my dog bed atop the covers in the big bed. I looked at the approximately 2' x 3' soft bed located near the foot of the bed curiously when it was first put in place. As Mom and Dad drifted off to sleep, I leapt into the bed like usual and searched for the ideal position to sleep. After circling a few ... ok, several ... times and stamping my feet to work the bed into an ideal resting place, I allowed my body to cuddle up to Dad with only my head resting on the dog bed. This was the lap of luxury! How perfect.

For the next several months, I nestled into Mom or Dad as if they were a giant teddy bear. Meanwhile, my head got the extra layer of support from my dog bed. This seemed to take up an inordinate amount of room on the bed for just my head, but that's how I chose to make use of it. I sensed that it wasn't what Dad had envisioned when adding the dog bed to an already crowded mattress, but we made it work.

My leaps onto the bed became more of a challenge at my steadily increasing age. I paced around all edges of the bed to look for the lowest spot on which to land. Although it looked relatively even, I usually picked Mommom's side of the bed after several minutes of reviewing each angle. I was barely making it up onto the bed surface, and it took my full effort to do so. Any time I tried to make the vault, one or both of my rear paws would slam against the side of the mattress. The struggle to get into bed became a late night ritual. When I finally hurtled onto the mattress, I would often hear sighs of relief from both sides of the bed after I made it. But, something had to change. Dad decided to place my pillow ... er, dog bed ... back on the floor as an option for sleeping. After one particularly frustrating night when I could not find a spot that I deemed low enough to jump into the bed, I despondently abandoned the nightly leap and opted for my much thinner dog bed on the floor. Dad got onto the floor next to me and put his arm around me in an attempt at consolation. I was not pleased with this aspect of my new reality as an older dog. Aging sucks.

Dad even tried to pick me up to place me on the bed, but that became a non-starter for me. Any time that he lifted me up, I would nose his face, but never bare my teeth. It's Dad ... I knew he was trying to help. However, I wanted him to know just how scared I was of this motion. After a few lifting attempts over the course of a week, he got the hint. Don't lift Newman. Check. Got it. Message received. Anybody that says dogs can't train humans is dead wrong.

Once Dad gave up on that option, Mom and Dad set up a series of portable steps leading from the floor to the edge of the bed. This freaked me out more than anything. Dad tried to train me to use these steps to get on and off the bed. I was extremely reluctant to even test these steps to support my weight. I had a death grip with my toenails on the steps any time that Dad would try to make me navigate the four steps. If left to my own devices, I wouldn't touch any of the damned things. I couldn't explain why I felt such fear about doing those steps, but even if Dad would get me up one or two steps, I did my best to jump off them without getting anywhere near to touching the surface of the mattress. It was a very frustrating experience because Dad kept harping on the training. I was not giving in to climb the steps. They were too scary, and I wanted no part of them no matter how many treats you fed me during our instructional attempts. My stubbornness eventually won out, with Dad giving in to the adage that you can't teach an old dog new tricks.

My trips down the stairs from our second floor to the first floor have always been ... interesting, to say the least. If the doorbell had rung or if I was in a particular hurry, it was never a sure bet that I would touch each and every step. I absolutely needed to travel down the steps at lightning speed in order to be my nosey self and investigate.

As I grew older, Mom grew especially concerned about my ability to keep doing the wooden steps without the aid of something on which to grip. Dad didn't blow it off, but he correctly assessed the current situation that I had *always* landed on my feet even if I touched only four or five of the fifteen steps on the way down. Through nine of your human years, that held true.

The proactive parents determined that an ounce of prevention was worth a pound of cure ... or however that proverb goes. Along with new carpeting in our dining room that was plusher, stain-resistant, and a richer brown color, our steps were covered with a similar runner of carpeting.

I couldn't believe how different the trip was going up and down the stairs. I actually had traction and did not have to rely on my nimble muscles to recover and make a smooth landing at the foot of the steps when I was in a hurry. Gone were the days of my noisy toenails pounding steps. You were more likely to hear gentle paw-pounding thuds or my panting if I was making the trip "north or south." This simple layer of carpet could not have come at a more opportune time because of what was to come.

The Times They Are a Changin'

AS WINTER WAS WINDING DOWN and spring was about to finally be unleashed in 2014, Dad noticed that I was scuffing my left rear toenails on our daily walks. It didn't get better, it didn't get worse; it simply persisted. There was no pain in it for me. I continued to happily bounce along down the road, enjoying the smells as the winter season thankfully transitioned into spring. I loathe cold weather!

Dad talked it over with Mommom and they decided that it would be best to take me to the vet to make sure it wasn't anything serious. They were concerned that I might be developing arthritis or hip dysplasia. After all, I was considered a "senior," despite my infantile mindset and fun-seeking behavior.

I'll admit it, I loved going to the vet. Some dogs are wary of doctors. Not me! I usually got to see other dogs, my vet gave me treats and attention, and let's not forget all the new smells. It seemed as though a million dogs have been there, and I tried to decipher each canine's individual odor with my very active schnazola.

The vet showered me with praise and love as usual, along with feeding me treats in the form of sticky paste. Mmm, so delicious! On this particular visit, Dr. Bryce also did a lot of manipulation on my joints to see what was causing my toe drag. He hypothesized that it was not anything neurological because I didn't show any signs of pain. His theory was that there perhaps could be some mild cruciate ligament damage. Dad decided to have me undergo an X-ray the following week to learn more about my condition. Yippee! Another trip to the vet!

Well, this visit wasn't as awesome as my many other trips to the vet had been. I didn't realize that I was going to be knocked out for the X-ray. God only knows what happened to me during those hours because I don't remember a thing. After I awoke, Dad arrived to pick me up. I was feeling very lethargic and shaky. As usual, the after-effects of anesthesia sucked. I was trying hard to keep my eyes open as Dad and Dr. Bryce's partner reviewed the results. The very nice lady vet, Dr. Scoda, did not feel as though I had any ligament damage. While I had very mild signs of dysplasia, it was deemed not to be the root cause. Dr. Scoda told Dad to monitor my situation and keep her and Dr. Bryce posted with any new developments.

As we prepared to check out, a thought dawned on her. Dr. Scoda quickly printed off an article on a condition that was prevalent in us boxers. It was called degenerative myelopathy, or DM. As she talked about the disease, more concern appeared on both of their faces. She mentioned a few other vets who specialize in neurology to better diagnose me. This was exhausting. I was fidgety and I just wanted a nap. The bottom line was that Mom and Dad needed to talk about the next step in the process. As we drove home, I slept most of the way. But, when I was awake, Dad was uneasily looking at me. I had never seen that look in his eyes before; it was fear.

It didn't take long for my parents to decide: consult the best. We got a referral to Cornell University within the next two weeks. Dad took the day off work and just the three of us took a pleasant ride to Ithaca, NY, on a sunny, perfect-weather day. This place was massive! And the dogs? I don't remember seeing so many dogs together in one place before. I wish I knew how to behave better around my kind, so Dad would have trusted me to visit more of them. But, I did get to meet a pug that reminded me of Mosby; she wasn't nearly as nuts as him. So, the rumors are true: all pugs aren't humping lunatics. Maybe there was still hope for my cousin as he matures.

After a lengthy stay in the waiting room, we got to visit with a fleet of doctors, some more seasoned than others. The young guy was the lucky one because he was the most "hands on" with me, so we got to talk quite a bit. I licked him enough that it would take him several scrub-downs to fully remove my saliva from his skin. Dad and I traversed the hallway to demonstrate my toe scuffing for the medical professionals.

The doctors proceeded to take me to an interior office to do further evaluations on me, while Mom and Dad waited. As always, I loved the doctors. They were really nice to me, and I just wanted to know what my problem was. A few minutes later, the doctors and I emerged from the back room to see Mom and Dad. The M.D.s agreed that the infancy of DM was a distinct possibility, but it could not be diagnosed with 100% certainty by only looking at me. They provided three basic options to Mom and Dad: 1) Pay careful attention to my condition and note any deterioration immediately; 2) Take a blood sample today to determine whether I was a carrier for DM or not; 3) Make an appointment to have an MRI, which would more definitively determine the prognosis.

The men and women in white coats left the room so Mom and Dad could mull over their decision. Because of my age, all the new activity today had me panting like I had just completed a triathlon ... and I couldn't swim. Don't even mention a bicycle. Not gonna happen ... although I'm an excellent driver.

So, I lay on the cool, hard floor and rested, my jowls expanding and contracting vigorously as I tried to catch my breath. I listened intently as my two favorite people in the world discussed what the best approach might be. The good thing about my parents is ... they're smart (shh, don't tell them I said that).

Both of them had done research on DM, especially Mom. While their knowledge might not have matched that of a veterinarian who went to school for nearly a decade, they knew me and picked up on subtle changes in my patterns that others could not quickly assess. They were fairly certain that I had the degenerative condition. The severity of my left rear toe dragging had barely, but perceptibly, worsened. It used to occur every other step, or two steps out of every three. Now, it happened with nearly every step.

Mom and Dad thoughtfully considered what to do. They believed that they could learn everything they needed with the blood test. If I was a carrier for DM as they feared, we would follow the exercise protocol and try to lengthen each stage of the degenerative condition so that I could enjoy a much more meaningful life. If I was not a carrier, then they would reconsider whether it was worth putting me through anesthesia again, along with an exorbitant cost for me to have an MRI.

When the doctors returned, Mom and Dad mercifully told the doctors that a simple blood test was their preferred choice. For whatever reason, I never seemed to mind getting shots or having blood taken. Heck, my nub even wagged on occasion as I was getting injections. Then, there was that one time that the nurse helped to fully express my anal glands. Meh, no big deal. This time was no different. The doctors had to send my blood to the University of Missouri because that was the only facility in the country that could perform this particular blood exam. Within minutes, we were on our way back to the 585 area code. I didn't see much of the 100-minute ride because I was so fatigued. I was thankful to be going home.

Two weeks later, Mom and Dad got the results. Unfortunately, it did not come as a pleasant surprise; I was indeed a carrier for DM. I didn't know it yet, but DM was going to consume my remaining days, and at an exponential rate. I wish I had been given the choice of dealing with only BMs, not DM.

❖ AS SPRING TURNED TO summer, my left rear paw scuffing started to wear down my toenails. Another sign of the disease's progression was that the scuffing was no longer limited to my left rear toenails. Now, my right rear nails occasionally abraded whatever surface I was navigating. Dad tried to teach me to raise my knees higher with each stride. From time to time, he would walk behind me and push up on my knees, and thus my hips, to avoid scraping my toenails with each stride. Yeah … not happening, buddy. He also preached something he called "muscle memory" with no luck whatsoever. I walked how I always walked, or so I thought.

I still felt great with no physical ailments otherwise. I had a strong appetite, no surprise there. I could still run, bounce, and enjoy life. Mommom did something unique for me for my tenth birthday. She invited my cousins, Bailey and Mosby (and their humans) to celebrate with me.

Bailey and I now see eye to eye, metaphorically speaking. We don't really pounce on each other anymore. I think he gets that I'm older and can't afford to play with the same wild abandon as we had enjoyed in our more youthful days. Age has softened our hyperactivity.

But, then there was Mosby. He was only two years old. I could understand his perspective, although those days were far in my rearview mirror. He was just a pup, and he's a pug. So maybe he's got a little Napoleon complex. I get it, I do. But, good grief, could you PLEASE stop humping me? You've been "fixed," you're a guest at my celebration. Leave my leg and hip alone! Mommom told me that Bailey swatted Mosby on his first humping attempt. Mosby learned quickly never to try that activity again with Bailey. I guess that makes me the nice guy, but also the violated one.

Cue up the band, start singing "Happy Birthday" and I know what's coming. Mommom gave each of us canines a Frosty Paw treat. What a delicious way to start my eleventh year on the planet. Poor Mosby could not finish his ice cream because of the shape of his snout and the length (or lack thereof) of his tongue. I was the beneficiary of Mosby's physical limitations as the remainder of his ice cream cup was placed in front of me to polish off.

A few weeks after I turned ten of your human years, the whole family went camping at Jellystone Park. This is one of those rare places where people and dogs get to cohabitate and be on vacation. We camped in a cabin as we had done the previous year. The regrettable difference between our 2013 and 2014 vacations was that I could no longer walk the length of the park, so I missed out on watching some of the kids' activities. But, it was a wonderful experience to be outside, be with my family, and feel included as part of the crew. Aunt Ally, Uncle Cody, Emerson, and Bailey were in the adjacent cabin. So, Bailey and I decided to tag team the required barking fits to announce the presence of any newcomer near our digs for the long weekend. If he saw someone approaching, he'd bark to let me know that there was someone that required my attention, and vice-versa.

Jellystone Park is a Yogi Bear-themed park with a water park and old-fashioned fun with many of the characters roaming around the park like Yogi, Boo Boo, and Ranger Smith. One day while Mommom and I were relaxing on the front porch of the cabin, one of the park employees was carting Boo Boo to his next park appearance. The cart stopped directly in front of my cabin. What was going on? Before I could even react, Boo Boo came up to the portable gate across our porch and reached over to say "Hi" just to me! He rubbed my head and scratched my ears with his

I didn't watch cartoons, but Boo Boo was assuredly my favorite character now.

fuzzy hands, and was just really nice. I didn't even think to bark at him.

❖ SHORTLY AFTER I turned ten years old, my crew had departed for a few hours in the evening to visit some other family. I had been left home alone, as had typically been the case in my life as an adult dog. I was trusted with freedom to come and go as I pleased throughout the entire house. Since exiting the puppy stage of my life, I had always exhibited exemplary conduct in such situations. I guess that the phrase, "out of sight, out of mind" is a good way to introduce this one-time return to puppyhood.

Mommom had bought a 24-pack of toilet paper because ... well, buy in bulk, people! It just made sense. 'Nuff said. She had not yet restocked the bathrooms and storage shelves with the recent purchase, so there it sat on the dining room floor.

I usually slept the majority of the time when my family was elsewhere; but not with the toilet paper just sitting there with all the untapped potential for hours and hours of entertainment.

Each toilet paper roll was individually wrapped within a clear plastic package. I first tore into the plastic to free the first wrapped roll. Yes!! I shook it violently and vigorously from side to side. This caused the tissue-thin wrapping to tear a few inches. If I kept playing with roll #1, then the individual wrapper opened more and more. This was outstanding! I got my paws into the act to hold down the roll while tugging on the wrapper until it shredded onto the floor. Roll #1 was free!! I tossed it into the air to myself and sprinted laps around the dining room table. With no companions present, I decided to play fetch ... with myself. Tiny little strips of toilet paper were being deposited all along the dining room floor. Roll #1 was a bit on the stubborn side because the loose end of the toilet paper roll stuck to itself. This did not allow the toilet paper to unroll as I had hoped. The good news was that I had 23 more options available to me.

Some new toys (aka TP rolls) were more fun than others, or perhaps I was more effective at playing with certain toilet paper rolls. I couldn't even loosen the wrapper on some of them, while others were easy to liberate. The more cooperative rolls were the best toys. I could see the fringe starting to shred on a few of the rolls and I tried my hardest to decorate the floor with lengthy ribbons of toilet paper. It never quite worked out that way, but with a 24-pack, I was able to fill the void of time left by my loved ones' departure. It may not have been my best work[10], but the sight of nineteen toilet paper rolls in varying states of disarray was something to behold. Toilet paper wrappers and tiny shreds of clear plastic, wrapping, and toilet paper were strewn all over the dining room floor. I never quite got to those last five rolls.

---

[10] See the chapter, Smells Like Teen Spirit, for my crowning artwork achievement.

Livin' on a Prayer

OUR FAMILY HAD A typically hectic summer. Hanna and Rudy played soccer while Dad coached. I even got to watch one of the games with seemingly the entire town of Honeoye Falls present and accounted for. Hanna did some lacrosse camps while Rudy kept progressing in taekwondo. Then, all of my people went on vacation ... without me. How rude! The benefit to watching them head off to the beach for the better part of a week was getting some quality time with Bailey and his humans. I spent five days with some of my extended family.

Bailey and I might not have been able to coexist before, but we were each at very different stages in our lives. We interacted with comparative calm, and did our own thing individually. The saddest part of my time there was seeing Aunt Ally get so upset about my affliction with DM. I was still in good shape. I could trudge up and down steps, and was fairly mobile. Sure, I might not have been quite as perky as I used to be. But, my lovable personality was still there. We had lots of memories yet to make!

As the weather turned from warm, but not oppressively hot, summer days to pleasant autumn days, I enjoyed getting back into the habit of assisting with Hanna and Rudy getting on and off the bus. I could still make it outside and walk along the sidewalk and front yard to perform this duty.

It was getting more difficult, but we did exercises to keep up my strength. Dad would pick up my front paws and force me to use my back legs to hold up the rest of my weight. He also pushed my hips from side to side to use different parts of my rear leg muscles. The most frustrating exercise that Dad forced me to endure was him holding up my front left paw and rear right paw, in an attempt to get me balanced on the two remaining paws. Similarly, he lifted my front right paw and rear left paw to bolster the other two legs. Each of these exercises was intended to minimize the degradation that DM had on my physical abilities. We wanted to keep me as upright and mobile as possible for as long as possible.

The fall of 2014 saw the ice bucket challenge go viral to support amyotrophic lateral sclerosis (ALS), a human variant of my affliction, DM. Dad was obligated and honored to get doused with some 60 pounds of ice water to bring attention to my increasing challenges. I wasn't particularly interested in his efforts, but it's nice to know that my family has my back (and hindquarters).

Through the social media component of the ice bucket challenge, Dad learned that one of our friends we met from camping at Jellystone the previous summer had a boxer who ultimately succumbed to DM. Dad talked on the phone for nearly two hours, almost all of which were done with tears streaming down his face. I knew that Dad was a softie, but I had never seen him like this. I could only imagine what he was learning in this conversation. Maybe I didn't really want to know.

Our walks began getting shorter because I could not do the full duration without doing damage to my rear toenails. I preferred to walk on the road, perhaps out of habit. Every scuff of my toenail on the road surface made Dad cringe. Eventually, the quick[11] in my rear toenails got so worn down that it was a regular occurrence for Mom or Dad to tend to one or more of my bloody toenails. This had a twofold effect on my life.

1. Dad tried his best to get me to take our walks on grass, as opposed to the road. Ten years of walking along the street pavement was a hard habit to break. After a week or so, it became a pattern that I willingly followed. The ground was soft and I bled considerably less. It made sense. We often took other routes where I didn't have a choice but to walk on the soft ground. My strength was beginning to dwindle, as I would often take breaks or cut short our typical walk length of a half mile to something that more closely approximated a quarter mile.
2. Mom did some research into making my walks easier and more rewarding. She found a company that would customize carts, or doggy wheelchairs, based on a dog's measurements. They specialized in aiding dogs that were missing limbs, had neurological disorders, or had temporary issues that would eventually heal, like broken bones or ligament damage.

It wasn't only the abrasive surface of the road that started the blood trickling from my quick. Unfortunately, the hard surface of the kitchen and entry tile also had the same effect. Mom and Dad laid down some temporary carpeting to avoid me scraping my toenails needlessly. Maybe they were worried that I was running low on blood, but their solution seemed to keep the blood from flowing freely.

Steps started to become a real issue for me, so trudging up the fifteen stairs to go to bed became an impossibility. I

---

[11] The quick is a prominent blood vessel that extends almost to the tip of each of a dog's toenails. If a dog's toenail is trimmed, ripped, or otherwise shortened by too much, the quick can be exposed and bleed out. This condition is rather painful for a dog and it often takes several minutes to clot the blood flow.

would watch Mom and Dad head up to bed, and they would leave me on either the couch or love seat to slumber. They would even cover me up if the night proved to be too frigid. I never stayed in one position throughout the night, so any blanket that initially covered me ended up acting as an extra layer of padding beneath me.

Mom, Dad, and I made a weekend trip to Massachusetts to check out Eddie's Wheels. We dropped off Hanna and Rudy at Bailey's house, then went on our way. I still loved to travel. Car rides soothed me like nothing else. I loved snoozing on Mommom's lap with my head against the chilly glass of the passenger window while Dad put miles behind us on the New York State Thruway. We drove about three hours on Friday night and got to spend the night at a hotel. It had been forever since we had done that. The dog area at the hotel was tiny, but big enough for me to poop and pee.

I was a bit uneasy because of my new surroundings. Thankfully, Mom and Dad were right there every step of the way so I felt more comfortable. We all slept just fine and continued on our journey the next day. It was a chilly October morning with frost on the ground, which is unseasonably early for anything frozen, even in the northeast US. Another two and a half hours in the car and we arrived.

As we walked through the door of Eddie's Wheels, we saw a handful of dogs of different breeds, both with carts and without carts. I did not act with the standard spazzy energy as I encountered other dogs with disabilities. Seeing other dogs in carts brought about an apprehensive calm in me. My outward personality had dulled for the moment. I could not easily detect the typical dog signs on these canines, and that was upsetting to me. The nice lady who ran the business made several measurements on me. I complied as she, in conjunction with Mom and Dad, pushed and pulled me in various directions to see what a big boy I was.

The woman brought out a metal device that was about three feet long and 18 inches high. She grabbed hold of me, and the whole situation. She lifted my hind legs and thrust them into pre-made gaps and quickly snapped two set screws in place, along with fastening a strap around my neck. My hind legs were then lifted into stirrups so that they did not touch the ground. In a few short seconds, I went from a dog that had two good legs and two mediocre legs to a canine where the function of my hind legs was irrelevant.

I took a step or two then rapidly realized that I could pull myself along using just the muscles in my front shoulders. You might think that I would have joyously bolted out the door and bounded down the ramp, running like I could a few short months ago. However, I methodically plodded along, taking each step at a steady pace. I was grateful that my toes were not obliterated thanks to the cart; however, I did not like feeling like an invalid. I was a bit grumpy because I had never needed this level of assistance before now.

After a few minutes of tooling around the lawn in the cart, I showed that I could do some normal functions without assistance. I didn't squat; I didn't even think to do so. No huffing and puffing. I stood there proudly, not looking at anything in particular and took a shit. Multiple large turds easily slid out of me and pelted the ground. Of course, Mom quickly cleaned them up so that it didn't cause a mess for me or anyone else. Well ... I guess that still works. It still didn't feel quite right even moving in the cart, but I was appreciative to have this option available to me.

We returned to talk with the nice lady. Mom and Dad ordered the cart that would be custom-fit to my specific measurements. Once they got me out of the cart following roughly 20 minutes, boy did my back legs feel weak. I felt as though they were dragging behind me. Getting them back and acceptably mobile was admittedly a challenge, but I got them going after some encouragement (aka treats) from the parental units. Mom and Dad also purchased a harness that would offer a more portable way to keep me upright with handles on both the front and back portions. While this series of straps and restraints may ultimately help me, I was not a proponent of its design. There was one strap that inevitably ground my "canine-hood" against my underbelly. I suppose I would grin and bear it. After all, they're just looking out for my best interests.

It would be another two weeks before my cart would arrive. Thank God that it was pre-assembled because Dad wasn't the handiest guy around. We tested it out and it didn't feel all that different from the floor model that I had tried in Massachusetts. Mommom made some tweaks to the strap that circumnavigated my neck. I could still walk steadily on my own, although my rear legs had begun to falter slightly despite our exercise regimen. Most days, we spent a few minutes getting in and out of the cart and allowing me to become more familiar with how to operate the beast. I did not completely capitalize on its capabilities in the early days because I was dismissive of the darned thing. I'd rather use all my legs while I still could. The one thing I was adamantly opposed to doing in the cart, at least fully, was peeing. I'd feel that urge coming, and would just shut down the notion. Much to my parents' consternation, the most you would ever see out of my urination efforts would be a few drips or a brief spray.

The cart was helpful, but it made maneuvering in the house more challenging. I never quite got the hang of accounting for the extra width of the wheels. Mom was always impressed by my ability to bound down a set of two steps to go from the house to the garage. I never exhibited any sign of trepidation, but instead I bolted for the out-of-doors. Mom or Dad definitely needed to use the leash and collar when I was strapped into my cart. The invisible fence boundary was the furthest thing from my mind when I was carted. I thought that the world was my oyster. After all, Mommom got me a license plate to show that I meant business in my cart.

In my new wheels, I could even take a gander at what was cooking.

Autumn wore on, and the chill of winter was not far off. The onset of DM began to plague my endurance. When we went on walks, I would be fine at the outset. After a few hundred feet, though, I often crossed my hind legs, essentially tripping myself. I also occasionally dragged them on the ground because I could no longer feel the positioning of my paws. When this occurred, Dad convinced me to stop and take a short break to rejuvenate my strength before continuing. It was frustrating to feel my athleticism deteriorate. But, Dad was insistent on keeping as much to our walking ritual as possible.

❖ MOM AND DAD typically celebrated their November wedding anniversary by going on a vacation. That wasn't going to happen this year because my health was a growing concern. They didn't feel comfortable leaving me in someone else's care for an extended period of time.

However, Aunt Lindsay and Mike were getting married. Mom, Dad, Hanna, and Rudy were headed out of town for a night, along with everyone on Mom's side of the family. We checked with Dad's parents, and they happily agreed to take care of me for a day or two. This was by far the best option for everyone's peace of mind. If you may recall, the last time one of my aunts got married, I attempted to destroy the basement where I was confined. Being crated was not an option at this stage of the game.

Grandma was especially distraught at seeing my degenerative condition because it had been a few months since she had last seen me. The day-to-day changes were minimal, but over the course of time, my abilities had lessened noticeably.

Thankfully, my weaknesses had not deteriorated my spirit, so we had a fun time together. I may have had an accident or two; but Grandma did not begrudge the need to clean up after me because I was unaware of some needs until it was too late.

Despite Dad's specific instructions to take me for at

least one walk over the weekend, I was relegated to remaining in and around the house, without the opportunity to venture down our quiet lane. I don't know why I wasn't asked to go for a walk. Maybe they just forgot; that's ok. They always took such wonderful care of me. We could let it slide this one time.

The weather was rather nice for November in suburban Rochester, which meant we would have an easy winter, right? It felt like Indian summer on the Sunday that my crew returned home. I could not contain my enthusiasm to be back with my parents. I had a spring in my step and an excess of untapped energy. Within minutes of their arrival, Dad thought it would be wise to take me for a little stroll. Yeah, no shit, Sherlock.

Dad smartly opted to keep the cart in the garage and just let me go with the leash and collar. I walked like I did when I was a puppy ... inspecting everything in sight ... and out of sight. It was a glorious fall day. We made it halfway to the end of our street. Dad carefully monitored my progress as we stayed on the grass that lined our street. He thought that we could go a bit further, as I had not shown any signs of slowing or fatigue.

I hadn't been to the circle at the end of our cul-de-sac in several weeks, cart or no cart. We took a short break and pondered the decision. By now, you know me and what my choice would be. However, I'm not the one operating the leash. I'm *on* the leash. My supposedly responsible Dad got to make this decision. He gauged my desire, my fitness, and my lack of weariness. We walked onward and trudged through each neighbor's yard as I absorbed the sights, sounds, and smells of the far end of the street. We made it to the circle at the opposite end of the road, woo hoo! We were about halfway home before those God-forsaken back legs that I barely recognized as my own started to give way to lethargy. Dad invited me to lie down in the grass to catch my breath. We spent a few minutes there before resuming our walk home.

The remaining portion of our trek was a series of fits and starts with a few short breaks to allow me to rest my increasingly weary and wary muscles. Finally, the finish line was in sight. My legs felt squishy as we crossed into my yard and plodded up the driveway, but I had done it. The two days without a walk with Grandma and Grandpa had given me a reserve of energy enough to make it around the block ... barely. Dad knew it then, but I had no clue – that venture was the last time that I would use all four legs to walk the full length of our street.

December

BY NOW YOU KNOW that I didn't like winter. Never have, never will. When November bled into December, the feeling in my lower back and legs aligned with that of the bitterly cold weather: numbing. Just before Thanksgiving, there were areas of western New York that saw seven feet of snow fall in a 48-72-hour period. Sixty miles away from the epicenter of the worst snowfall, we had the good fortune of seeing only a coating of snow, but it was still cold as hell, well cold as ... ice. Hell's not cold.

When I did my business, I didn't have the warning that I was accustomed to. It was more like a fire drill. Hurry up, get out of the house! Hurry! Now! Do it! Oh boy! Oh no! Crap, crap, crap! Mommom! Dad! Hurry, help!!! The urgency became the standard until I was relaxing one day in the dining room while Mom was paying some bills. I looked behind me and was mortified to see that I was pooping *in the house*. Oh no, oh no, NO!!! A look of disappointment and self-loathing was all I could muster to Mom when I realized what I had just done. I didn't sense it coming at all. The feeling of guilt and shame was overwhelming. Mom was surprised, but not mad or upset with me. She unquestioningly cleaned up the mess, then tried to reassure me and relieve my anxiety over the accident. I felt awful and wondered what the more dictatorial parent would think about this new development.

As hard as I tried to go potty outside every time, that was no longer the reality of my life at age 10 ½ of your human years. There were occasions when I had zero idea that my bowels were going to let loose. The pangs of guilt subsided over time because it appeared that Mom and Dad were not furious, but rather, were in a hurry to clean up the mess and eliminate as much of the odor as possible. Hanna and Rudy were initially completely grossed out that I was becoming incontinent. Who can blame them? What adult dog poops in the house? Unfortunately the truth is, it's me, that's who. I was sure that Bailey and Mosby didn't do this crap, literally.

I didn't like disappointing my humans, but as my condition worsened, I think everyone understood that I wasn't dropping deuces inside to be malicious. Hanna and Rudy even pitched in to help get paper towels, rags, baggies, and appropriate cleaning products depending on where I made my deposit. Mom and Dad were very careful to not have the kids actually clean up anything, but they were good little assistants.

I know it's gross, but there were occasions when I tried to ... how do I put this delicately ... clean up the mess myself. Hey, I wanted to do my part, ok? I thought I was being helpful despite the rather harsh admonishments that I would get when I even sniffed my own crap, let alone attempted to orally dispose of the evidence.

One chilly, but not frigid winter Tuesday, Dad was working from home while Mom was at work and the kids were in school. He received a call from the heater repair company that they were due to arrive shortly. Dad decided that it was an opportune occasion to take care of me before the repairman came. I couldn't go up and down steps quite as easily as in the past, so Dad chose to pick me up to carry me out the front door. As he often did, he held me tightly around my barrel chest with our heads close together, allowing my hind legs to dangle freely. Let's just say that gravity took over. Dad shouted, "What the hell?" My rear legs instinctively rose to avoid what was happening down below. It shocked me that my bowels released twelve, count 'em, TWELVE, turd nuggets onto the porch, steps, and sidewalk. Some of them bounced off Dad, some just plopped without any deflection. Holy shit ... literally! Who knew I had that much poop inside me, especially considering that I had already crapped three times that morning without eating a meal. Dad worked furiously to clean up both of us, and each of the bombs. Within a minute of Dad concluding his sanitation duties, I announced the arrival of the heater technician with a loud series of barks and howls. Dad had a fun time recounting this story to Mom. Thus, the term "nuggetize" was born.

The winter turned out to be the coldest in Rochester ... EVER! I can only account for eight of those years, and the 2014-2015 winter sucked the most for sure! It seemed like every week we got bombarded with another bout of heavy snow (6-12 inches in less than 24 hours) to further bury us. I never wanted to spend more than the necessary moments outside, just enough to tinkle and, if I hadn't turded inside, then I'd give that a shot outside before scampering to come back inside the warm house. Mom and Dad used to make sure that I got daily walks, but I had no interest in walking (cart or not), on slushy, icy, or snow-covered roads. So, the bitter cold primarily kept us inside.

Due to advancing DM, my rear leg muscles started to atrophy and lose significant tone. All the flexibility workouts became a losing proposition. I could no longer perform any of the balance or strength exercises without squatting on my back side. My musculature had worsened each day despite our best efforts. The "D" stood for degenerative for a reason. Walking had become more of a challenge without the aid of my cart or someone holding up my rump. I still maintained some mobility and could travel a few paces without assistance, but not for any meaningful duration of time or distance. When the kids got off the bus, I could pry myself off the couch or floor and waddle to the door to greet them. When Dad (or Mom) returned home from a long day at work, I put forth max effort to go see them as they entered the house through the garage.

Around the house, Mom or Dad would put me in the cart more often, presumably to allow me improved mobility so that I could eat, follow my humans around, or bark at something of keen interest. However, I honestly preferred not to be bound to the cart. Lying around was considerably more desirable.

I experienced the next stage of DM as winter hit its stride. A dog's urine flow is a funny thing. When you have four able and active legs, you don't even think about it. But, as two of those appendages become far less than able, peeing in the right spot became a paramount concern. As with number twos, the timeliness of the internal warnings disappeared. With limited agility, I could scoot, waddle, and occasionally make steps in the direction I wanted to go. The first time I peed in the house was as alarming as the first time I had pooped. In short, I panicked. I flailed about wildly, which only made the stream scatter in a random yet circular pattern due to my freaked out 360-degree turns. The spray dotted the carpet, my belly, front paws, and simply everywhere. Mom and Dad knew that I was not going to make it outside, so they tried to get me to remain stationary to limit the damage and clean-up. No such luck people. This was NOT happening. No, no, NO!! I despised this disease, and what it was doing to me. The feel of shame was unbearable.

I saw a new battery of cleaning products appear and an additional cleansing ritual began. I got wiped down, the months-old carpet was wiped, blotted, sprayed, vigorously scrubbed, and checked for moisture and odor. My eyes gloomily focused on the area of the incident, trying to wish away the ounces of pee that I had expelled with zero warning. Curse you, DM. If I could cry, I think I would. The reassurances I received from Mom and Dad were present, although I detected that they were laced with aggravation. Whether they were frustrated with me, the disease, or both, I could not discern. The only thing I felt was disgust.

Christmas came and went with little fanfare. I used to receive toys, treats, and other goodies every year. My family chose not to give me a new toy this year ... and rightfully so. My toys were now largely ignored. Sure, I can chew on them, but that isn't as entertaining as fetching, doing a poor job of catching, or playing keep away with my opponent ... er, I mean, family member. I no longer possessed the mobility to do any of those joyous activities.

Nights were more fitful and sleep began to elude me. Everyone was upstairs, and I was stuck downstairs, moping in my sullen attitude. If I was lonely or perhaps had an accident in the middle of the night, I would ease off the couch, effort toward the stairs and whimper audibly until someone acknowledged my wake-up calls. The kids sleep like the dead, so they never heard any of my soliloquys. My parents would tag team responding to the clamor by venturing downstairs to determine what I needed. After a week or so of this, it became evident that something needed to change.

Suddenly, I started to see blankets and pillows coming downstairs each night. More often than not, Mom or Dad would sleep on the couch to be in the living room with me.

They ensured that I did not encounter any issues while everyone was sleeping. I am ever so grateful for their comfort and love. It made all the difference in the world. No longer was whining required for anything; I had company and did not feel lonely.

I would have accidents on occasion. The good news was that I never peed overnight, but those pesky bowels had a mind of their own. I even slept through some of the movements only to be awakened by one of my dear, sweet humans cleaning up the mess that had escaped me. Apparently, the stench awoke them because I failed to realize that something so disgusting had occurred.

The majority of my last year was focused on what most puppies deal with: #1 and #2. I was not a puppy; I was approaching eleven of your human years old. If we were going to have any meaningful time left together, Mom or Dad would have to come up with a creative solution to overcome constantly dealing with my accidents. The first step was sleeping in the same location. Check. Done. One alternative to the aforementioned living room sleeping arrangement was Dad carrying me up the steps each night and downstairs the following morning. I no longer refuted this option because I desperately desired to be with Mom and Dad, especially when I slept. Since we had moved into this house nearly eight years ago, I had always slept in the master bedroom. So, my parents did their best to make me as comfortable as possible.

Dad initiated a routine so that I knew when he was going to lift me. He whispered in my ear, "I'm going to pick you up, okay?" Then, he would pat my side so that I knew he was about ready, followed by a "1-2-3" and Dad would wrap his arms around me just behind my front shoulders. My head would inevitably end up right next to his so that he could continue talking to me. I suppose this was to put me at ease while my hind legs vacillated uselessly.

Unfortunately, Dad had to leave for work most mornings before the sun rose. If he woke up far earlier than Mommom, we'd spend our nights downstairs so as to keep the household undisturbed. But, I did get the opportunity to sleep on my dog bed on the floor next to my parents' bed a few nights each week: on weekends, and on the days when Dad could work from home. It made for a more restful night for me because I loved being up where I belonged.

The trip up and down the stairs was a crap shoot. I nuggetized Dad more than a few times. It's gravity, what can I say? Once in a while, I would also need to pee. Mom and Dad quickly learned to have a towel or some other cloth or wrap covering my crotch, just in case a geyser-like spray of urine was ready to erupt.

My gas was frequent, often unexpected, and more audible than in years past. As we dined one night, I let one fly that was loud and reverberated quite audibly, to which Rudy's quick wit retorted, "Fire in the hole." Mommom got quite a kick out of that.

Everything started to get into a routine for me once again because that's what I thrive on: a schedule, a pattern, something that I can follow with regularity. We would go outside at the necessary times to try and go to the bathroom. This was done in an effort to adjoin those periods of my physical "uprightness" with meals. It seemed to minimize the accidents and make life somewhat easier. However, there was one failure with this plan. I was hurting Mommom.

When I went outside, either Mom or Dad would hold me up to allow me to perform my bodily function because I refused to pee while in my cart. As I tried to support some of my weight, I would inevitably feel my hind legs buckle, thus relying on a parent to hold up the weight that I could not bear, endeavoring to keep me mess-free.

One of the methods that Dad adopted was rapidly squeezing and releasing the insides of my hips to force the pee right out of me. It may not have worked every time, but it certainly did the job better than leaving me to my own devices. Dad's maneuvering of my hips appeared to have a priming effect on my bladder. He also became rather skilled at aiming the urine flow off to one side of me so that neither of us got wet during our potty stops. Mommom picked up on Dad's tricks of the trade, too. It was like a little game for us to make it out and in without adding to the clothing that required laundering. Dad coined yet another new term for our ventures outside: a blessed occurrence. I don't know what was so holy about it. Maybe he thought it was a blessing when I didn't have an accident in the house. Who knows?

An added complication of my degenerative disease was that Mom's back was aching and really starting to become an ongoing issue. Dad decided to step up to the plate to handle as many of my bathroom needs as possible. Combine the back soreness with the biting cold of the 2014-2015 winter, and it was not exactly inviting for Mommom to make several outside trips each day with me. She loathed the cold, especially this blasted winter, so who could blame her? As the winter weeks went by, Mom's pain subsided or her lumbar muscles toughened, I'm not sure which one. Fortunately, the constant pain receded and we were in a holding pattern with my affliction.

My maneuverability had leveled off to a rather low plateau. I could no longer walk on four legs and rarely used the cart in the winter. But, I could certainly scoot with the best of 'em. When I was properly motivated, I could move very quickly through the house. I feel the need to emphasize that I was not in pain. My hindquarters simply had next to no sensation.

Think of me as though I was paralyzed from the crotch down. Couldn't really feel much of anything back there. I didn't have arthritis, hip dysplasia, cancer, or anything that made each step torture. I just couldn't move my hind legs. But, dragging them along was not a difficulty because my front shoulders remained strong from all the scooting. I still used those shoulders to attempt 180-degree rotations on the couch (to find the cool side of the cushion).

That's a little bit of a white lie. There were occasions when I could feel things back there. They were very specific occasions when I contorted my body to be "sitting like a person" as Mom or Dad would say. My body from my rear hips forward would be slightly hunched, and not quite vertical. My front paws were at shoulder width with my front paws supporting some of my weight. Meanwhile, my hind legs lay helplessly flat on the floor facing directly forward.

This was an awkward position for a multitude of reasons. It was incredibly challenging to get out of this position, either by myself or relying on assistance. My weight is that of a corpse in this stance, and utterly useless. The other byproduct of being stuck in this position was a physiological one. Nearly without fail, I would get an erection. I was on complete display here, people, unable to move and with this growing problem ... it was embarrassing (for my parents, not me)! Mom or Dad would either dead lift me, or try to roll me more onto my side before scooting me to my next location. One of the only benefits of my affliction with DM is that we could patent a non-pharmaceutical replacement for Viagra and the like. We would just need to find the human equivalent of my blood flow while "sitting like a person" to induce a male's erection.

Mommom came up with the ingenious idea to wrap a towel immediately in front of my hind legs to assist trans-

Sitting like a person induced a "condition" for me. But, I was still too modest to show you.

porting me from point A to point B. The parent would lift up on each end of the towel to get me outside so that most if not all of my urination would occur on the snow-covered deck or the spot that Dad plowed for me to use in the yard. This was helping to keep the house as clean as possible from Newman-related messes. We were working through DM. It wasn't a good hand to be dealt, but I was so blessed to have such a loving family to see me through this progressively worsening neurological disorder.

Higher Ground

ON FRIDAY, February 13, 2015, Mom and Dad announced to Hanna and Rudy that they were going to have a little sister. Talk about another blessing! No, not the blessed event that my neutering was more than ten years ago. Not the blessed occurrence of going to the bathroom outside. A *real* blessing. The looks on everyone's faces were brilliantly beaming. Hanna even cried because she was overflowing with happiness. Rudy didn't even object, which was rather unlike him. He had a goofy grin of pride and joy. My parents shared that the little girl would be coming from China, likely by the end of 2015.

My coexistence with the new addition to the family (who will have the name Charlotte) was questioned. With tears in their eyes, Mom and Dad both suggested that it was unlikely that Charlotte and I would ever have the opportunity to meet. It appeared that both kids understood this inescapable reality.

I watched as Hanna's sensitivity about my disease grew. There were occasions when she teared up with sorrow about my aging process. I wished I could tell her that I wasn't in pain. Maybe that would make her feel better. She had grown up so much and understood the circle of life better than she got credit for. Although she had matured to approach her teenage years, I was far her senior. I had gone through the hormonal phase that is only a short trip forward for her in the time machine that we call life. I see her being a caring, sweet woman who has the typical life flow including marriage and children. I suspect that one day in her adult life, she'll think of me and have a boxer of her very own.

Then, there's Rudy. He cared for me in a different way. I know that he loves me, but he was more preoccupied by worldly things. I could tell that he cared about me when he patted me on the head, called me Newmie, and helped the parental units with my cleanup and previous walking duties. Dad has often said to me that he hoped my spirit would enter Rudy when I'm no longer here physically. If my essence is drifting around in the ether, I suppose that Rudy is about the best spot it could land. I hope that the little dude can find some focus in life to make something of himself. He's got potential, but I don't picture him with a boxer; rather, a pet monkey ... or maybe a snake. If you do that, little buddy, don't expect to have Mom visit you EVER! Do you remember how she freaked out about the one snake that she saw in the yard?

❖ IN MARCH, my family had a social worker pay us a visit. This was done to complete the home study requirement as part of Charlotte's upcoming adoption. In preparation for the social worker's arrival, I proceeded to gas up the entire house. Not the typical one and done, thirty-second intervals of foulness. More like a constant cloud that may require an industrial strength fan to blow the filth out of the house. It wasn't spiteful on my part; rather, I occasionally felt very flatulent. Today was just our lucky day. Mom was furiously trying to eliminate the odor up until minutes before Anita, the social worker, arrived. Windows were opened, Febreeze was sprayed. Meanwhile, the source (aka my rear end) should have been fumigated.

As Anita arrived, I greeted her calmly and she did not appear to notice any of my stink. I curled up on the floor at Anita's feet as she interviewed my family, much to Mom and Dad's dismay. What if I farted or pooped? How bad would that look in her eyes?

Thankfully it was a relatively brief visit. As Anita went through the house to survey Charlotte's future home, I needed to be part of the action. As Mommom showed Anita the upstairs portion of the house, my rowdiness (DM did not affect my ability to vocalize any concerns that I had) caused Dad to move me from the dining room to the living room so that I could see what was transpiring. As he did so, *it* happened. The pee zigzagged across the tile of the entrance to our home. Dad was mortified at the timing of my urination. He quickly got me situated in the living room, then sprinted to the kitchen to retrieve paper towels and Clorox spray to clean the mess, on the sly, of course. Dad was in such a hurry that he missed a spot. As everyone returned to the main floor, Dad mouthed silently to Mom, "Pee!" She looked around and quickly identified a small missed piddle and pointed this out to Dad. Meanwhile, she smartly led Anita to the basement for further inspection (away from the offending area). Dad cleaned up the last remaining dribbles to prevent Anita from discovering what I had done.

All's well that ends well. We passed the home study visit and the early stages of the adoption process with flying colors. The documentation was being finalized to head overseas and our family was becoming hopeful of a fall homecoming for Charlotte, perhaps a month or two earlier than initially expected.

One night after the kids went to sleep, Dad talked to Mom more intimately about my condition. He felt as though my degeneration had seemingly stalled. He hypothesized, "What if we bring Charlotte home, and Newman's still doing relatively well." Mom and Dad discussed this for quite some time, coming up with several names of family and friends who might be able to take care of me while my crew went to the Orient for approximately two weeks.

I knew that it was unfair to expect any one person or group of people to take care of me for that duration of time. My parents have gotten me into such a routine that we have a manageable and still enjoyable time together. Of course it would be better if I had four operating limbs as well as a controllable bladder and bowels. People not used to the routine could encounter more accidents because they mistakenly didn't follow the schedule to a tee, or if they didn't pick up on my increasingly subtle cues to indicate what I needed.

I could look out of the corner of my eye at the pantry and my parents knew that I was hungry. When I glanced in the general direction of the kitchen, Mommom rushed right over to grab a treat from the container next to the fridge. If I was relaxing on the couch and I started to even lean toward the floor, one of my parents would help me get down and allowed me to lead the way on where I wanted to go; it may only have been to perch at one of the windows, or perhaps I had an inkling that I need to go outside. These subtleties, among many others, were daily improvements in communication so that I didn't have to resort to being more vociferous.

However, I had started the habit of moaning at Mom and Dad when I wasn't fully satisfied with the current situation. There were times when I was merely restless as I lay on the floor; perhaps my water dish was not in a desirable location, maybe I just wanted my 206th treat for the day, or I felt as though I'd been wronged. Moaning became my "go to" response for any injustice. This often confounded my crew. I wish I could have told them what was bothering me so that they would understand that I wasn't trying to piss them off. Mom or Dad would ask me a litany of questions in an attempt to decipher what I needed. As it turned out, Mom or Dad would often respond by picking me up and placing me on the couch next to one of them. This action usually put me enough at ease for the moans to cease, although it was not a sure-fire solution at all times.

This was a winter that refused to yield ... so much so, that Dad took me outside on Easter morning to discover a half-inch of fresh white slushy snow covering the yard and deck. Good grief, it was April already! I needed spring. I longed for the days when I could lie in the yard and enjoy the aroma of the new greenery and flowers in bloom.

Mother Nature decided to relent and allow that Easter morning snow to be the last accumulation I would ever see. After a week or two, the spring weather finally broke through with bright, sixty-degree days with grass starting to grow. We still had some downright crisp days, but I could feel warm weather trying to invade our corner of the country.

Dad would play lacrosse and baseball with the children, while I supervised the activity from the front sidewalk on my dog bed. It is so peaceful to take everything in ... people, weather, and the familiar sight of our quiet road with few comings and goings.

I had my annual well-pet visit, this time with Dr. Scoda. It had become like clockwork for Mom and Dad to lift me into the back of the minivan and get me out to place me into my cart so that I was mobile for my appointment. After subtracting the weight of my cart, Dad and the nurse determined that I weighed a meager 57 pounds. My muscles had withered away so much that I had lost fifteen pounds in the past year. My rear legs were a shell of their former selves. Previously, I had had solid, taut musculature that held up my rear end. Now, the minimal meat that I had on my rear legs was spongy in nature. You could roll around the flesh of my thighs in your hand. My trunk had lost some girth although my appetite had never waned. I still enjoyed a good meal of lamb and rice.

After getting weighed, two very boisterous, yippy dogs greeted me with deafening barks. I know, I know—I have a cart. You can't understand why I have wheels. But, SHUT UP! I barely made a whimper in return and the nurses hurriedly steered the two loud nutjobs into an exam room.

Dr. Scoda and the nurses remarked how happy I was, considering my condition. I certainly still loved life and the vet administered the regular battery of tests (eyes, ears, teeth, heart) and said that I was doing great, all things considered. To check my heart, Dr. Scoda had to stifle my panting due to my excitement from the day's activity. She covered my snout for two or three seconds. Guess what I gave her? A big ol' muffled burp. Dr. Scoda didn't understand what everyone else had come to understand: I always get the last word.

I also had the pleasure of receiving a shot in my hind leg. Dr. Scoda squirted cold water on the target before administering the injection. Both the water and the shot caused my hind leg to jump. Yes, you read that right – I still had a smidgeon of feeling back there, even a year after the initial onset of the neurological disease.

Dr. Scoda thought that the cart was great, and especially enjoyed my custom license plate that simply read "NEWMAN." The army of adults (Dr. Scoda, Mom, Dad, and a nurse) held me in place in my cart so that I could also get my nails trimmed. The doctor sounded optimistic about my current condition and I got a clean bill of health for the next twelve months unless I needed immediate attention.

❖ ONE WARM SPRING NIGHT, Mommom was my downstairs sleeping partner. At about 4:00 a.m., I dropped from the couch and fell onto the floor in a less than graceful way. Although I rarely displayed elegance, this confirmation that gravity still worked was especially thudding in nature. I was rolling around on the soft carpet in bizarre, contorted patterns as Mommom shined her cell phone light on me in a panic in the otherwise dark living room. She called my name and I was unresponsive. I didn't feel a thing or know anything that was transpiring. It looked as though I could have been having a stroke or seizure.

I stopped writhing on the floor and remained still for a bit. My heart was still beating and I was breathing normally. Mommom lay by my side and tried to get my attention. Now with the ceiling light fixture on, she tried to force me to make eye contact. My gaze was consistently elsewhere. Mom touched, prodded, and moved my usually overly sensitive front paws. I offered no response, which proved worrisome. She thought that full paralysis may have been underway. My bowl of water was placed directly in front of me. I had no interest. Mommom retrieved a treat and waved it in front of me. I sleepily took the small biscuit and methodically chewed and swallowed it. Mommom surmised correctly that I felt no pain. She cuddled me on the floor and watched me like a hawk because she was unsure of what this meant.

It was the middle of the night, so both of us were drowsy and eventually fell back asleep. Within a few minutes, a light dawned on me that I would be far more comfortable on the couch. As such, I rose up enough to tower over Mommom and began to whimper. She roused and got me back onto the couch with little effort. She touched my front paws and I quickly retracted them. Apparently, things were back to "normal" following this scary episode.

I had lived a long, full life. I had been surrounded by such wonderful people. My time in this earthly realm was coming to a close. We have had some fantastic fun together: running and playing, sharing secrets, being partners in crime. I knew that the last year had been an effort on everyone's part. Mom and Dad didn't want me to go, but they wanted a sign from me that I was done.

I couldn't give anyone that sign. Number one: I am a boxer. Dr. Bryce describes my breed as perennially "shitting unicorns." Although I don't approve of this imagery (and the pain that the singular, long horn may do to my sphincter), I begrudgingly admit that he has a point.

Number two: I am stubborn. I will hang on because I can and I will. I didn't give up on ANYTHING even if it was for my own good.

Number three: I love life! Even the simplest pleasures were a treasure to me. Waiting for Dad to get home from work. Looking upstairs, anticipating Mommom to return from some sort of household chore. Seeing the kids get on and off the bus or returning from sports or dance. Everyone always greeted me with such vigor and love.

The problem was that I had become accustomed to *watching* life's events unfold instead of actively participating, especially as the springtime weather began to transition to summerlike conditions. Sure, I ate, drank, peed, pooped ... but rarely was I able to be thoroughly involved. I never played with my toys anymore at all. Car rides became tough because I loved getting in, but I HATED getting out, to the point that my whole body shook with anxiety about exiting the vehicle. I knew that Dad would never drop me, but it did not allay my fears.

We had to back off one of the things that made me happiest. I was going to remain downstairs to sleep each and every night. This was a decision that Dad made primarily because I had started to experience awful shakes each morning when anticipating the fifteen dreadful steps we had to take downstairs to the first floor to start the day. As I just mentioned, I knew that I was safe in Dad's arms; that didn't prevent the tremors from stopping. He had picked up on this cue of mine to eliminate any activities that cause my shakes. So ...no more upstairs for me. Reality was getting exceedingly harsh. It was for the best, but it was still a disappointment.

Walks had even become a lot of work. In late spring, I was rarely going further than the perimeter of my own yard. My front leg stride had begun to diminish to the point where it really wore me out to walk for a few hundred feet. My breathing had become more labored when exerting myself, whether during a walk, or scooting inside the house, or when being amped up to see someone or something. It was incredibly frustrating but I never publicly showed that emotion.

My family had perfectly taken care of me and showed me such amazing love. However, my life had become incredibly small. I almost always stayed within the realm of the living room. At mealtime, I scooted under the dinner table to be with the fam. Occasionally, I would find my way to the dining room if something was of particular interest there. Also, Mom or Dad would take me out on the deck or onto the front lawn for potty breaks. It's great to get some fresh air, but this was only a biological effort. I seldom took time to smell the proverbial roses, so to speak. Although I would never say so, the time had come.

I still loved to be out in the sunny weather.

One More Night

AS THE CALENDAR ROLLED OVER to June, my eleventh birthday was imminent. Mom, Dad, and the kids were talking quite often about my birthday. It was not because there was going to be a big blowout celebration. Rather, they were unsure if I would still be here to see eleven. I was old by any standard: for a dog, for a boxer, for a DM-afflicted canine, all of the above. As such, I treated my birthday as any other day that was not June 6th; I slept, lounged, tried not to have an accident, and begged for treats early and often.

When it came time for my mini-party with just the immediate family, Dad gave me a mental exam. Instead of singing "Happy Birthday" to me, which immediately elicits my barks and my foresight that I was about to receive a Frosty Paw treat, Dad had another thought. He asked the family to sing the same tune in Spanish to see if I would recognize it just the same. It only took the first line, "Feliz cumpleaños a ti," for me to realize what was about to happen. I happily barked because I was certain of what was to come: ice cream! I was presented with my frozen dairy treat, which I gratefully and promptly scarfed down.

As the days following my birthday wore on, I noticed that Dad was especially weepy. I tried to comfort him by

Getting older does indeed have its privileges.

licking his face to make him feel better. It temporarily worked, but the tears continued to stream down his face in a torrent a few times each day. The rest of the crew showed signs of the same sorrow on occasion. I even saw some of my extended family including Aunt Ally, Uncle Cody, Emerson, and Aunt Lindsay come to the house and many more tears were shed especially when visiting with me.

I didn't get it. I was fine. I was sitting here, shitting my unicorn. Movement had become harder. So what? Accidents were now commonplace (I'm sorry. I really am, but ...). So what? Sleeping was not as restful as it used to be. So what? Breathing was at times a challenge. SO WHAT?

So ... if I didn't live in the moment, I would realize that each DM-related deterioration over the past year had gradually slivered away at my life as a dog. It had been seven months ago that I made my last venture to the end of the road and back. I took my last poop outside last week, and that was a mere "happy accident." I couldn't go for car rides, couldn't go upstairs, needed Mom or Dad to hold me up to pee, and needed a cart to go around the yard for what now served as a "walk" before I became exhausted. I couldn't even leave the property under my own power because my body was simply too weak to go any further.

I still had a wonderful spirit and terrific personality, but my days as a fully functioning canine were unfortunately a thing of the past. We went through the next few days before a proclamation was made to the kids. It was with sheer agony that Mom told Hanna and Rudy that I was going to heaven tomorrow. This caused a subdued, sorrowful energy at the family dinner hour. I lay under the table hearing the words, but not fully digesting their meaning.

I guess I should have realized that only I was going on a special trip, one that the others couldn't make quite yet. Normally when we went on trips, we did it as a family. I should have been struck by the fact that only Newman was making this venture. Any time I heard the word "go," I was game. You could have told me that I was going to go on a canoe ride over Niagara Falls. My response would be full-on anticipation and working my way to one of our vehicles because most trips began there. I supposed that I would just have to wait and see what this trip to heaven entailed.

Later that night, Mom and Dad let the kids stay up late so that they could all video chat with Charlotte. I wasn't the center of attention, so I started to whimper and whine audibly. As my agitation level rose, so did the volume of my disruptiveness. That's when Dad briskly hoofed it downstairs to get me a Frosty Paw. I slid off the couch awkwardly and thudded to a comfortable spot on the carpet to enjoy the treat. I inhaled it quickly and picked right up where I had left off, whining with annoyance in my voice. The family was not yet done Skyping with Charlotte, so I was being scolded aggressively yet silently by Dad for my rude manners. He glared at me through gritted teeth and wagged his finger at me off camera. Dad's efforts to keep me reasonably quiet were unsuccessful. I sensed that it wasn't as big a deal as it would have been in the past. Maybe that had to do with my upcoming adventure.

After the family signed off with Charlotte and the kids went to sleep, Mom and Dad wept openly and often. I always got attention from my parents, but it was bordering on the obsessive amount as the quiet portion of a typical weeknight unfolded. Mom talked about accompanying Dad to sleep with me downstairs. Ultimately, she decided to go upstairs so that we all had a chance at getting some sleep.

Mom tearfully bid me good night and headed "north" to turn in. Dad coerced me off the couch by opening a bag of Doritos. Mmmm ... nacho cheese. The guy knows how to get my attention. He used these as a treat to bait me into a trip outside to urinate on the deck one more time before bedtime. Doritos were once again the treat of choice to motivate me to return to the love seat for my final night of earthly slumber.

Dad stayed up with me for another two hours. He stared at me, talked with me, took a few pictures of me, and sobbed into my fur as I dozed off and on. Dad asked me to give him a sign tomorrow that I got where I belonged. Despite my weariness from the day's events, I took this in and tried to understand what he meant.

As I drifted off to sleep for the night, Dad left the lamp

on the end table illuminated on the lowest setting. It provided a soft light for the room that would not keep either of us awake, but allowed us to see one another. I was getting a sense that everything was about to change, but I didn't yet know how.

It's the End of the World as We Know It

JUST BEFORE 6:00 A.M., my eyes shot open with terror. My body was betraying me once more. I had to pee ... now. I forced my body off the love seat and sprayed streams of urine as I tried to hustle away from my own mess. It was uncontrollable and incredibly irritating. As Dad woke to the sound of my rump hitting the carpet, he gathered the necessary cleaning products. He was beginning to blot, spray, and scrub, when my bowels erupted without any notice. I scooted along the floor leaving a second trail that required cleaning. It felt like I lost several pounds following this expelling of excrement. What a wicked way to awaken. I watched helplessly as Dad spent the dawn hours scrubbing and furiously cleansing the affected areas.

After he had completed this brutal task, Dad gave me a curious look. He questioned, "Buddy?" to which I responded with a half head-cock as if to say, "What?" He then said the words that had always been pure magic for me, "Do you want to go for a walk?" I got up on two paws and shimmied closer to him to show how excited I was at the prospect of heading out for a morning jaunt.

Dad brought my cart into the house and labored position me in the cart so that I could roll along the tile to head outside. I needed very little provocation to bound down the two steps into the garage. After doing so, we walked down the driveway and I sniffed all the smells following yet another spring rain shower. I stood still and simply took it all in. Dad asked where I wanted to go. I led us to the intersection of our quiet lane and the state route where very light weekday road traffic was only beginning. My front shoulders were beginning to tire, so I turned around and plodded toward home, meandering between the wet grass and fairly dry pavement of the road. It's my world, right? Of course, Dad kept watch to ensure that no cars were approaching, even when my cart and I were enjoying the smooth surface of the middle of the road.

I trudged up the driveway and Dad lifted me out of my cart at the corner of the driveway and sidewalk and coerced a few drops of pee out of me before picking me up and presumably heading back inside the house. However, he carried me in his arms toward the backyard and allowed me to view the sights that used to be the most familiar to me. Dad blubbered openly and not quietly. After a minute or so, we were back in the house and I was chowing down Science Diet chicken and rice for the last time.

Shortly thereafter, the household came to life with Mom and the kids arriving downstairs to begin their day. Rudy was preparing for school and Hanna was heading to Aunt Ally's for the morning. Mom and Dad asked Rudy to come talk to me ... which he did as I lounged in the dining room. Rudy and I shared our last moments together while he petted my head and scratched my ears. He talked casually with me and said his goodbyes while making minimal eye contact. As the start of another school day beckoned, Rudy departed through the garage to catch the bus. As the sound of the diesel engine idled in front of our driveway, I offered up a few expectant woofs to let the driver know that I didn't miss her. I *never* missed the comings and goings of the kids' school bus.

Hanna was also getting ready, but she was not going to school today. She felt that it would be too difficult on this day to sit in the classroom and be expected to focus. So, Aunt Ally had offered to take her for the morning. While Hanna was completing her final preparations for the day, I received an unexpected morning Frosty Paw from Dad. I could deal with dessert with my breakfast each and every day, that's for sure!

A few moments later, Hanna could not hold back the tears. She was asking Dad what to say and how to talk to me. He offered the suggestion to just keep it short and sweet, to simply say how she felt. Dad decided to leave the room to give us a moment of privacy, which Hanna preferred. She gave me a lot of love and talked briefly about what I have meant to her and how much she would miss me. Without turning back because it would be too painful for her, Hanna was gone. I watched out the window as Aunt Ally drove them out of sight.

I was left with my two favorite people in the whole world, Mom and Dad: the two best parents a pooch could ever want. They hovered by me, often touching me and appearing very sad. They talked to me and appeared on the verge of an emotional breakdown when a small hatchback pulled into our driveway. I barked feverishly as the silver vehicle approached more closely. As the car got closer, I scooted as close to the front door as possible without touching the tile.

I watched as a woman and a young man came across the sidewalk toward the front door. It was ... Dr. Scoda?! What in the world was she doing here? We're not at the vet's office. That was nice of her to come pay a visit to me. The young man was apparently her helper.

I was trying to scoot across the tile because I was so eager to greet my two guests. My labored breathing filled the room. Dr. Scoda saw my activity and confided to Mommom, "It's definitely time." We all visited a little while as I gave the young man, Brandon, the Newman greeting. This consisted of lots of licks, trying to make a new friend. He was receptive, so I was more enthusiastic about sharing my well wishes. The grown-ups spoke in subdued tones as preparations were made. I smelled the doctor's bag including a stethoscope, syringes, and all sorts of other goodies.

Dr. Scoda and Brandon drifted off to the kitchen as I tried to figure out where they were going. Mom and Dad spent a few minutes with me, loving on me and barely giving me any room to maneuver, or even breathe.

Dad departed to bring the vets back to see me. Dr. Scoda explained that she was going to inject me with a shot of anesthesia in one of my hind legs. This was going to make me very sleepy. Mom and Dad were freely bawling now and holding me as I continued to lick Brandon's face.

Dr. Scoda was fiddling around with a needle and syringe as I lay on my living room carpet. She poked and prodded in my left rear leg, then looked up to Mom and Dad. The kind, young vet said that I had minimal blood pressure in my hind legs and she would have to try a different leg. She repositioned to be near my face. I looked upon her inquisitively then saw the needle approaching my front leg.

My front paws remained overly sensitive up until these, my last moments. I was not a huge fan of anyone messing with them. Dr. Scoda lightly trimmed a minimal amount of fur with battery-powered hair clippers off the target area as Mom and Dad soothed me. A few tiny clumps of fawn fur dropped away as the injection location was prepped. Dr. Scoda was able to get the needle in place as I tensed due to my front left paw's hypersensitivity. Mom and Dad held me close to reassure me, as they had for nearly eleven years.

The anesthetic had not yet been administered. Dr. Scoda and Brandon excused themselves once more to give us some privacy. Mom and Dad held me closely, told me that I was the best dog ever, cuddled me, and made me feel very much at ease although I still had no idea what was about to occur. We spent these last few minutes together in a quiet, peaceful heap on the floor. They took away any apprehension that I may have felt from getting poked with a needle.

Dad returned with Dr. Scoda and Brandon and Mom continued cuddling my face and bawling her eyes out. I could feel Dad's body heaving with sobs on my back as Dr. Scoda injected the anesthetic that probably could have taken down an elephant. Within moments, I felt my body start to lose feeling although I could still hear and see Mom and Dad. The upper portion of my body was no longer upright as I dropped onto my right side and looked cloudily toward Mom and out my "Newman" window.

It was about this time that I understood that my adventures on Earth were coming to a close. All the crying from the family, all the goodbyes. My body betraying me over the past year. Nothing lasted forever here on Earth, not even me.

My life proved to be a perfectly symmetrical picture. In my infancy, I had a birth mother (and presumably birth father) with siblings. Perhaps my fur family and I were not close, but we started our journey together. I had to learn so much as a youth, but my puppy behavior prevented me from comprehending everything until my teenaged hormones settled to a manageable level. With adulthood, I proved to be as steady as a rock while having a fun, happy life surrounded by people who made every day worth living. As I became a senior, my body began to betray me to the point that I could no longer perform some of the routine lessons that I worked so tirelessly to learn. My days became a struggle, not because life lacked direction, but rather, because of a dreaded disease. In my final days and moments, I had the opportunity to recollect all the memories of my human parents and siblings, who I absolutely adored.

If I had to go out, this was the way to do it: with my parents encouraging and loving me every step of the way. I was not scared, nervous, or in pain. A few last kisses, hugs, and tears, and a second drug was administered. Just like that, with my parents' arms around me and my eyes remaining half open, my heart that was always so full of love, ceased beating on June 18, 2015.

Welcome to Paradise

WHEN MY EYES OPENED, I look around to hear the deep bellows of some massive canines and higher-pitched yips from smaller breeds. Hmmm ... I've never been here before. This is brand new. I get up on all fours to inspect my bright, new surroundings. Wait a minute. I got up!! On my own!!! My legs work again!!!! I don't have DM anymore?! "Holy shit, boss." Or shouldn't I say that here?

I sprinted in no particular direction. "Yes, yes, yes!" I ran in circles. I ran laps. I leaped. I jumped. "Woo hoo!" I lay on my back to scratch it as I rolled side to side. Oooh, that feels so good. I sat down and used my hind legs to scratch the insides and outsides of my ears, and then smelled my toenails to enjoy the odor of my ear wax for the first time in nearly a year.

I saw a few dogs slowly meander over to me to check me out. I heard a yellow lab say, "Hey Newman." I have never had the pleasure of seeing this friendly face before or the two black labs that accompanied him. They greeted me to let me know that I'm here because I had a great family and they taught me right from wrong. My new friends are Flax, Max, Duchess, among many others that are spread everywhere. They tell me that we are all part of a giant extended family. Max was my mom's childhood black

Labrador retriever, while Flax and Duchess were Dad's boyhood yellow and black labs.

My eyes turn to my surroundings and there appears to be no boundaries anywhere. There are thousands, maybe even millions of dogs sniffing one another and cavorting. It is a giant puppy play time, with dogs as far as the eye can see (with no cats anywhere to be seen). There are bins of food and water dishes scattered throughout the sunny pasture. People appear from time to time to throw toys for those dogs who are interested. Others are tossing sticks for the less refined pooches. We have a grand, old time doing whatever we want. I'm struck by the fact that any barks that I hear are playful. There are no menacing snarls, no scolding tones from any humans. We are at complete harmony with one another.

We played with unceasing energy. I felt as though I could run forever and ever when I noticed many dogs just staring at me in wonderment. I paused and approached them. "What?" I questioned simply with a slight head cock.

A German shepherd remarked with a chuckle, "New pup on the block."

I exclaimed, "YEP!" and began sprinting with renewed invigoration. I recalled my younger days and renewed my haphazard running style with neither rhyme nor reason. My new friends howled with laughter.

I felt an urge come over me and I squatted to do my business. I felt it coming! It didn't just slide out of me without warning. Thank you, God! As I walked away and pranced with each paw playfully digging into the ground and showing off my rediscovered ability to poop, I turned back and my feces was already gone. Holy crap. The saying takes on a new meaning here.

Off in the distance, a set of bells rang. Everybody slowly halted their activities and they all began walking at varying speeds in a fairly uniform direction. I caught up with my new friends and asked about the purpose of the bells that sounded like church peels tolling in the neighborhood. Flax told me, "Puppy play is over for the time being. Never fear, Newman. We'll have more time tomorrow."

"So where are we going?"

Max replied, "It's family time."

I got a little sad. "My family is not here yet, I don't think."

Flax, Max, and Duchess all chime in. "We know what you mean. Your humans aren't here yet," Duchess thoughtfully replied. "Neither are ours. We are our own family right now. The great part about this place is that there are so many humans that want to be around us. We have plenty of people to spend time with us until our humans arrive." I looked around a bit skeptically.

Max, the bulkiest yet meekest of the bunch, said, "It's your first day. You'll be fine. Don't worry about a thing; let us show you the way." We continued walking until we reached my new residence. My three new buddies showed me around. It had all the comforts of home. Whatever I needed or wanted seemed to be within view. I saw couches with thick plush cushions. There were bags full of treats within reach, not up on the counters like they were in my earthly home. I instinctively leaped onto the couch, circling five, ten, twenty times like I used to, before settling in for a little rest. My friends told me that they would remain close by in case I needed anything. When I awakened from a short nap, I headed upstairs to the bed and felt as though my beaming, toothy smile could brighten the darkest storm. I just walked up the steps without any help from Dad. And now I can jump onto the bed!?!? My vault onto the mattress left me breathless, so much so that I forgot to circle, and promptly fell asleep for the night.

As the dawn of a new day broke, I bounded off the bed

with an extra giddy-up in my step because I realized that I had had no accidents overnight. Duchess was the first to greet me. "How was your first night?" I told her that I slept great and I was ready for what today would bring.

We all playfully bounced off one another as we headed back to play time. As we neared the supersized green field, I asked for a moment of privacy. The dogs walked a few paces ahead of me and I found a quiet spot to collect my thoughts.

I said to myself, "If this is my reward for my time on Earth, I owe it to my family, to Mom, Dad, Hanna, Rudy, even Charlotte, everybody. Earth was awesome because of you, but this place is incredible. I can't wait to show it to you. Take your time, though, and appreciate everything that your planet has to offer. Get another boxer when you're ready. When each of your times on earth is up, we'll be waiting for you. Then we'll have forever together." I took a long pause and realized that my current experience is very similar to my first night with Mom and Dad. I have a lot to learn from my new family so I can make the most of eternity. I might even pick up a pointer or two for when the rest of my family arrives.

I yelp, "Hey, wait up!" and ramble with my jowls rhythmically flapping in the wind to catch up with my new pals. Flax playfully paws me. I jump off Max's back to spring up into the air because he seems like the sturdiest. I fall to the ground with a dull clunk. Oooh, that smarts but only a little. Dogs can evidently be clumsy in heaven ... well, at least I can. Lesson learned. What's the adage? "You can't teach an old dog new tricks." Yeah ... I'm still in training.

Acknowledgments

I MUST FIRST THANK my mom for putting the seed into my mind that a book about Newman was a possibility. You always mentioned how often we "spoke for him," offering his thoughts. To Mom and Dad, you have always offered an unwavering support system for me and my sisters throughout all the twists and turns that our lives have taken.

This book would have been one of those unfinished projects if not for the love and devotion of my wife, Laura. You have been a steady and sweet companion as we have taken life's voyage together. I cannot contemplate what my life would be without you in it. I could always count on you to recall delightful memories of Newman. Your input and feedback helped to shape Newman's story.

Our kids, Hanna, Rudy, and now Charlotte, keep us hopping each and every day. Our lives feel like a giant, blindfolded rollercoaster ride because of your ever-present personalities. The steep drops, steady climbs, and sharp turns that we experience are our family's journey.

To Newman: you were, and continue to be, an inspiration to me. I only hope that this is a sufficient tribute to how great a partner-in-crime you have been to us. We love you always, big boy. It's not fair, but you will be the standard by which all future pets will be measured.

To the rest of my family and friends, you are an integral piece of this story. Some of you were extraordinarily close to Newman (like Alison and Cody), while others were separated by a greater distance. But, all of you have had an impact on the person that I am. If you had not shaped my life in some way, who knows how this story would have turned out ... or if it would have been told at all?

Appendix

WE HAVE CALLED NEWMAN by a seemingly endless stream of nicknames over the years. Admittedly, some of these were not very inventive and others were downright embarrassing. Newman would respond to each of these, with varying degrees of interest (or aloofness):

Baby, Big Boy, Big Brown, Bloomin' Onion, Boober, Boom, Boom Boom, Boomer, Buddy, Dog, Doofus, Fart-knocker, Filthy Animal, Four-Legged Vacuum Cleaner, Mr. Brown, Newm, Newm Newm, Newmerator, Newmie, Patches, Poop, Pooperston, Pup, Puppy, Quilt, Scooter, Señor Woof, Shelock Lock, Shocka Locka, Stink Butt Crotch Lick, Stink Dog, Turd Burglar (or, in Latin: Turdis Burglaris), Waddles, Waddles McGee, Woodrow, Woody.

Afterword

SINCE THE STORY of Newman's life concluded, the family has welcomed home little Miss Charlotte. She shines with such joy in her heart that she makes us laugh each and every day. We allowed Charlotte a few months to get comfortable in her new environment before chaos returned to the household with a male boxer puppy named Bosco. Heaven help us all.

www.ingramcontent.com/pod-product-compliance
Lightning Source LLC
Chambersburg PA
CBHW071559080526
44588CB00010B/959